The Critics' Choice

"This Fledgling Series May Soon Do For Travel Guides What Hitchcock Did For Film." —Chicago Tribune

"Sharp Writing And A Thrilling Layout Make It A Guidebook You Can Read From Cover To Cover Without A Yawn." —San Francisco Examiner

"Dripping With Attitude... Cutting Edge..." —Atlanta Journal-Constitution

"It's Hip To Be There -- All The Usual Topics From History To Hotels To Shopping But With A Welcome Cutting-Edge Spin." —Chicago Sun-Times

"No Other Guide Captures So Completely And Viscerally What It Feels Like To Be Inside The City." —San Francisco Bay Guardian

"Razzle-Dazzle Design." —USA Today

"An Insider With Attitude." —Newsday

"For Travelers Who've Outgrown The Shoestring Budget Of Their College Days, There's Avant-Guide, A New Series From Itinerant Genius Dan Levine." —Elle Magazine

"Ultra Hip Travel Tomes." —Atlanta Journal-Constitution

"If It's Cutting Edge You Want In A City That Teeters Between Conservative And Revolutionary, This Is The Book To Buy." —Toronto Sun

PICK OF THE MONTH – "Refreshingly Sharp Entertaining Advice." —Consumer Reports

"Opinionated, Mildly Caustic And Very Stylish" —Baltimore Sun

"Wealth Of Local History And Color." —US News & World Report

"One Guide That … essing Opinions." —Boston Glo…

fiercely independent!

Each Avant*Guide is created by independent experts who never accept discounts or payments in exchange for positive coverage.

Our visits to restaurants, clubs and other establishments are anonymous, and expenses are paid by Avant*Guide.

FEW OTHER GUIDEBOOKS CAN MAKE THIS CLAIM.

AVANT GUIDE

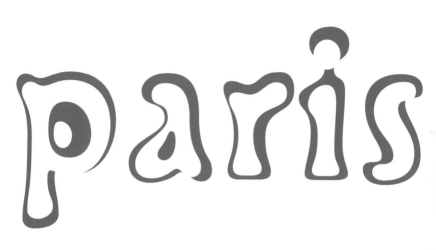

paris

Empire ~ New York

EMPIRE PRESS MEDIA
444 Madison Avenue
35th floor
New York, NY 10022

E-mail: editor@avantguide.com
Web: http://www.avantguide.com

Editor-in-Chief: Dan Levine
Photo Editor: Cornelis Van Voorthuizen

Design: >0< Mowshe
Gregorini (mig); Kleček (1i6®); Matyáš (On)

Writers: Robert Blackshaw, Gary Lippman, Stephen Mudge, Christopher Oldcorn, Jacques Moinnerau, Alain Corre, Tabitha Hartman, Stewart Tobias, Rik Thomason, Mickey Henri-Thomas, Dominique Vernier.

Copy Editor: Jeannette Vota
Research Editor: Lilith Cowan
Copy Editor Français: David Pajot
Fact checker: Heather Stimmler-Hall
Photography: Cornelis Van Voorthuizen, Kristoff Halversham
Photo Imaging: Julie Denesha
Cover Digital Imaging by Li6® & fido
Back Cover Photo: Liz Steger

Dog Animation: Petr Morkes
Web Design: Ivan Gosić
Fonts: **Cobra** by Franta Štorm

Very Special Thanks
Fran and Alan Levine, Petra Lustigová, Pluto, Dr. Shedivka, Jonathan Pontell, Chronic and Marilyn Wood, Vláďa Strejček, Filip Blažek, Kamilala Mrak and Mike G. Money

ISBN: 1-891603-19-1
Second Edition

Printed in the Czech Republic.
Distributed in North America by Publishers Group West

also from Avant•Guide
Avant•Guide New York City
Avant•Guide San Francisco
Avant•Guide New Orleans
Avant•Guide London
Avant•Guide Prague
Avant•Guide Toronto
Avant•Guide Las Vegas
Avant•Guide Disney World & Orlando
Avant•Guide Chicago
coming soon...
Avant•Guide Amsterdam
Avant•Guide Cuba
Avant•Guide Italy

Contents

№ 01

PARIS ENLIGHTENED

FRANC-O-FiLE

There are almost a quarter of a million dogs in Paris, collectively producing over four thousand pounds (1800 kilos) of crap per day. Most of it seems to end up in the middle of the sidewalk. How paradoxical, for a people whose culture places so much importance on good form, that their capital is so fouled by feces.

The sorry state of the city's sidewalks is a glaring manifestation of a collective cultural selfishness and, yes, arrogance. Fact is, Parisian dog owners just don't care if other people end up stepping in their pet's poo. Like it's some kind of inalienable right to be able to crap anywhere one pleases. *Liberté, Egalité, Fraternité* is the French national slogan after all.

Modern France is increasingly defined by its paradoxes. The nation that has known centuries of global dominance has had the tables turned and now fears losing its cultural independence. But they bash McDonald's with one fist while holding a Big Mac in the other. They create the *Académie Française* to shield the French language, then admire English for its freeform flexibility. They pass protectionist legislation against American cinema, and are first in line to see the latest Hollywood trash.

But that's the small stuff. More importantly, French people know that keeping up with material-obsessed America comes at a price; namely the wonderful, leisurely approach to all the aspects of life they have come to call "*l'exception Française.*" In practice, this means that Paris no longer comes to a screeching halt each August, and Parisians are increasingly uncomfortable letting mail go unanswered for a month.

The French have a nagging sense that, with the onslaught of consumerist culture and Great Satan-led globalizaion, they will become incapable of maintaining their own admirable play-ethic.

Somewhat depressed, and impotent about their future, the French increasingly look to their past for solace. The result are nationalists like Jean-Marie Le Pen, protectionist legislation, and heavy arts-funding, proscribed like doses of cultural Viagra.

Everywhere you turn in Paris are reminders that the city's heydays have passed; the greatness of Napoléon, the heady days of the Revolution, and the burst of creativity between the wars that nurtured everyone from Ernest Hemingway and Pablo Picasso to Gertrude Stein and Coco Chanel.

Even the exalted *Paris Review* has been edited from New York City for the last dozen years. Despite our ranting, we are actually

very upbeat about Paris and feel infused with love for the city. It's the swirl of monuments, cathedrals, bridges and buildings. The quirky cobblestone lanes and the grand boulevards. It's Baron Haussmann's imposing fountains, hydrants, and sewers, and the urinals which are nicknamed after him. It's the omnipresence of art and culture. It's that *le coq* is the national symbol, and that baths are still viewed with suspicion. It's the striking French truckers, the 35-hour work weeks, and the five weeks of paid vacation. It's the cultish loyalty to Louis XIV and Emperor Napoléon, both of whom imposed absolute rule and fought a series of wars trying to dominate the world. It's Marianne, the muse of the country, whose bust is in every city hall. It's the rich history that permeates the air. It's the nudity on TV. It's the *cafés*, the bistros and the boutiques. And that nobody minds if you smoke. And not even the smog-belching automobiles can dispel the city's intoxicating aura of romance. That is the "movable feast" that what's-his-name once called Paris.

So resign yourself to soiled soles. The City of Light is so beautiful that you can hardly keep your eyes on the sidewalk.

fACTS & FiGURES

Percent of babies born out of wedlock	40
Age of Consent	15
Ratio of soap consumption, as compared to the European average	3:4
Percentage of French adults who smoke at least one pack of cigarettes a day	40
Year in which women were first allowed to vote:	1945
Percentage of married French women who admit to extra-marital affairs:	38

Sources: Ministère de l'Intérieur et de l'Aménagement du Territoire
The Economist Magazine

Population

France	58,416,500
Île-de-France	11,161,000
Paris	2,158,918
Marseilles	850,550
Lyon	465,487

Age

Under 20	25.8 %
20-59	53.8 %
60 and Over	20.4 %

Religions

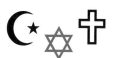

Catholic	90 %
Protestant	2 %
Muslim	1 %
Jewish	1 %
Other	6 %

Ethnicity

Portuguese	700,729
Algerian	585,846
Moroccan	441,000
Italian	268,047
Spanish	246,342
Tunisian	178,217
Turkish	147,558
British	59,790
Belgian	57,574
German	57,670
Polish	46,193
North American	27,053
Irish	4,778

Most common family names:

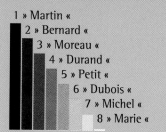

1 » Martin «
2 » Bernard «
3 » Moreau «
4 » Durand «
5 » Petit «
6 » Dubois «
7 » Michel «
8 » Marie «

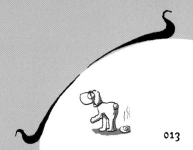

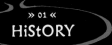

PARiStORiC: HiStORY iN A HURRY

c250 BC	Celtic Parisii tribe founds Lutétia on the Ile de la Cité.
52 BC	Romans conquer Paris.
260	St-Denis martyred on Mount Mercury (Montmartre).
361	Governor Julian of Lutétia becomes Roman Emperor.
451	Attila the Hun retreats before attacking Paris.
496	King Clovis baptized at Reims.
508	Paris becomes the regional capital.
543	Monastery founded at St-Germain-des-Prés.
800	Charlemagne becomes first Holy Roman Emperor; capital Moves to Aix-la Chapelle (Aechen).
845–880	Vikings sack Paris.
987	Count Hugues Capet becomes first king of France.
c1100	Famous French lovers Abélard and Héloise meet.
1163	Notre-Dame Cathedral begins construction.
1181	market established at Les Halles.
1190–1202	New city wall constructed.
1207–29	Cathar heresy brutally suppressed by King Philip Augustus.
1215	Papal Charter recognizes University of Paris.
1226–70	Capetian king Louis IX (St-Louis) wages 7th and 8th Crusades.
1248	Sainte-Chapelle consecrated.
1253	Sorbonne founded.

c1300	Conciergerie rebuilt.
1309–77	Papacy established in Avignon.
1340	Hundred Years' War with England begins.
1364	Charles V moves royal court to the Louvre; Vincennes and Bastille fortresses built.
1420–36	Paris under English rule.
1463	Paris gets its first printing press.
1515–47	Reign of François 1er; Renaissance in Europe.
1528	Rebuilding of Louvre begins.
1572	Protestants killed in St-Bartholemew's Day massacre.
1593	Wars of Religion end when Henri IV becomes Catholic.
1598	Edict of Nantes recognizes Protestants and ends Huguenots persecution.
1605	Construction of Place des Vosges begins.
1610	King Henri IV assassinated.
1634	Cardinal Richelieu founds *L'Académie Française*.
1643–1715	Reign of Sun King (*Roi Soleil*) Louis XIV ushers in French "golden age."
1648–53	La Fronde rebellion occupies Paris.
1661	Louis XIV declares personal rule.
1667	First street lights illuminate Paris.
1672	Grands Boulevards built along the lines of old city wall.
1680	La Comédie Française founded
1682	Louis XIV moves court to Versailles.
1685	Edict of Nantes revoked provoking mass Huguenot exodus.
1685	Place des Victoires commissioned by Jean-Baptiste Colbert.
1700	War of the Spanish Succession begins.
1715–74	Reign of Louis XV.
1751	Diderot's *Encyclopédie* published.
1753	Place de la Concorde begun.
1785	Tax Wall built around Paris.
1789	Mob attack on the Bastille begins French Revolution; Louis XVI forced to leave Versailles for Paris.
1791	Louis XVI attempts escape from Paris.
1792	September Massacres; Republic declared.

1793	Louis XVI & Marie-Antoinette executed; Louvre museum opens to the public.
1794	Jacobeans overthrown; Robespierre and other revolutionary leaders executed.
1799	Napoléon Bonaparte stages coup and becomes First Consul.
1800	Population 550,000.
1804	Napoléon declares himself Emperor
1806	Arc de Triomphe begun under Napoléon's orders.
1812	French troops capture Moscow before retreating from Russia.
1814	Russian army defeats Napoléon, occupies Paris.
1815	Napoléon regains power (the "Hundred Days"), raises a new army and is defeated at Waterloo; Bourbon monarchy restored under Louis XVIII.
1821	Napoléon dies in exile on St-Helena.
1828	Horse-drawn buses begin service.
1830	Charles X overthrown in revolution, Louis-Philippe becomes king; population 1 million.
1830–48	France conquers Algeria.
1832	Cholera kills 20,000 Parisians.
1836	Arc de Triomphe completed.
1837	First railway line in Paris opens.
1848	Louis-Philippe overthrown in revolt; Second Republic begins under President Louis-Napoléon Bonaparte; most men get the vote.
1852	Louis-Napoléon declares himself Emperor Napoléon III, Second Empire begins.

1853	Georges Haussmann appointed Prefect of Paris.
1862	Palais Garnier begins Construction.
1866	*Le Figaro* newspaper founded.
1870–71	Napoléon III abdicates after Prussian victory at Sedan; Alsace and Lorraine ceded to the victors.
1871	Revolutionary "Paris Commune" takes the government and is then violently suppressed.
1874	First Impressionist exhibition on Blvd. des Capucines.
1875–87	Vineyards ravaged by phylloxera epidemic.
1889	Eiffel Tower built for Paris Exhibition; Moulin Rouge opens.
1890	Population 2 million.
1894–99	Jewish officer Alfred Dreyfus falsely convicted of treason.
1895	Lumière brothers premier first public cinema.
1900	First Métro line opens.
1904	Pablo Picasso comes to Paris.
1914	World War I begins; Germans defeated near Paris at Battle of the Marne.
1918	Armistice signed in forest of Compiegne.
1919	Treaty of Versailles returns Alsace and Lorraine to France.
1934	Fascists demonstrate in Paris.
1936	Socialists lead "Front Populaire" government; banks, railroads and factories nationalized.
1939	World War II begins.
1940	Germans take Paris; collaborationist government installed at Vichy.
1941–42	Mass deportations of Jews.
1944	Allies liberate France; de Gaulle forms provisional government; broad nationalization begins.
1946	Fourth Republic established; Women get the vote.
1949	Simone de Beauvoir's *The Second Sex* published.
1955–56	Algeria revolts supported with mass demonstrations in Paris.
1957	CNIT opens in new La Défense corporate district.
1958	Charles de Gaulle elected President; Fifth Republic established.

1959	France helps found European Economic Community.
1968	Workers strike and students riot.
1969	Pompidou elected President; Les Halles market closes.
1973	Boulevard Périphérique around Paris opens.
1977	Centre Georges Pompidou opens; Jacques Chirac becomes Mayor of Paris.
1981	François Mitterand elected President; death penalty abolished.
1986	Musée d'Orsay opens.
1989	Louvre pyramid completed; Opéra Bastille opens.
1992	Disneyland Paris opens.
1995	Jacques Chirac elected President.
1996	Bibliothèque Nationale François Mitterand opens.
1997	Lionel Jospin's socialist government elected.
1998	France wins football World Cup in Paris.
1999	Wind storms wreck havoc on city.
2000	Euro becomes legal tender; Centre Georges Pompidou reopens after two year renovation.
2004	French lounge/ electronica music explosion continues with the release of Air's newest, Talkie Walkie.

Nº 02

ThE LAY Of THE LAND

NAViGATiNG

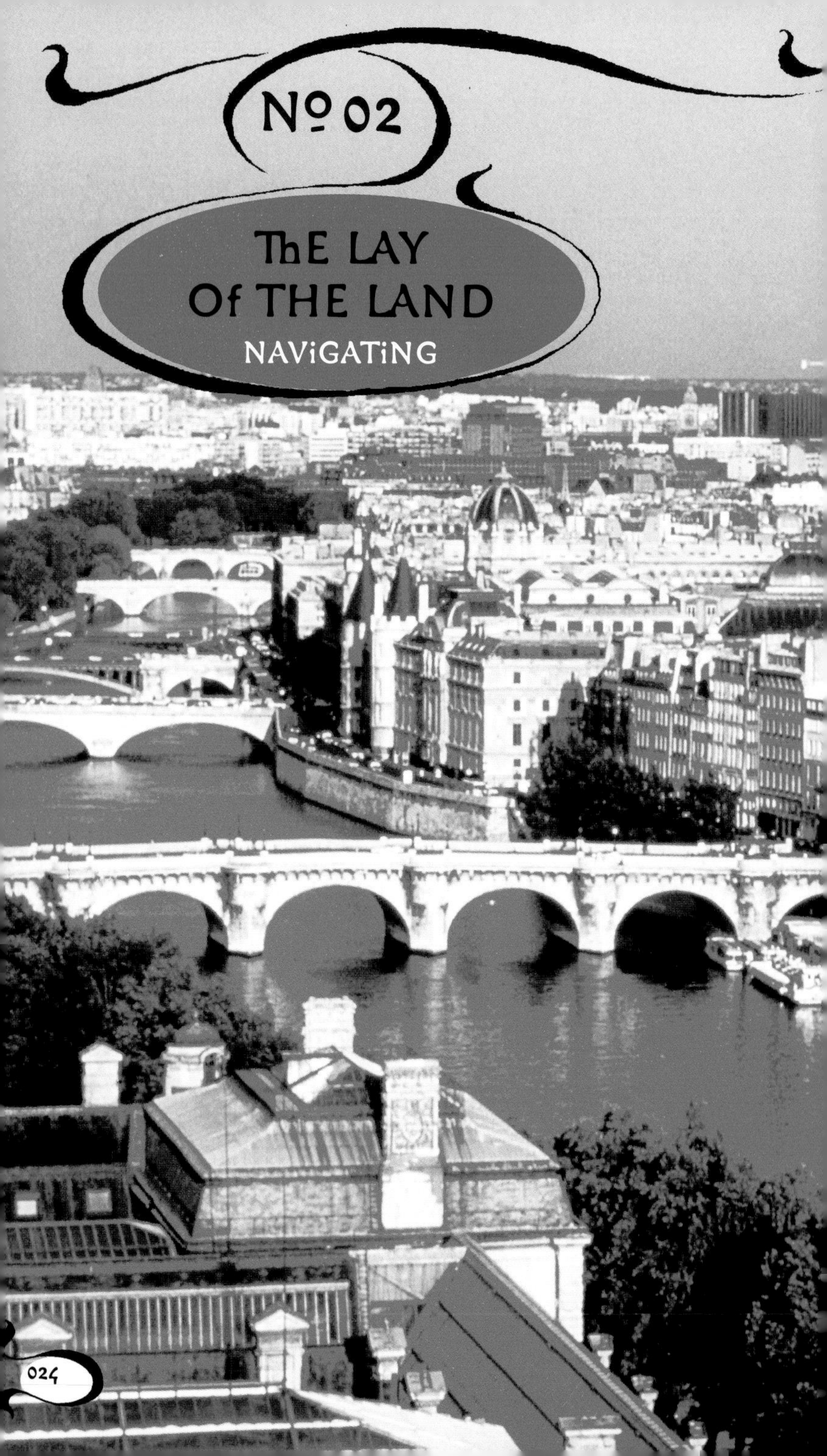

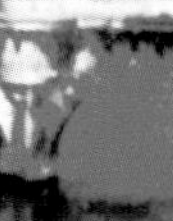

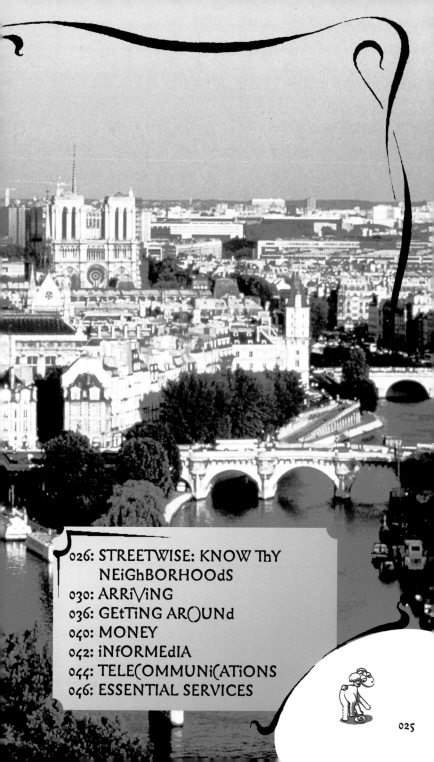

STREETWiSE: kNOW ThY NEiGhBORHOOdS

Paris is in the center of the **Île-de-France**, a historic region which once belonged to the Capet family who, in 987, became the royal family of France. From the 15th century until the Revolution, the Île-de-France was a separate province of the country; but today this *appellation* basically refers to the city and its suburbs.

The River Seine bisects the Capital, creating the northern **Right Bank** (*Rive Droite*) and southern **Left Bank** (*Rive Gauche*). Parisians once had a strong sense of Right Bank and Left Bank living. The Left Bank (as the river flows) is more than a simple geographical position, it refers to a lifestyle that is traditionally more left-brained, intellectual and politically left than its neighbor. The Right, by contrast, represents the business community, and one feels as though here the emphasis should be on the word "bank," as in money.

Nowadays the division between Left and Right has blurred and, due to the rising cost of real estate, Parisians of either persuasion will live anywhere they can find affordable housing.

ARRONDiSSEMENtS & POST CODES

Paris is divided into 20 *arrondissements* which spiral like a snail's shell beginning from the Louvre Palace in the heart of the city. While these administrative districts don't correspond directly with individual neighborhoods, they are helpful in locating addresses. The *arrondissement* immediately follows every address listed in this guide.

Postcodes always begin with "75." If the postcode is 75001, the address is in the 1st *arrondissement;* if the code is 75020, it's in the 20th. And the 16th *arrondissement* is divided into two codes, 75016 and 75116.

ThE iSLANdS

Île de la Cité and adjacent Île Saint-Louis are the two small islands in the heart of Paris between the Left and Right banks.

Paris began on the Île de la Cité in the 1st century AD when the Romans established a regional capital there. Notre-Dame is here, along with Sainte-Chapelle and the Concièrgerie, both of which were part of the original Royal Palace.

QUARTIER LATIN & ST-GERMAIN

Since the founding of the Sorbonne in the 13th century, the Latin Quarter has been synonymous with university life and the lifestyle it engenders. The adjacent St-Germain-des-Prés quarter is crammed with restaurants, cafés, shops and entertainment venues.

MONTPARNASSE

Montparnasse was the turn-of-the-century capital of cubism. Its heydays long gone, the area has settled into a decent residential and entertainment area, punctuated by a very ugly skyscraper.

CHÂTELET & LES HALLES

The area around Place du Châtelet, once dominated by the powerful butchers' guilds, is now a busy commercial district that includes La Samaritaine department store and Hôtel de Ville (City Hall). Les Halles, a produce market for over 800 years, was razed in the 1960s to make room for the horrible, underground shopping mall that dominates the area today. We prefer the (above ground) sex shops on Rue St-Denis.

LE MARAIS

Part Jewish, part gay, the Marais is one of the most fashionable neighborhoods in town. The quartier remains riddled with small, ancient streets filled with cafés, bars, shops and sights.

BASTILLE

Due east of the Marais, this former blue-collar neighborhood has become a bastion of Parisian nightlife, with more restaurants and cafes per capita than any other district.

THE LOUVRE & ENVIRONS

The monarchy is long gone, but the architecture of this neighborhood has survived as a reminder of centuries of royal rule. Formerly the king's residence, the Louvre is now one of the largest and greatest museums in the world. The adjacent Jardin des Tuileries still provides a respite from the maddening Right Bank bustle.

CHAMPS-ELYSÉES & ThE 8tH ARRONDISSEMENT

Overwhelmed with fast-food and megastores, the Champs-Elysées has become something of an outdoor shopping mall. Still, you can't avoid this mythical avenue capped by the Arc de Triomphe. The 8th Arrondissement, by contrast, is the heart of *haute couture* and filled with elegant shops and art galleries.

LES GRANDS bOULEVARdS

Created in the 19th century, these broad streets from the Madeleine to the Bastille are home to the Opéra, theaters and some of the city's largest department stores.

THE 16tH ARRONdISSEMENT

Across the river from the Eiffel Tower, the 16th is a rich residential area with a wealth of museums, banks and expensive hotels. There's a high concentration of art nouveau and art déco buildings here too.

THE 7TH ARRONDISSEMENT

One of Paris's most prestigious addresses, the 7th is an elegant area dotted with government ministries, embassies, antique shops, and lots of beautiful private homes. The Eiffel Tower is here too, along with Les Invalides and the Musée d'Orsay.

MONTMARTRE

Known for its village charm, and its overdose of tourists, Montmartre is a hillfull of lyrical, winding streets that work their way up to the landmark Sacré-Coeur Basilica. Just below, neon lights alert punters to the sex and commercialism of Pigalle.

THE GRAND BIBLIOTHÈQUE & THE 13TH

The soon-to-be-gentrified 13th is home to the city's largest Chinatown, set amongst bleak 1960s apartment buildings, and the new Bibliothèque Nationale François Mitterand.

THE NATION & VINCENNES

Place de la Nation is a grand open space that's an infamous French Revolution-era guillotine site. Nearby are some interesting museums and the Parc de Vincennes, a vast green that's home to a Buddhist temple, a zoo and the imposing Château de Vincennes.

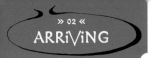

ARRiVING

BY PLANE

Paris is served by two major and two minor airports, all of which have good public transport links to the city center.

ROISSY-CHARLES-DE-GAULLE (CDG)

19 Miles (30 km) North of Paris
Tel. *01.48.62.22.80 (English)*
www.parisairports.com

Paris' smoke-filled main airport is a decent place to land. Signage is abundant, services are plentiful, and luggage carts are free. Getting into the city is relatively cheap and quick, providing you don't travel during rush hours (7-10am and 4-7pm). There are two terminals, the second of which is divided into five sections: 2A, 2B, 2C, 2D and 2F. Bureaux de Change, located near the exit on the arrivals level, are open daily from 630am to 1030pm. There is also a 24-hour cash exchange machine.

A bus connects Roissy-Charles-de-Gaulle with Orly Airport every 20-30 minutes daily, from 6am to 11pm. The journey takes about an hour. Taxi between the two airports is about €46.

By Taxi Except during rush hours, when the RER rules (see below), a taxi is the quickest way to your destination. It's also the most convenient, especially when you have big bags in tow. Well-marked taxi queues are located outside each terminal. The fare to central Paris ranges from €38-€61, depending on traffic. Big bags and little dogs cost an additional 80¢ each. A €2 tip is normal.

GOiNG	TO TOWN
Metered Taxi	€36–€50
RER-B	€7.70
Shuttle Van	€15-€20
Air France Bus	€10-€11.50
RoissyBus	€8
Limousine	€100-€250

By RER-B RER (tel. 01.53.90.20.20) is terrific because it lets you avoid the ubiquitous road traffic. However, trains come with their own hassles. There are two stations—one in Terminal 1 and another in Terminal 2—to which you may have to travel, on a free shuttle bus. Once in the city center you'll either have to flag down a cab, or schlep your bags onto the Métro to reach your final destination

(see the public transport map on the inside back cover of this book). The most convenient city-center RER stations are Gare du Nord (10th) and Châtelet (1st). Watch your bags, as thieves have been known to prey on jet-lagged tourists. Trains depart every 10-20 minutes from about 5am to midnight. Travel time is 45 minutes.

By Shuttle Van Airport Shuttle (tel. 01.34.45.81.33) has a large fleet of 8 passenger vans offering door-to-door service between the airport and city. Service runs daily from 4am to 7pm and costs €19 per person; €15 each for two or more. **PariShuttle** (tel. 01.43.90.91.91) and **Airport Connection** (tel. 01.44.18.36.02) offer the same service for €23 per person; €15 each for two or more. The journey to central Paris takes between 30 and 90 minutes, depending on traffic. For trips back to the airport, it's best to reserve two days in advance.

By Air France Bus **Air France Buses** (tel. 01.41.56.89.00) connect the airport with Porte Maillot (17th) and Place Charles-de-Gaulle (8th). They depart from designated stops outside each terminal every 20 minutes between 550am and 11pm and take anywhere from 30 to 90 minutes, depending on traffic. Air France buses also run to Gare de Lyon (12th) and Gare Montparnasse (14th) daily, every 30 minutes from 7am-9pm. The fare is €10-€11.50.

By RoissyBus Operated by **RATP Public Transport** (tel. 01.48.04.18.24), the RoissyBus travels between Roissy Terminal 2 and the corner of Rue Scribe and Rue Auber, near Place de l'Opéra (9th). The bus departs every 15-20 minutes from 545am to 11pm, and travel time is between 30 and 90 minutes, depending on traffic. Pay upon boarding. The fare is €8.

By Limo Les Berlines de Paris (tel. 01.41.40.84.84) and **International Limousines** (tel. 01.53.81.14.14) provide various meet-and-greet services from the airport to the city center for €100–€250. All major credit cards are accepted.

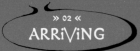

ORLY AIRPORT (ORY)

9.5 miles (15 kilometers) South of Paris.

Tel. *01.49.75.15.15 (6am-1130pm). wwwparisairports.com*

Orly has two terminals: Orly-Sud (South) and Orly-Ouest (West). Airport Bureaux de Change are open daily from 630am to 10pm.

A bus connects Orly Airport with Roissy-Charles-de-Gaulle (€11) every 20-30 minutes daily, from 6am to 9pm. The journey takes about an hour. Taxi between the two airports is about €46.

GOiNG TO TOWN

Metered Taxi	€15-€31
Orlyval & RER	€8.75
Shuttle Bus & RER	€5.50
Shuttle Van	€13-€23
Air France Bus	€7.50
OrlyBus	€5.50
Limousine	€100-€250

By Taxi Except during rush hours, when the RER rail flies past the competition (see below), taxi is the quickest way to your destination, taking about 30 minutes to the city center. It's the most convenient too, especially when you have big bags in tow. Well-marked taxi queues are located outside each terminal. The fare to central Paris will range from €15 to €31, depending on traffic. Big bags and little dogs cost an additional 80c each. A €2 tip is normal.

By Orlyval & RER The high-speed Orlyval rail line shuttles passengers to the Antony station on RER line B, from which you can reach central Paris. Service runs every 7 minutes, Mon-Fri 6am-10pm and Sat-Sun 7am-11pm. The two-part ride from the airport to the city center takes about 40 minutes and costs €8.75.

By ShuttleBus & RER A courtesy bus connects the airport with Pont de Rungis station on RER line C, where you can board a train to central Paris. Buses depart every 15 minutes from 530am to 1115pm. The two-part ride to the city center takes about an hour and costs €5.50.

By Shuttle Van Airport Shuttle (tel. 01.45.38.55.72) has a large fleet of 8-passenger vans offering door-to-door service between the airport and the city. Service runs daily from 6am to 6pm and costs €21 per person; €13 each for two or more.

archive photo

PariShuttle (tel. 01.43.90.91.91) and **Airport Connection** (tel. 01.44.18.36.02) offer the same service for €23 per person; €15 each for two or more. The journey to central Paris takes between 30 and 60 minutes, depending on traffic.

By Air France Bus Special **Air France Buses** (tel. 01.41.56.89.00) leave both Orly terminals every 12 minutes from 550am to 11pm. They stop at Gare Montparnasse (14th) and Invalides (7th). The fare is €7.50.

By Orlybus This bus offers direct service to the Denfert-Rochereau Métro/RER stop in the Montparnasse district (14th) and departs every 15 minutes daily, from 535am to 11pm. The trip takes about 45 minutes, and costs €5.40.

By Limo Les Berlines de Paris (tel. 01.41.40.84.84) and **International Limousines** (tel. 01.53.81.14.14) provide various meet-and-greet services from the airport to the city center for €100-€250. Major credit cards are accepted.

Pontoise-Cormeilles Airport

25 miles (40km) from Paris.

Tel. *01.30.31.13.25*

Smaller European carriers land at this small airport. Since there's no direct public transportation, most airlines offer bus transfers to a nearby train station from which you can reach the city.

Beauvais-Tillé Airport

44 miles (70km) from Paris

Ryan Air (tel. 03.44.11.41.41) and other budget airlines fly into this regional airstrip. A bus link (€8) connects to Porte Maillot (17th) in 60-90 minutes.

ARRIVING BY CAR

Driving in Paris is just as hairy as in any other major city; and parking is at least as difficult and expensive.

All roads into the Capital lead to the *Périphérique*, a "ring road" that circles Greater Paris and connects to *portes* (gates) into the city center.

Few hotels offer on-site parking. Parking meters have been replaced on most streets by pay-and-display machines (*horodateurs*), which accept only cards ("Paris Carte") that are available from tabacs (shops licensed to sell cigarettes) in €10 and €30 denominations. Parking is usually free after 7pm during the week, all day on weekends, and throughout the entire month of August. Underground parking garages are abundant; most charge about €2.50 per hour and €12.50 to €25 per day.

See Chapter 11/Before You Go for more info on driving in Paris.

ARRIVING BY COACH

Paris-bound buses almost always terminate at the Gare Routière (20th) in northeastern Paris (M Gallieni). For English-language reservations call **Eurolines** (France tel. 08.36.69.52.52; UK tel. 01582/404511).

ARRIVING bY tRAiN

There are six train stations in Paris, all of which have excellent taxi, bus and Métro connections (*see the transport map on the inside back cover*). Pulling into Paris under the metal hooded roofs of the Gare du Nord, Gare de Lyon or Gare Saint-Lazare is an emotional Old World experience. But reality checks-in fast and furious once you get swept up by the commuter crowds. There are few baggage trolleys, but porters with large carts can sometimes be found (€1 per bag). Major train stations all offer currency exchange services and transport information centers.

GETTiNG AR()UNd

The Métro, buses and RER trains are all run by RATP (*Régie Autonome des Transports Parisiens*). Paris and its suburbs are divided into five travel zones—you pay for each zone you cross. Most visitors usually only travel within zones 1 and 2, which cover the city center.

Métro and bus tickets cost the same flat fee per ride, no matter how far you go. RER is cheapest within the two central zones, then increases the farther you go from the center. Single tickets are sold at Métro stations and from bus drivers. Hold on to your ticket for the entire journey as you may be stopped by a controller.

Several money-saving options are available from most Métro station ticket booths:

If you're staying in the city for a few days, it makes sense to buy a ***Carnet*** of 10 tickets. It costs about €10 and is available at Métro stations, tourist offices and tabacs.

A weekly pass, called ***"Carte Orange Semaine,"*** is an even more economical way to go. The card is valid for unlimited travel in the city center from Monday to Sunday. These cards expire at the end of each weekend, no matter what day you began to use them. You'll need a wallet-size photo for it, but there are photo booths near the ticket office in most stations. Write your card number on the magnetized ticket.

Multi-day ***Paris Visite*** passes, offering unlimited travel on Métro, RER and buses, are also available from Métro stations. But unless you travel a lot in a very short amount of time, they offer very little value for the money.

Public transport prices usually rise slightly each July or August.

BY BUS

Although Paris' bus system is comprehensive, service remains at the mercy of the city's famously dense traffic. Most buses operate Monday to Saturday, from about 6am to 1230am, with limited service on Sundays and holidays. When standing at a bus stop, signal the driver that you want to be picked up. Either pay upon entering, flash your *carte orange*, or stamp your ticket in the machine.

Routes can be confusing. Get a free bus map from the tourist office or try to decipher the route diagram at each bus stop. When you're not in a hurry to get anywhere, bus riding is a great, budget sightseeing adventure.

Like the Métro, regular bus service stops before 1am, after which **night bus** (*Noctambus*) service kicks-in. Night buses have different routes and numbers from their daytime counterparts and most depart only once an hour from the hub on Avenue Victoria, by Châtelet-Hôtel de Ville (4th). You can't miss it, just look for the mob.

BY MÉTRO

Opened on July 19, 1900, the Paris subway has grown into one of the most extensive underground networks in the world. The *Métropolitain* system has 124 miles (199 km) of track along 15 lines and 368 stations. No building in Paris is more than 500 meters from a Métro station. There is a Métro map on the inside back cover of this book.

Trains run every few minutes, daily, from about 6am to 1230am. Exact closing times vary at each station and "last-train" times are posted at Métro entrances. Tickets can be purchased from the station ticket window or from coin-operated machines nearby. Hold on to your ticket throughout the ride in case you run into a controller. Navigate your way around the Métro by identifying line numbers and termination points, i.e. #4: *Direction Porte de Clignancourt* or, in the opposite direction, *Direction Porte d'Orléans.* Look for orange signs marked "*correspondance*" when transferring between lines. "*Sortie*" means exit.

If by some odd chance a controller catches you without a ticket, remember to speak only English and that your name is Smith or Doe. You are not carrying any identification or money. Refuse to pay a fine on the spot (you forgot your wallet) and the controller will write you a ticket upon your promise to send payment in full.

Although the Métro is relatively safe, always be on the alert for pickpockets. It's the same old scam: somebody "accidentally" drops something in front of you while his or her partner pushes you from behind. Watch your ass.

BY RER

Réseau Express Régional (RER) is basically a suburban train line that moves below ground when it reaches central Paris. Because it has fewer stations than the Métro, the RER moves faster through the city and is especially handy for longer trips, like to the airport, Versailles and Disneyland Paris.

There are five lines (A, B, C, D and E), most of which fork out into numerous directions. Video monitors on platforms indicate each train's destination; and also the length of each train (*train long* or *train court*). This will keep you from making a mad dash down the platform when a short train stops at the far end. Also, keep an eye on the blackboards to make sure that the train you're about to board will indeed stop where you want it to.

The fare for trips wholly within the city center is identical to the Métro and buses. If you plan to travel outside the central zone, an additional ticket is required. Check the zone map located in all RER stations, or ask a ticket-book clerk if an additional fare is necessary.

The RER operates daily from about 530am to 1am.

BY TAXI

Parisian taxis are no more expensive than in any large city, but they seem fewer and farther between. Theoretically, you can hail cabs in the street; when the roof light is lit, the car is available for hire. However, drivers often refuse to take passengers to destinations they're not in the mood to visit. They hate very short trips too.

Taxis line up at stands throughout the city. Alternatively, phone for a cab (or ask the restaurant to call for you) to pick you up. When phoning, expect to find €3-€5 already on the meter when the car arrives since taxis start the clock from the minute they set out to fetch you. Note that drivers will usually take no more than three passengers. For groups of four or five, call a company and tell the dispatcher what you need.

When crossing the *Périphérique* into the suburbs—and then only—the driver will set the meter to Fare C, a higher rate.

The digital display on the back ledge of each taxi indicates how many hours and minutes a driver has been on the job that day. Cabbies are limited by law to ten-hour work days.

TOP TAXI COMPANIES

Taxis Bleus
08.25.16.10.10

Taxis G7
01.47.39.47.39

Taxis 7000
01.42.70.00.42

BY BiCY(LE

Bike lanes are almost unheard of and cars are unyielding, so very few daredevils pedal around the city as a means of transportation. Things get less hectic in the outer suburbs, where wheeling through quaint lanes and massive parks is a thoroughly pleasant day's outing. The best rental places are:

Maison de la Roue Libre (RATP), Forum des Halles, 95-bis Rue Rambuteau, 1st (tel. 08.10.44.15.34). Touring bikes cost about €12 per day €18 for the weekend. You'll need ID and a credit card deposit. AE, MC, V. M Les Halles.

Paris-Vélo, 2 Rue du Fer-â-Moulin, 5th (tel. 01.43.37.59.22), rents mountain bikes and 21-speed touring models for about €15 per day. ID and deposit are required. They're open daily, 10am-1230pm and 2-6pm. MC, V. M Censier-Daubenton.

BY fOOt

Paris is not for windshield tourists; walking is the best way to discover the city's diverse neighborhoods. The city is big. It takes 60 to 90 minutes to walk from the Eiffel Tower to the Marais, depending on how many slow-moving "Meanderthals" are in your way.

Maps A good map is essential—even Parisians carry them. You can find excellent accordion-type maps and in-depth map-booklets at almost every newsstand. The best pocket-sized map is *Paris Par Arrondissement*, which has an excellent index and costs about €6.

MONEY

CHANGE MONEY?

Exchange places in the city center are almost as common as sidewalk dog doo, but commissions can be as shocking as the contents of an andouillette sausage. Don't be fooled by an attractive exchange rate; always ask what the *commission* is first and refuse to pay more than two percent. Most banks in the city center offer currency exchange services and the best rates.

But American Express and some private exchange offices are not far behind. Beware of late-opening exchange places, like **Chequepoint,** that charge nearly ten-percent commissions.

Banking Hours are usually Mon-Fri 9am-5pm, though many close for lunch between 1230pm and 230pm. A few banks are open Saturdays; and all are closed on public holidays and from noon the previous day. **Crédit Commercial de France** (see below) has 24-hour cash exchange machines that accept most major currencies.

American Express, 11 Rue Scribe, 9th (tel. 01.47.14.50.00). Open Mon-Fri 9am-430pm. **Bureau de Change** (tel. 01.47.77.77.07) open Mon-Fri 9am-630pm; Sat 9am-530pm; Sun 10am-5pm. M Opéra.

Barclays, 6 Rond Point des Champs-Elysées, 8th (tel. 01.44.95.13.80). Open Mon-Fri 915am-430pm. M Franklin D Roosevelt.

Chequepoint, 150 Ave. des Champs-Elysées, 8th (tel. 01.42.56.48.63). Open nonstop. M Charles de Gaulle-Etoile.

Citibank, 125 Ave. des Champs-Elysées, 8th. (tel. 01.53.23.33.60). Open Mon-Fri 10am-6pm. M Charles de Gaulle-Etoile.

Crédit Commercial de France (CCF), 28 Rue de Rivoli, 4th (tel. 01.44.54.58.20). Open Mon-Fri 9am-5pm. M St-Paul. **Branch** 103 ave. des Champs-Elysées, 8th (tel. 01.40.70. 30.70), open 9am-430pm. M Georges V.

Thomas Cook, 52 Ave. des Champs-Elysées, 8th (tel. 01.42.89.80.33). Open daily 820am-1030pm. M Franklin D Roosevelt. Also at the following train stations:
Gare d'Austerlitz (tel. 01.53.60.12.97), open daily 715am-845pm;

Gare Montparnasse (tel. 01.42.79.03.88), open daily 8am-655pm (until 8pm in summer); **Gare St-Lazare** (tel. 01.43.87.72.51), open daily 8am-7pm; **Gare du Nord** (tel. 01.42.80.11.50), open daily 615am-1125pm; **Gare de l'Est** (tel. 01.42.09.51.97), open Mon-Sat 645am-950pm, Sun 645am-650pm; **Gare de Lyon** (tel. 01.43.41.52.70), open daily 7am-1030pm.

TiPPiNG

The French are the worst tippers in the western world. That's why they love Americans. Here is the rule of thumb: in restaurants, bars and taxis, just round-up the bill a euro or two.

ATMs

There is absolutely no need to carry a bundle of cash when traveling to Paris, or any other major European city for that matter. In fact, you can travel here without a penny in your pocket and obtain all the dough you need from hundreds of ATMs that work seamlessly with banks around the globe. Connected to the Cirrus and Plus networks, Paris' cash machines allow 24-hour access to your accounts and offer excellent midpoint exchange rates. Your bank will charge between $1 and $3 (or £1-£3) for each withdrawal. Almost half of the city's ATMs also accept Visa or MasterCard (make sure you have a PIN).

ViSA LA FRANCE

Credit cards are widely accepted in the city's restaurants, hotels and shops, and often the exchange rate is far superior to what you'd get from banks when trading cash. Cash advances on your Visa and MasterCard can be obtained from most banks.

TRAVELERS ChEQUES

Travelers cheques are obsolete. You don't use them at home, so why embarrass yourself with these clumsy dinosaurs when you're away? Any company claiming their cheques are as good as cash is lying. Even the tellers at **American Express** may refuse to exchange *their own* checks without your passport in tow. Stick to ATMs and credit cards. If you still insist on giving interest-free loans to multinational companies, you'll find the best exchange rates at American Express, 11 Rue Scribe, 9th (tel. 01.47.14.50.00) M Opéra, where checks from all issuers are exchanged commission-free. Some restaurants and many hotels will exchange traveler's cheques, but their rates are always much worse than banks.

WhEN ALL ELSE FAiLS

Western Union Money Transfer, CCF Change, 4 Rue du Cloître-Notre-Dame, 4th (tel. 01.46.33.80.22). Open daily 9am-5pm. M Cité. 48 post offices also provide Western Union services, call (tel. 08.25.00.98.98) for details.

What's a euro worth?
For today's exchange rates, check-out the Avant-Guide Cyber Supplement at **www.avantguide.com**

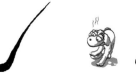

iNfORMEdIA

The www.avantguide.com CyberSupplement is the best source for happenings in Paris during your stay.

Once in the city, head to the nearest newsstand, stock-up on the city's listings magazines, and check out the surprisingly lean English-language mediascape.

Pariscope, published Wednesdays, is an indispensable listings magazine offering a comprehensive inventory of current cultural events. Unfortunately it's all in French, except for the last few pages which are prepared in English by Time Out magazine. It's available at newsstands throughout the city.

Novamagazine, a French-language monthly, has the Capital's most avant bar and club listings.

Time Out Paris Free Guide, published quarterly, is an excellent cultural update. It's distributed in hotels, bars and shops frequented by Anglophones.

Paris Voice is a decent arts and entertainment monthly that usually has a juicy nugget or two tossed into an otherwise lackluster mix of upcoming cultural events. **FUSAC** (France-USA Contacts) is a free fortnightly, jam-packed with English-language classified ads offering everything from travel tickets and appliances to apartment rentals and jobs. Both magazines are available at bookshops and bars around town.

Of all the city's newsagents, none tops **OFR Systeme,** 30 Rue Beaurepaire, 10th (tel. 01.42. 45.72.88), for its huge selection of national and international newspapers and magazines. They're open Mon-Fri 10am-7pm, but close for lunch at a time which varies slightly from day to day(!). M République. **WH Smith,** 248 Rue de Rivoli, 1st (tel. 01.44.77.88.99), also has a great selection. They're open Mon-Sat 930-7pm, and Sun 1pm-7pm. M Concorde.

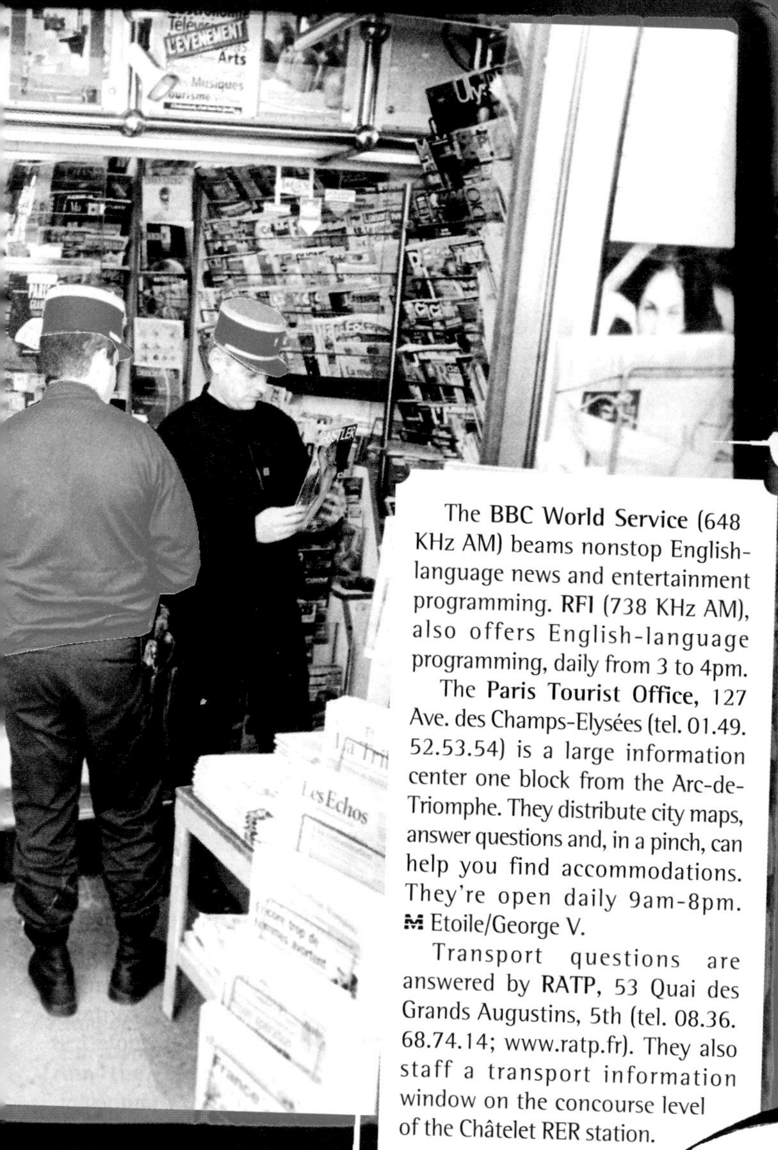

The **BBC World Service** (648 KHz AM) beams nonstop English-language news and entertainment programming. **RFI** (738 KHz AM), also offers English-language programming, daily from 3 to 4pm.

The **Paris Tourist Office,** 127 Ave. des Champs-Elysées (tel. 01.49.52.53.54) is a large information center one block from the Arc-de-Triomphe. They distribute city maps, answer questions and, in a pinch, can help you find accommodations. They're open daily 9am-8pm. M Etoile/George V.

Transport questions are answered by **RATP,** 53 Quai des Grands Augustins, 5th (tel. 08.36.68.74.14; www.ratp.fr). They also staff a transport information window on the concourse level of the Châtelet RER station.

TELECOMMUNICATIONS

TELEPHONES

French phone numbers have ten digits. Those in Paris begin with 01. Cell phones start with 06. When phoning France from abroad leave off first "0." Free or discounted calls begin with 08.

There are two kinds of **pay phones.** The first (and more rare) accepts coins, while the other operates exclusively with credit cards and *Télécarte* phonecards, available from post offices and tabacs in various denominations. Cardphones are especially handy if you want to call abroad as you don't have to continuously feed in euros. You can change cards in the middle of a call.

Paris phone information, a.k.a. **directory inquiries** (tel. 12) is free from public phones. For the Operator, dial (tel. 13). You can often get an English-speaking operator.

The **international operator** for the UK is (tel. 00.33.12.44); for the US (tel. 00.33.12.1) .

For **international calls,** dial 00 followed by the country code (US/Canada, 1; Britain, 44; Australia, 61; Republic of Ireland, 353; New Zealand, 64; South Africa, 27), the city code, and the telephone number of the person you wish to call.

AT&T USA Direct (tel. 0.800.99.00.11); **MCI** (tel. 0.800.99.00.19); **Sprint** (tel. 0.800.99.00.87); **Canada Direct** (tel. 0.800.99.00.16).

Be forewarned that hotel surcharges on both long-distance and local calls can be astronomical. Think about using a public pay phone in the lobby.

Cell phones in Paris, as in the whole of Europe, operate on a GSM frequency that is not compatible with the American system. You can rent a top-of-the-line Motorola cell phone in Paris and pay only for usage, which is about 95¢ per minute for local calls. Contact **Rent A Cell Express,** 116-bis Ave. des Champs Elysées, suite 440 (tel. 01.53.93.78.00). They will even deliver the phone to you.

COMPUTERS / iNTERNEt

America Online (access tel. 0.826.026.000; service tel. 08.92.02.03.04; www.aol.fr); **CompuServe** (access tel. 01.72.25.00.00; service tel. 03.21.13.49.49; www.compuserve.fr).

Rendez-Vous Toyota, 79 Ave. des Champs Elysées, 8th (tel. 01.56.89.29.79) is a particularly well-located automobile showroom that doubles as a free-of-charge Web zone. M George V. **Café Orbital,** 13 Rue de Médicis, 6th (tel. 01.43.25.76.77), in the Latin Quarter, is another cyber spot with Web access that's the choice of Paris' student digerati. M Luxembourg.

Rentals Laptops and accessories can be rented from **A'Loc Informatique,** 141 Blvd. Montparnasse, 6th (tel. 01.53. 10.09.40). Souped-up Pentiums cost about €72 for two days. M Vavin.

ESSENTiAL SERViCES

CREDIT CARDS

American Express	(tel. 01.47.77.70.00)
Diners Club	(tel. 08.20.82.05.36)
MasterCard	(tel. 08.00.90.13.87)
Visa	(tel. 08.36.69.08.80)

DENTISTS/DOCTORS **Centre Médical Europe,** 44 Rue d'Amsterdam, 9th (tel. 01.42.81.93.33). M St-Lazare. A variety of practitioners under one roof charging minimal fees. Appointments Mon-Fri 8am-7pm, Sat 8am-6pm.

DRUG STORES Unlike their American counterparts, French pharmacists can bandage wounds and diagnose minor illnesses. **Pharmacie les Champs,** 84 Ave. des Champs-Elysées, 8th (tel. 01.45.62. 02.41) fills prescriptions nonstop, including holidays. M George V. **Pharmacie Européenne de la Place de Clichy,** 6 Place de Clichy, 9th (tel. 01.48.74.65.18) is also open 24/seven. M Place de Clichy.

EMERGENCIES **Police** (tel. 17); **Ambulance** (tel. 15); **Fire** (tel. 18).

EYEWEAR/CONTACT LENSES New lenses in a hurry? Phone, or ask at your hotel for the nearest branch of the ubiquitous **Alain Afflelou,** 104 Ave. des Champs-Elysées, 8th (tel. 01.43.59.87.99) or **Lissac,** 207 Blvd. St-Germain, 6th (tel. 01.45.48.16.76), two of the largest optometry chains in Paris. They stock hundreds of styles and can have prescription glasses ready within the hour. **SOS Optique** (tel. 01.48.07.22.00) is an ultra-handy 24-hour repair service that makes house calls.

EMBASSIES/CONSULATES
(See Chapter 11/Foreign Essentials for French embassies abroad)

Australian Embassy, 4 Rue Jean-Rey, 15th (tel. 01.40.59.33.00). Open Mon-Fri 9am-6pm; Visas Mon-Fri 915am-1215pm. M Bir-Hakeim.

British Embassy, 35 Rue du Fbg-St-Honoré, 8th (tel. 01.44.51.31.00). Open Mon-Fri 930am-1pm and 230-6pm. M Concorde. **Consulate/Visas** 18-bis Rue d'Anjou, 8th (tel. 01.44. 51.33.01 or 01.44.51.33.02). Open Mon-Fri 230-530pm. M Concorde/Madeleine.

Canadian Embassy, 35 Ave. Montaigne, 8th (tel. 01.44.43.29.00). Open Mon-Fri 9am-noon and 2-5pm. **Consulate/Visas** 37 Ave. Montaigne (tel. 01.44.43.29.16). Open Mon-Fri 830-11am. M Franklin D Roosevelt.

Irish Embassy, 4 Rue Rude, 16th (tel. 01.44.17.67.00). Open Mon-Fri 930am-noon; by phone Mon-Fri 930am-1pm and 230-530pm. M Charles de Gaulle-Etoile.

New Zealand Embassy, 7ter Rue Léonard de Vinci, 16th (tel. 01.45. 01.43.43). Open Mon-Fri 9am-1pm. M Victor-Hugo.

South African Embassy, 59 Quai d'Orsay, 7th (tel. 01.53.59.23.23). Open by appointment Mon-Fri 830am-515pm. M Invalides.

US Embassy, 2 Ave. Gabriel, 8th (tel. 01.43.12.22.22). Open by appointment Mon-Fri 9am-6pm. M Concorde. **Consulate/Visas** 2 Rue St-Florentin, 1st (tel. 01.43.12.22.22). Open Mon-Fri 845-11am; Passport service Mon-Fri 9am-3pm. M Concorde.

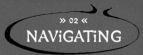

FILM PROCESSING/PHOTOGRAPHY There is an abundance of 30-minute developing spots in and around the Champs Elysées and other high-volume tourist areas. If you can't find a speed-processor on your block, try **Kodak Express**, 2, rue Marsoulan, 12th (tel. 01.43.07.67.08) M Picpus.

For **professional service** and equipment head to **Hasselblad France**, 5 Pass Piver, 11th (tel. 01.43.55.16.26).

LAUNDRY/DRY CLEANING In some neighborhoods there are launderettes and dry cleaners on nearly every block. Ask at your hotel or check the yellow pages under *laveries* and *blanchisseries.*

LOST PROPERTY If you lost it in Paris, it's probably gone forever. Cross your fingers and visit **Bureau des Objets Trouvés**, 36 Rue des Morillons, 15th (tel. 01.55.76.20.20). M Convention. They're open Mon, Wed and Fri 830am-5pm; Tues and Thurs 830am-8pm.

PHARMACIES See Drug Stores above.

POLICE **Emergencies** (tel. 17) from any phone; no money is needed. For other matters phone the **Préfecture de Police** (tel. 01.53.73.53.73).

POSTAL SERVICES/EXPRESS MAIL The **Main Post Office**, 52 Rue du Louvre, 75001 Paris (tel. 01.40.28.20.00) is open nonstop. M Les Halles/Louvre-Rivoli. To mail letters or packages, queue at a window marked *Envoi De Lettres Et Paquets* or *Toutes Opérations.* Most local post offices are open Mon-Fri 8am-7pm, Sat 9am-noon. You can also buy stamps at the tabac shops you see all over town. **DHL** 59 Ave. d'léna, 16th (tel. 08.00.20.25.25 or 01.45.01.91.00); **Federal Express**, 63 Blvd. Haussmann, 9th (tel. 01.40.06.90.16); **UPS**, 107 Rue Réaumur, 2nd (tel. 08.00.87.78.77).

TIME Paris is one hour ahead of Greenwich Mean Time (GMT+1); 6 hours ahead of US Eastern Standard Time. **Daylight Savings Time** moves the clock ahead one hour, from the last Sunday in March through the last Saturday in September.

TUXEDO/COSTUME RENTAL **Les Deux Oursons**, 106 Blvd. de Grenelle, 15th (tel. 01.45.75.10.77) charges about €65 to rent a basic tux. They've got costumes and accessories too. M La Motte Picquet Grenelle.

VIDEO PAL standard. English-language tapes, discs, and multi-format machines can be rented from **Prime Time**, 24 Rue Mayet, 6th (tel. 01.40.56.33.44) M Duroc.

No 03

Where to Stay

Sleeping

Compared to most other European cities Paris offers an unrivaled selection of hotels in all price ranges. Fierce competition not only boosts quality, it keeps a ceiling on prices. And it's just part of French nature to keep even low-rent places looking pretty good—even the standard of bed linen is consistently high.

The long arm of French bureaucracy reaches deep into Hoteland with long lists of criteria for categorizing establishments according to a "star" system—the more stars, the greater the services and facilities. But that doesn't necessarily mean a better hotel, as cleanliness, location, functionality and decor have zero influence with the *governmentos* (unless you bribe them, we suspect).

The hotels in this guide represent the very best in each price category that Paris has to offer. Every establishment meets our strict criteria for service, facilities and value. All offer something special in the way of local color and character. And we have gone to great lengths to flush out the very best of the city's budget hotels.

All rates include service and VAT, but a minuscule *taxe de séjour* of around €1 per day may be added to your bill. When breakfast is not included in room rates, it's usually better to forego the hotel's overpriced offering and head out to a local café.

The Truth About Pricing

The "rack" is the highest rate that a hotel charges for its rooms. These are the prices printed on the hotels' rate cards, and it is the rate usually quoted when you simply phone and ask "how much do you charge?" Because of travel agent commissions, discount reservations services (see below), and corporate and club discounts, most hotel rooms are sold for substantially less than rack—sometimes more than 50%. Rates are most elastic in August, and on weekends throughout the year. A stay of one week or more is also worthy of a reduction. The best way to reserve a hotel room is to phone, fax or email and ask for their "best corporate rate." To compare prices and save time, contact several hotels concurrently and then immediately cancel the ones that don't work for you.

Apartment Rentals

Several companies rent apartments to short-term visitors when their owners are away. These range from corporate-owned flats to highly-personalized places belonging to vacationing locals. Amenities vary, but every apartment is carefully pre-screened and priced far below a comparable hotel room.

Contact **Paris Appartements Services**, 20, rue Bachaumont, 2nd (tel. 01.40.28.01.28; fax 01.40.28.92.01; http://www.paris-appartements-services.fr) or **France Appartements**, 97 Ave. des Champs Elysées, 8th (tel. 01.56.89.31.00; fax. 01.56.89.31.01; www.rentapart.com).

HOtELS bY AREA & PR*CE

The cost (*) reflects the average price of a double room.

*	= Under €60
**	= €65-€100
***	= €110-€210
****	= €265-€400
*****	= Over €475

Page		Price
	1st Arrondissement	
062	Britannique	***
057	Costes	****
070	Hôtel du Cygne	**
053	Ritz	*****
	2nd Arrondissement	
070	Baudelaire Opéra	**
077	Sainte-Marie	*
	3rd Arrondissement	
061	Pavillon de la Reine	****
	4th Arrondissement	
063	Hôtel Saint-Louis Marais	***
072	Hôtel Saint-Merry	**
076	Jeanne d'Arc	*
068	Jeu de Paume	***
079	MIJE le Fauconnier	*
072	Place des Vosges	**
072	Sansonnet	**
073	Septième Art	**
	5th Arrondissement	
075	Esmeralda	*
065	Hôtel de Notre-Dame	***
067	Jardins du Luxembourg	***
	6th Arrondissement	
062	Angleterre	***
063	Artus Hotel	***
062	Hôtel de l'Abbaye	***
078	Hôtel de Nesle	*
074	Hôtel du Globe	**
067	L'Hôtel	***
058	Lutétia	****
059	Relais Christine	****
	7th Arrondissement	
071	Hôtel d'Orsay	*
065	Hôtel Duc de Saint-Simon	***
068	Hôtel Thoumieux	***
060	Montalembert	****

Page		Price
	8th Arrondissement	
054	Bristol	*****
054	Crillon	*****
055	Four Seasons George V	*****
056	Plaza Athénée	*****
	9th Arrondissement	
073	Hôtel Langlois	**
	10th Arrondissement	
068	Libertel Terminus Nord	***
	11th Arrondissement	
076	Mondia	*
	12th Arrondissement	
069	Le Pavillon Bastille	***
	14th Arrondissement	
070	Istria	**
	16th Arrondissement	
059	K Palace	**
064	L'Hotel Pergolèse	***
060	Raphaël	****
	18th Arrondissement	
074	Ermitage	**
079	Le Village	*
077	Prima Lepic	*
069	Terrass Hôtel	***
	20th Arrondissement	
079	Auberge de Jeunesse d'Artagnan	*

VERY EXPENSIVE

Hôtel Ritz

15 Place Vendôme (1 st). **Tel.** *01.43.16.30.30.* **Fax** *01.43.16.36.68. www.ritzparis.com* **Rate** *€580–€675 single/double. Suites from €800.* **Parking** *€34 per day. AE, DC, MC, V.* **M** *Opéra/Concorde*

Opened in 1896, the Ritz is the epitome of a romanticized version of *fin-de-siècle* Paris. Swathed in heavy silk and tapestries, and dripping with crystal chandeliers, the city's ultimate palace hotel is so over-the-top flamboastful that it's almost a parody of itself. Even the in-house fitness center sports a couple of frescos. Still, it's hard to argue with a hotel whose name has become synonymous with "swank." Guestrooms are fabulously intimate and the suites, many of which are named after former residents such as F. Scott Fitzgerald, Marcel Proust and Coco Chanel (who died here) are positively awestriking. Start the day with breakfast by the pool, where regulars swear by the scrambled eggs and french fries. And if you're lucky enough to get a room during Fashion Week, install yourself in the hotel's Bar Vendôme, which transforms itself into the event's unofficial headquarters. The lack of a lobby discourages sightseers, but you can get a peek at the over-privileged when you visit the famous Hemingway Bar, which the writer claimed to have "liberated" in 1944 (*see* chapter 9/Nightlife).

175 Rooms: *Air conditioning, cable TV, VCR (on request), telephone, modular jacks, fax (on request), hairdryer, minibar, 24-hour room service, concierge, restaurant, 2 bars, business facilities, fitness center, swimming pool.*

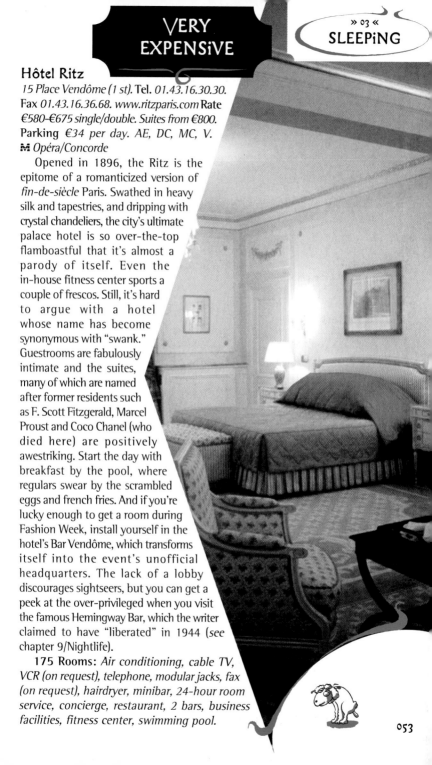

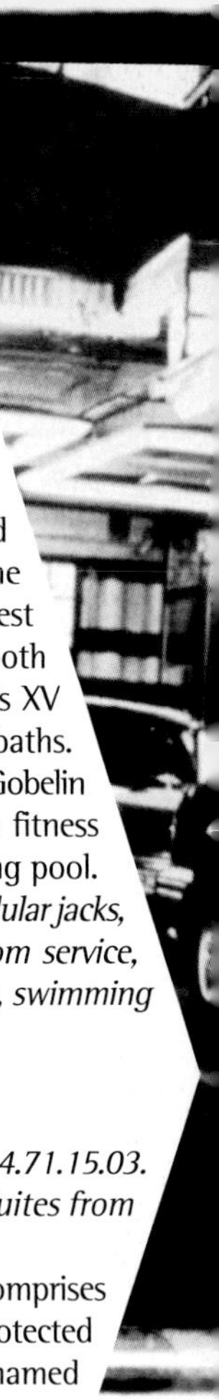

Le Bristol

112 Rue du Faubourg Saint Honoré (8th). **Tel.** *01.53.43.43.00.* **Fax** *01.53.43.43.01. www.hotel-bristol.com.* **Rate** *€580-€730 single/double. Suites from €750. Free parking. AE, DC, MC, V.* M *Miromesnil*

Members of the New Guard looking for privacy, and those from the Establishment who don't want to encroach on friends, hole up at the Bristol, long the bastion of privilege. This is where thick-walleted globobosses stay, along with entertainment-industry *arrivistes* looking for opulent anonymity. Although it's situated on the exclusive Faubourg St-Honoré, the Bristol exudes a quiet elegance, as opposed to the over-the-top gaudiness of some of its rivals. Behind the understated facade is a luxurious hotel that ranks amongst the best in Paris. And it should, since it's the most expensive. Rooms are both spacious and elegant. Some are decorated with authentic Louis XV and Louis XVI furniture, and all come with lavish marble-clad baths. The Bristol's public areas are filled with Old Master paintings, rich Gobelin tapestries and sumptuous Persian carpets. And the in-house fitness center comes with a terrific, glass-enclosed rooftop swimming pool.

173 Rooms: *Air-conditioning, cable TV, VCR, telephone, modular jacks, internet access, fax, hairdryer, minibar, radio, 24-hour room service, concierge, restaurant, bar, business facilities, fitness center, swimming pool.*

Hôtel de Crillon

10 Place de la Concorde (8th). **Tel.** *01.44.71.15.01.* **Fax** *01.44.71.15.03. www. crillon-paris.com.* **Rate** *€480-€855 single/double. Suites from €945. Free parking. AE, DC, MC, V.* M *Concorde*

Majestically lording over Place de la Concorde, the Crillon comprises two opulent, 18th-century palaces that are now government-protected national treasures. One of the original *grands appartements* is named for Marie-Antoinette, who took singing lessons there. The Crillon is the best place in Paris to pretend you're royalty, as many of the politicians who stay here are inclined to do. A fabulously marbled lobby leads into lavishly decorated guestrooms crammed with Directoire and Rococo antiques. There are plenty of gold fittings, and crystal-and-gilt wall sconces as well. And it doesn't hurt that the whole of central Paris is within walking distance. If you've got the cash, reserve the Leonard Bernstein Suite where you can breakfast on a terrace with a view of the Champs-Elysées and the Eiffel Tower. Even if you don't stay here, it's worth popping in just to marvel at the sheer quantity of marble in the downstairs public areas and Les Ambassadeurs restaurant (see Chapter 8/Top Food).

147 Rooms: *Air-conditioning, cable TV, telephone, modular jacks, internet access, video rental, hairdryer, minibar, radio, 24-hour room service, concierge, bar, res-taurant, business facilities, fitness center, wheelchair access.*

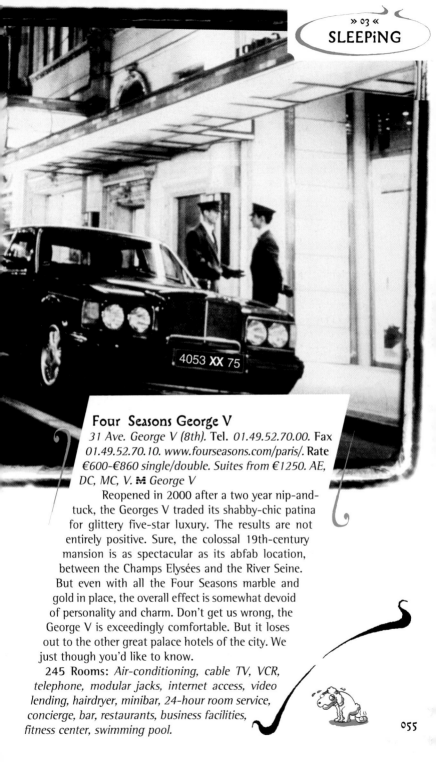

Four Seasons George V

31 Ave. George V (8th). Tel. *01.49.52.70.00.* Fax *01.49.52.70.10. www.fourseasons.com/paris/.* Rate *€600-€860 single/double. Suites from €1250. AE, DC, MC, V.* M *George V*

Reopened in 2000 after a two year nip-and-tuck, the Georges V traded its shabby-chic patina for glittery five-star luxury. The results are not entirely positive. Sure, the colossal 19th-century mansion is as spectacular as its abfab location, between the Champs Elysées and the River Seine. But even with all the Four Seasons marble and gold in place, the overall effect is somewhat devoid of personality and charm. Don't get us wrong, the George V is exceedingly comfortable. But it loses out to the other great palace hotels of the city. We just though you'd like to know.

245 Rooms: *Air-conditioning, cable TV, VCR, telephone, modular jacks, internet access, video lending, hairdryer, minibar, 24-hour room service, concierge, bar, restaurants, business facilities, fitness center, swimming pool.*

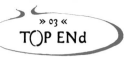

Hôtel Plaza Athénée

25 Ave. Montaigne (8th). Tel. 01.53.67.66.65. Fax 01.53. 67.66.66. www.plaza-athenee-paris.com. Rate €498-€720 single/double. Suites from €792. Parking 150F (€23) per day. AE, DC, MC, V. M *Alma-Marceau*

One of Paris's most *à la mode* hotels, the Plaza Athénée is where the fashion elite hole up when visiting the nearby *haute-couture* houses. Needless to say, bedrooms are faultlessly well-dressed with large, firm beds, executive-size desks, good lighting and quality art. Situated near the Champs Elysées, the hotel is also known for bullet service and buzzing public areas. Plenty of deals have been sealed at Le Régence, the hotel's Michelin two-star restaurant. In summer, the romantic, ivy clad courtyard becomes a social hub for chicly dressed ladies who lunch.

143 Rooms: *Air-conditioning, cable TV (some rooms have flat screen TVs), VCR, telephone, modular jacks, internet access, hairdryer, minibar, stereo with CD player, 24-hour room service, concierge, restaurant, bar, business facilities, fitness center.*

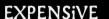

Hôtel Costes

239 Rue St. Honoré (1st). Tel. *01.42.44.50.00.* Fax *01.42.44.50.01.* Rate *€350-€700 single/double. Suites from €1200. Parking €20 per day. AE, DC, MC, V.* M *Tuileries*

Jean-Louis and Gilbert Costes' eponymous hotel is the hippest place in town. It's an ultra-trendy hotspot that's as intensively-designed as it is relentlessly marketed. At its core, the Costes is a beautiful boutique hotel that conjures up Napoléonic palaces for a decidedly music-video crowd. There always seem to be beautiful models running around, and most guests appear to be single. Children are discouraged. Guestrooms go for Baroque with rich bronze and blush tones and luxurious patterned fabrics dripping with brocade and fringe. And the bathrooms are truly extraordinary. Hotel Costes is the choice of rock royalty and the media elite (think Red Hot Chili Peppers and Wallpaper magazine). The hotel restaurant remains one of the city's premiere scene spots and is a great place to linger over a cocktail (*see* Chapter 8/Dining).

85 Rooms: *Air-conditioning, cable TV, VCR (on request), telephone, modular jacks, fax, hairdryer, minibar, radio, room service, concierge, restaurant, bar, fitness center, swimming pool, wheelchair access.*

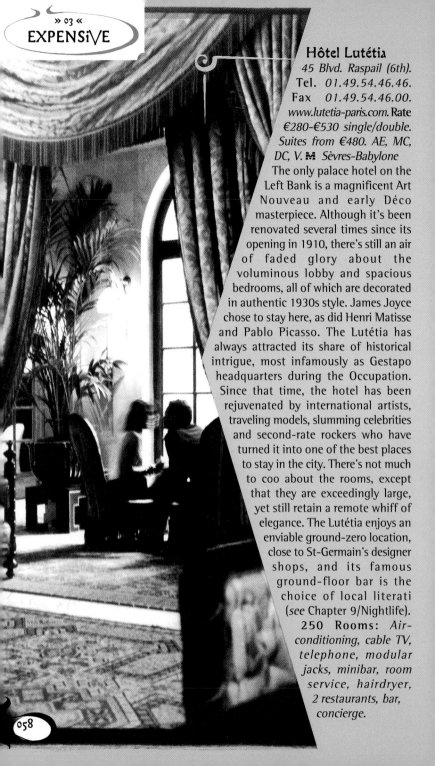

Hôtel Lutétia

45 Blvd. Raspail (6th). Tel. *01.49.54.46.46.* Fax *01.49.54.46.00. www.lutetia-paris.com.* Rate *€280-€530 single/double. Suites from €480. AE, MC, DC, V.* M *Sèvres-Babylone*

The only palace hotel on the Left Bank is a magnificent Art Nouveau and early Déco masterpiece. Although it's been renovated several times since its opening in 1910, there's still an air of faded glory about the voluminous lobby and spacious bedrooms, all of which are decorated in authentic 1930s style. James Joyce chose to stay here, as did Henri Matisse and Pablo Picasso. The Lutétia has always attracted its share of historical intrigue, most infamously as Gestapo headquarters during the Occupation. Since that time, the hotel has been rejuvenated by international artists, traveling models, slumming celebrities and second-rate rockers who have turned it into one of the best places to stay in the city. There's not much to coo about the rooms, except that they are exceedingly large, yet still retain a remote whiff of elegance. The Lutétia enjoys an enviable ground-zero location, close to St-Germain's designer shops, and its famous ground-floor bar is the choice of local literati (*see* Chapter 9/Nightlife).

250 Rooms: *Air-conditioning, cable TV, telephone, modular jacks, minibar, room service, hairdryer, 2 restaurants, bar, concierge.*

K Palace

81 Ave. Kléber (16th). Tel. *01.44.05.75.75.* Fax *01.44.05.74.74. www.Kpalace.net.* Rate *€300-€380 single/double. Suites from €460. Parking €16 per day. AE, DC, MC, V.* M *Trocadéro/Boissière*

Über-fashionable K Palace is the latest offering from the brothers Costes, Paris' hoteliers-to-the-stars. You can easily locate the entrance by the stylishly-dressed actor/model/doorman standing on the sidewalk. Inside is all about minimalist decor and maximalist prices. In the lofty lobby there are white walls, white furnishings, white flowers... everything seems to be white except the staff, who are dressed in black. Designed by celebrity architect Ricardo Bofill, the hotel's accommodations are like chic-simple film sets with lots of natural light and streamlined furnishings that make much ado about nothingness. Lay your passport and wallet on the dressing table and you have made an impossible mess. The fitness center includes a wonderful teak Jacuzzi with a view; but the small swimming pool is more about form than function.

83 Rooms: *Air-conditioning, cable TV, VCR (on request), telephone, modular jacks, fax (some), hairdryer, minibar, radio, room service, concierge, restaurant, bar, business facilities, fitness center.*

Hôtel Relais Christine

3 Rue Christine (6th). Tel. *01.40.51.60.80.* Fax *01.40.51.60.81. www.relais-christine.com.* Rate *€325-€425 single/double. Suites from €510. AE, DC, MC, V.* M *Odéon*

One of the first boutique hotels in the *Quartier Latin*, Relais Christine shares the elegant style and luxurious comfort of its sister hotel, Pavillon de la Reine (below). Much imitated but seldom bested, the hotel remains an oasis of tasteful good living between the Seine and Boulevard St-Germain. Built as a religious college and abbey, this 16th century mansion benefits from a bucolic garden and a rare sense of spaciousness in an area cluttered with narrow twisting streets. That goes for the unusually large guestrooms too, which are simply styled with rich upholsteries and mahogany antiques. The best ones have exposed ceiling beams and overlook the garden. Breakfast (included) is served in a wonderful stone vaulted dining room. A spa and fitness center occupies the 13th-century vaulted cellars.

51 Rooms: *Air conditioning, cable TV, telephone, modular jacks, hairdryer, minibar, room service, concierge, bar.*

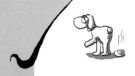

Le Montalembert

3 Rue Montalembert (7th). Tel. *01.45.49.68.68.* Fax *01.45.49.69.49. www.montalembert.com.* Rate *€820-€360 single/double. Suites from €480. AE, DC, MC, V.* M *Rue du Bac*

Grace Leo-Andrieu's sleekly avant Montalembert is the Left Bank's original choice for entertainment industry folk and fashion fiends. Behind a pretty Beaux Arts facade are 56 luxurious guestrooms dressed in one of two distinctive styles: traditional *à la* Louis-Philippe with beautiful inlaid wooden beds, or high tech with chrome and spotlights. Both are united by clean lines and deluxe extras that include Frette linens, marble bathrooms, and lots of detailed signature design elements. The lobby, bar and restaurant attract a regular smattering of celebs, some of whom are just popping down from their room to fetch a video from the hotel's extensive library. Montalembert is more sophisticated and stylish than the similarly-priced L'Hôtel Pont-Royal, next door; but you'll probably want to visit their legendary bar, once a favorite of Sartre, Sagan and Styron.

56 Rooms: *Air conditioning, cable TV, VCR, telephone, modular jacks, hairdryer, minibar, room service, concierge, restaurant, bar.*

Hôtel Raphaël

17 Ave. Kléber (16th). Tel. *01.53.64.32.00.* Fax *01.53.64.32.01. www.raphael-hotel.com.* Rate *€435-€520 single/double. Suites from €690. AE, DC, MC, V.* M *Kléber*

The consummate model of overstated luxe, the Raphaël attracts everyone from presidents and rock stars to old-money guests who, themselves, are not necessarily old. From the cozy red-velvet-and-wood-paneled bar to the turquoise-and-gold lounge, this is a beautiful hotel that is at once elegant and upbeat; cultivated and cool. Festooned with high-quality frescoes, delicately painted moldings and Louis XV furnishings, the hotel oozes with Old World charm that's frequently lacking in larger establishments. There's even an original Turner in the lobby. The huge bathrooms alone make the Raphaël one of the best places to stay in town. And if you're lucky enough to camp in their top suite (as did George Bush the elder and Lenny Kravitz), you'll be treated to a private garden with terrific views over Paris.

90 Rooms: *Air-conditioning, cable TV, VCR, telephone, modular jacks, hairdryer, minibar, 24-hour room service, concierge, restaurant, bar, business facilities.*

Pavillon de la Reine

28 Place des Vosges (3rd). Tel. *01.40.29.19.19.* Fax *01.40.29.19.20. www.pavillon-de-la-reine.com.* Rate *€335-€470 single/double. Suites from €520. Free parking. AE, DC, MC, V.* M *Bastille*

The ivy-covered Pavillon de la Reine wows with dramatic elegance and a perfect location, behind the romantic arches of Place des Vosges in the Marais. It's an ultra stylish, five-story mansion reconstructed from original 17th-century plans. Depending on whom you check-in with, the hotel can feel either amorous or clubby—the atmosphere is equally appealing to honeymooning couples or rockers like U2, who've been spotted roaming the halls. The hotel is fitted with *faux* Louis XIII furnishings, leather armchairs, working fireplaces and rich-toned fabrics. Guestrooms are beautifully bathed in warm colors and frequently include an ornate four-poster bed. The best are duplexes, with French windows that open onto a leafy courtyard. And breakfast is served in a historical vaulted cellar.

55 Rooms: *Air-conditioning, cable TV, telephone, modular jacks, hairdryer, minibar, radio, room service, concierge, bar.*

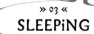

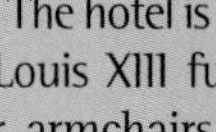

MOdERAtE

Hôtel de l'Abbaye

10 Rue Cassette (6th). **Tel.** *01.45.44.38.11.* **Fax** *01.45.48.07.86. www.Hotel-Abbaye.com.* **Rate** *€185-€292 single/double. Suites from €345. AE, MC, V.* **M** *Saint-Sulpice*

With tourism at its peak and religion on the outs, several former convents and abbeys have found new life cloistering weary travelers. Hôtel de l'Abbaye is one of the best of its kind; indeed, it's one of the very best small luxury hotels on the Left Bank. Guests pass through a stone-vaulted entrance into a gorgeous country-house environment designed with warm earth tones and stylishly rustic antiques. Standard guestrooms are equally inviting but are on the small side; a negative that's countered by a beautiful rear garden and spacious public areas offering several plush seating options. Rooms on the upper floors have exposed oak beams, while those below open onto the garden. Duplexes are larger, and each comes with a private terrace overlooking the rooftops of Paris.

46 Rooms: *Air-conditioning, flat-screen satellite TV, telephone, fax access, modular jacks, hairdryer, minibar, radio, room service, concierge, bar.*

Hôtel d'Angleterre

44 Rue Jacob (6th). **Tel.** *01.42.60.34.72.* **Fax** *01.42.60.16.93. anglotel@wanadoo.fr.* **Rate** *€140-€230 single/double. Suites from €280. AE, DC, MC, V.* **M** *Saint-Germain-des-Prés*

There's still a whiff of Englishness about the Angleterre, a former British Embassy in which the Treaty of Paris, guaranteeing US independence, was prepared. Well situated for Left Bank day- and night-life, the hotel is built with an exquisite staircase with *trompe l'oeil* murals, a comfortable salon with a grand piano, and just over two dozen well-appointed rooms decorated in a variety of styles. There are three room sizes, priced accordingly, with the largest containing massive bathrooms and Baroque four poster beds. Most overlook a peaceful and leafy central courtyard.

27 Rooms: *Air-conditioning, cable TV, telephone, modular jacks, hairdryer, bar.*

Hôtel Britannique

20 Ave. Victoria (1st). **Tel.** *01.42.33.74.59.* **Fax** *01.42.33.82.65. www.hotel-britannique.fr.* **Rate** *€130-€180 single/double. Suites from €280. AE, DC, MC, V.* **M** *Châtelet*

Conveniently situated by the Châtelet Theater, the Britannique offers a very French take on a clubby English hotel. In other words, Parisian stylishness has replaced Dickensian shabbiness. From the cozy, post-Colonial downstairs study to the well-appointed, smallish bedrooms, everything is immaculate. Windows are soundproof, breakfasts are ample and, although we might not choose such weighty decor for our own homes, the Britannique nonetheless remains a comfortable and useful address in the price range.

39 Rooms: *Cable TV, telephone, modular jacks, internet acces, hairdryer, minibar.*

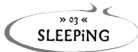

Hôtel Saint-Louis Marais

1 Rue Charles V (4th). **Tel.** *01.48.87.87.04.* **Fax** *01.48.87.33.26.* **Rate** *€90-€120 single/double. MC, V.* **M** *Bastille/Sully Morland*

In a quiet street on the Bastille side of the Marais, the Saint-Louis is a tasteful, mid-priced boutique hotel. A spacious reception, set with Louis XIII-style furnishings on a terra-cotta floor, gives way to warm guestrooms decorated with beamed ceilings, antiquish furnishings and upmarket colors. Bathrooms are sparkling. And breakfast is served in an ancient, stone vaulted basement.

16 Rooms: *Cable TV, telephone, hairdryer, 24-hour room service, wheelchair access.*

Artus Hotel

34 Rue de Buci (6th). **Tel.** *01.43.29.07.20.* **Fax** *01.43.29.67.44. www.artushotel.com.* **Rate** *€190-€300 single/double. Suites €320. AE, DC, MC, V.* **M** *Mabillon*

A quirky designer hotel, Artus Hotel eschews floral charm for post-modern chic. Tuscan-red walls, colorful non-figurative art and built-in wood furnishings are the hallmarks of this stylish youth magnet. The zebra-skin sofas in the lobby and graffiti-art in the corridors are good counterpoints to the ancient building that overlooks a lively St-Germain street market. Original decor in each room is loosely inspired by either a modern or a contemporary artist. Most rooms are wanting for space, but there's a terrific duplex suite on the top floor, and a Jacuzzi suite with a private terrace.

27 Rooms: *Air-conditioning, cable TV, telephone, modular jacks, hairdryer, minibar, room service, bar, wheelchair access.*

L'Hôtel Pergolèse

3 Rue Pergolèse (16th). **Tel.** *01.53.64.04.04.* **Fax** *01.53.64.04.40. www.paris-charming-hotel.com.* **Rate** *€175-€280 single/double. Suites from €310. AE, MC, V.* M *Porte Maillot/Argentine*

Behind a conventional stone facade and stylish blue steel door is a voguish, design-driven hotel built with clean lines, polished woods and plenty of avant style. Guest rooms are stunningly functional and free of frou-frou, with huge, comfortable beds and stylish sitting areas, all wrapped in primary colors. The high-tech baths make use of lots of chrome and glass-brick, while public rooms are set with soft leather sofas and Philippe Stark-designed furnishings. The hotel's location, between the Champs-Elysée and the Palais des Congrès, ensures an equal mix of suits and sightseers.

40 Rooms: *Air conditioning, cable TV, VCR, telephone, modular jacks, minibar, hairdryer, room service, bar.*

Hôtel de Notre Dame

19 Rue Maître-Albert (5th). **Tel.** *01.43.26.79.00.* **Fax** *01.46.33.50.11. www.hotel-paris-notredam.com* **Rate** *€139-€154 single/double. AE, DC, MC, V.* **M** *Saint Michel Notre-Dame/Maubert-Mutualité*

An excellent comfort/price ratio, and a terrific location, on a narrow street close to the Seine, earns Hôtel de Notre Dame a listing here. The ancient building has been competently restored with large plate glass windows, exposed stone walls, original beams and well-chosen antique furnishings. Guestrooms are on the small side and decorated with an eye toward function rather than form. Rooms in front are a bit larger than the others, while the ones in back benefit from dead silence.

34 Rooms: *Air-conditioning, cable TV, telephone, modular jacks, hairdryer, minibar, radio, bar, fitness center and sauna.*

Hôtel Duc de Saint-Simon

14 Rue Saint-Simon (7th). **Tel.** *01.44.39.20.20.* **Fax** *01.45.48.68.25. duc.de.saint.simon@wanadoo.fr.* **Rate** *€215-€270 single/double. Suites from €335. AE, MC, V.* **M** *Rue du Bac/Solférino*

This very beautiful little hotel, in a historic street off the Boulevard St-Germain, is all about style. Laura Ashley style, that is. From the charming reception area to the chintzy public rooms, the Saint-Simon is filled with fine paintings, fresh flowers and enough brocade to drape the Champs-Elysées. The individually decorated guestrooms are just as rich. Doubles are smaller than twins, and the best ones open onto a terrace overlooking a beautiful back patio. If you're into minimalism, you've come to the wrong place. But if an immaculately dressed doll's house is your bag, cross your fingers and hope for an available room.

34 Rooms: *Air-conditioning (some), cable TV, telephone, modular jacks, hairdryer, bar.*

L'Hôtel

13 Rue des Beaux-Arts (6th). **Tel.** *01.44.41.99.00.* **Fax** *01.43.25.64.81. www.l-hotel.com.* **Rate** *€248-€625 single/double. Suites from €529. AE, MC, V.* **M** *Saint-Germain-des-Prés*

A-list entertainment types and run-of-the-mill hipsters have long been attracted to L'Hôtel's over-the-top floral decor and extravagantly camp style. From Mick Jagger to Robert de Niro, the hotel's reputation is legendary. Oscar Wilde lived here—in Room 16, under the assumed name of Sebastain Melmoth—until his death in 1900. The Hôtel d'Alsace, as it was then known, was a far more austere establishment than the fashion-conscious place it is today. L'Hôtel recently underwent extensive remodeling, but happily this eccentric Left Banker has kept some of its more outrageous rooms, like the double that's decorated almost entirely in leopard-print; and the Mistinguett Room, which pays tribute to the legendary French vaudeville star (and Maurice Chevalier's lover). Even if you don't stay here, it's worth popping in to see the rotund staircase and funky lounge.

27 Rooms: *Air-conditioning, cable TV, telephone, modular jacks, hairdryer, minibar, radio, room service, bar, business facilities.*

Hôtel Jardins du Luxembourg

5 Impasse Royer-Collard (5th). **Tel.** *01.40.46.08.88.* **Fax** *01.40.46.02.28.* **Rate** *€130–€140 single/double. AE, DC, MC, V.* **M** *Maubert Mutualité*

This very quiet and comfortable hotel, situated near the Luxembourg Gardens, offers good quality and decent prices in an enviable Latin Quarter location. Darkly elegant decor, a friendly staff, sparkling clean bathrooms, and a sauna for guests' use make this a very popular place to stay. Rooms are typically smallish so ask for one with a balcony overlooking the street, or Room 25, which has the best view. The hotel lays claim to its own bit of historical intrigue: Siegmund Freud stayed here in 1885, when he was a student in Paris, and reputedly had the green curtains in his room removed for fear they contained arsenic.

27 Rooms: *Air-conditioning, cable TV, telephone, modular jacks (some), hairdryer, minibar, room service, bar, sauna, wheelchair access.*

Hôtel Jeu de Paume

54 Rue Saint-Louis-en-l'Ile (4th). Tel. *01.43.26.14.18.* Fax *01.40.46.02.76. www.hoteldujeudePaume.com.* Rate *€164-€297 single/double. Suites from €486. AE, DC, MC, V.* M *Pont Marie*

This hotel takes its name from the 17th century stone-and-wood atrium which was originally built as a court for paume, a racquet game that pre-dated tennis. Today it's a breakfast room in one of the nicest hotels in Paris. From the exposed timber construction and soaring ceilings to the glass elevator and chic staff, this is a highly original, slightly off-beat, and very nice place to stay. The island location, in the middle of the Seine, is unique too. Guestrooms are uniformly smallish but very well maintained and stylishly dressed with quality linens. And there are two apartments with kitchen that sleep up to five, plus a small fitness room, Norwegian sauna, and billard room.

21 Rooms: *Cable TV, telephone, modular jacks, hairdryer, minibar, room service, bar, wheelchair access.*

Libertel Terminus Nord

12 Blvd. de Denain (10th). Tel. *01.42.80.20.00.* Fax *01.42.80.63.89.* Rate *€155-€203 single/double. AE, DC, MC, V.* M *Gare du Nord*

The Terminus Nord is a welcome oasis in a sea of seedy hotels hard by the Gare du Nord. The Libertel group, known for corporate-style boutique hotels, has done a good job with this relatively large property, dressing it in a self-consciously stylish way. The hotel's position, directly opposite the station, is ideal for those who want to go from bed to berth in a matter of minutes.

236 Rooms: *Cable TV, telephone, modular jacks, hairdryer, minibar, room service, bar, wheelchair access.*

Hôtel Thoumieux

79 Rue Saint Dominique (7th). Tel. *01.47.05.49.75.* Fax *01.47.05.36.96. www.thoumieux.fr.* Rate *€115–€130 single/ double. AE, MC, V.* M *Invalides/La Tour Maubourg*

Thoumieux is one of the most famous historic brasseries in the city. But few people know that, above it, the owners also run a small hotel. Both businesses have been in the same family since the 1930s. Besides the obvious advantage of having a great dining room below (*see* Chapter 8/Dining), the hotel offers large, comfortable guestrooms that are stylishly decorated with black lacquered furniture, white upholstery and beige carpets. The welcome can be rather perfunctory, and services and facilities are few. But you can wile away long evenings with a stroll around the nearby Eiffel Tower and Les Invalides.

10 Rooms: cable *TV, telephone, modular jacks, hairdryer, room service, restaurant, bar.*

Hôtel Pavillon Bastille

65 Rue de Lyon (12th) Tel. *01.43.43.65.65.* Fax *01.43.43. 96.52. www.france-paris.com.* Rate *€130 single/double. Suite €213. AE, DC, MC, V.* M *Bastille*

A starchy townhouse *façade* gives way to a comfort-filled interior designed with sexy curves and minimalist straight lines. Resolutely contemporary in style, the Pavillon takes its cue from the Bastille Opera house which it overlooks. The post-modern decor is all yellow and blue, endlessly reflected by innumerable mirrors. Bedrooms are clean and compact, and fitted with lots of accessories you don't normally see in a hotel in this price range. Service is attentive, complimentary wine is served each evening in the salon, and the breakfast buffet is generous.

24 Rooms: *Air-conditioning, cable TV, VCR, telephone, modular jacks, hairdryer, minibar, room service, bar, wheelchair access.*

Terrass Hôtel

12 Rue Josephe de Maistre (18th). Tel. *01.46.06.72.85.* Fax *01.42.52.29.11. www.hotel-paris-terrass.com.* Rate *€194-€256 single/double. Suites €311. AE, DC, MC, V.* M *Place de Clichy*

Contrary to what tourist brochures profess, Montmartre is not brimming with delightful hilltop hotels. In fact they are few and far between. Terrass Hôtel is the best of the bunch; and as its name suggests, has a magnificent patio restaurant that overlooks all of Paris. There's not much to the unengaging exterior, but once inside, it has all the warmth and coziness you'd want from a hotel in this romantic quarter. Guestrooms are richly decorated in a style that's too palatial for their size. But get one facing the city, and interior design becomes an afterthought. Only two-thirds of the rooms are air-conditioned, and Americans will be happy to know that an entire floor is designated smoke-free.

101 Rooms: *Air-conditioning, satellite TV, telephone, modular jacks, hairdryer, minibar, room service, restaurant, bar, business facilities.*

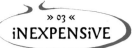

iNEXPENSiVE

Hôtel du Cygne

3 Rue du Cygne (1st). Tel. *01.42.60.14.16.* Fax *01.42.21.37.02.* Rate *€83-€106 single/double. AE, MC, V.* M *Etienne Marcel/Chatêlet*

Run by two charming sisters, the Hôtel du Cygne offers diminutive, simply-furnished bedrooms in a 17th century building on a car-free strip of Les Halles. Exposed beams and a charming salon/breakfast room are pluses. Secure the large room on the top floor and your tramp up the stairs will be rewarded with more than enough room to swing a cat.

20 Rooms: *Cable TV, telephone, hairdryer.*

Baudelaire Opéra

61 Rue Sainte-Anne (2nd). Tel. *01.42.97.50.62.* Fax *01.42.86.85.85. hotel@cybercable.fr.* Rate *€110-€140 single/double. Split-level rooms from €170. AE, DC, MC, V.* M *Pyramides*

The Anglo-French owners of this hotel near the Opera run a tight ship and appear to take a genuine interest in the well-being of their guests. Rooms are small but nicely decorated, with bright colors and immaculate baths. The larger duplexes are great for those who don't mind going up a spiral staircase to bed. And creative types might be inspired by the fact that Baudelaire slept here and Céline (the poet, not the singer) had a place next door.

29 rooms: *Cable TV, telephone, hairdryer, minibar.*

Hôtel Istria

29 Rue Campagne Première (14th). Tel. *01.43.20.91.82.* Fax *01.43.22.48.45.* Rate *€96-€106 single/double. AE, DC, MC, V.* M *Raspail*

Situated adjacent to the last purpose-built artists' studios in Montparnasse, this family-run hotel was the choice of Man Ray, Marcel Duchamp, Rainer Maria Rilke and other artists from the 1920s and '30s. Nowadays the decor of this comfortable little hotel is coyly conformist. But it's a pleasant enough place to stay with simple furnishings, a flower-filled courtyard, and a dynamite retro location near the brasseries of Boulevard du Montparnasse.

26 Rooms: *Cable TV, telephone, modular jacks, hairdryer, room service.*

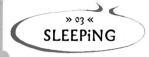

Hôtel d'Orsay

93 Rue de Lille (7th). **Tel.** *01.47.05.85.54.* **Fax** *01.45.55.51.16. hotel.orsay@wanadoo.fr.* **Rate** *€105-€138 single/double. Suites €225. AE, DC, MC, V.* **M** *Assemblée Nationale*

Hôtel d'Orsay offers perfectly recommendable rooms and an excellent 7th Arrondissement location across from the Musée d'Orsay, and within easy walking distance to the Quartier Latin. The entire hotel has seen a recent makeover. Floral coverings and tiled baths create a comfortable, if slightly bland, atmosphere.

41 Rooms: *Cable TV, telephone, modular jacks, hairdryer, minibar, room service, wheelchair access.*

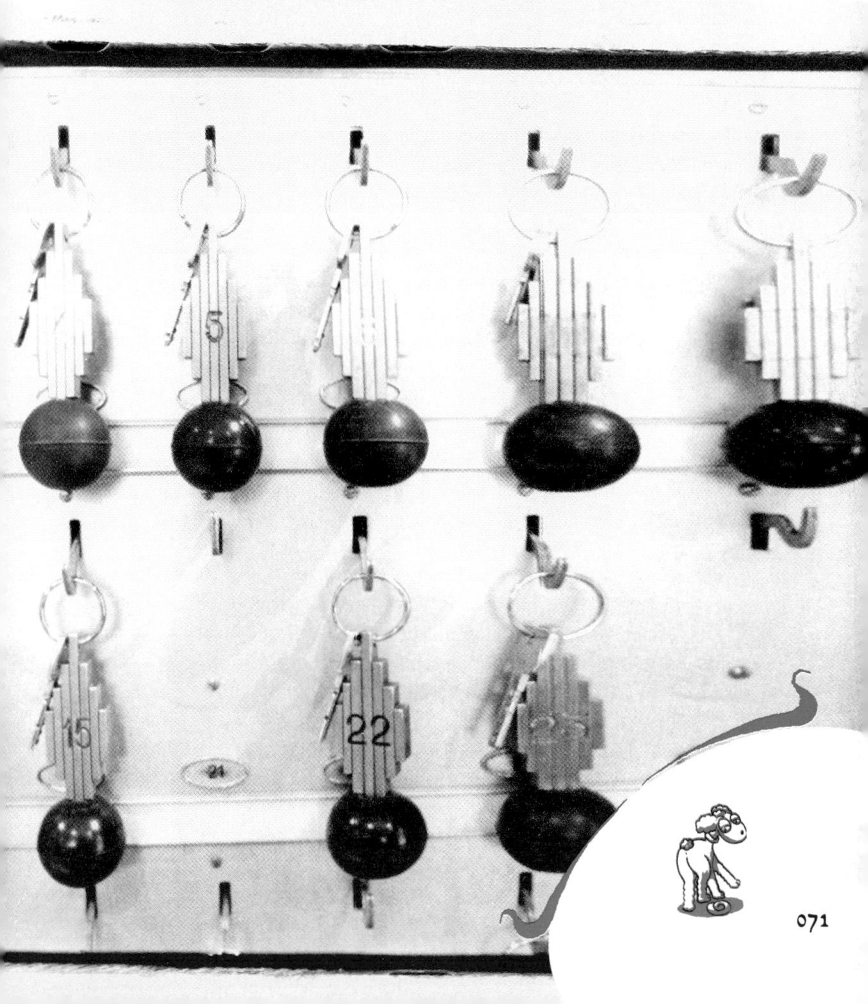

Hôtel Place des Vosges

12 Rue de Birague (4th). Tel. *01.42.72.60.46.* Fax *01.42.72.02.64.* Rate *€100-€137 single/double. AE, DC, MC, V.* M *Saint-Paul*

Its name may be a tad optimistic since, in reality, this pleasant hotel is located a full block away from Place des Vosges, one of Paris's prettiest squares. Nonetheless, this is a great place to stay, and the neighborhood is terrific. As with many hotels in this price range, the public areas are far more attractive than the bedrooms. A Louis XIII-style reception area gives way to simpler guestrooms, some of which are no larger than a walk-in closet. However, those on higher floors have romantic rooftop views. There's plenty of eye-candy inside too, including rough-hewn stone, oak-beamed ceilings and rustic furnishings. But in the end, guests pay for location.

16 Rooms: *Cable TV, telephone, modular jacks, hairdryer.*

Hôtel Saint-Merry

78 Rue de la Verrerie (4th). Tel. *01.42.78.14.15.* Fax *01.40.29.06.82. www.saintmerrymarais.com.* Rate *€146-€250 single/double. Suites from €305. AE, V.* M *St-Martin/Hôtel-de-Ville*

Adjacent to the church of Saint-Merri, this distinctive building began life as a presbytery before becoming a private residence, a brothel and, finally, a hotel. In its most recent incarnation, the Saint-Merry celebrates its medieval roots with a Transylvanian style that's perfectly suited for Goths. Stone, iron and wood are the materials of choice, creating an atmosphere that evokes either Middle-European charm or horror movies, depending on your point of view. Guestrooms, reached by a spiral staircase, range from small and somber to a spectacular theme suite. Draculas and other nightcrawlers be warned: TV plays no part in the Gothic lifestyle.

12 Rooms: *Telephone, modular jacks, hairdryer, TV (only in suites).*

Hôtel Sansonnet

48 Rue de la Verrerie (4th). Tel. *01.48.87.96.14.* Fax *01.48.87.30.46. www.hotel-sansonnet.com* Rates *€45-€78) single/double. MC, V.* M *Hôtel de Ville*

An unbeatable value in the tab-happy Marais, Sansonnet offers decent sized bedrooms that are well-kept with simple furnishings. The quieter back rooms have only showers; shared toilets are down the hall. Those in front have full bathrooms, along with double-glazed windows to keep street noise at bay.

25 Rooms: *Cable TV, telephone, hairdryer.*

Hôtel du Septième Art

20 Rue Saint Paul (4th). Tel. *01.44.54.85.00.* Fax *01.42.77.69.10.* Rate *€75-€130 single/ double. AE, DC, MC, V.* M *St-Paul*

Behind what looks like a typical Marais storefront is a simple and unorthodox hotel that doubles as a shop, bar, and art gallery. The hotel's name, "Seventh Art," is French slang for filmmaking, and the ground floor is a riot of old cinema posters and memorabilia, each of which sports a price tag. Although some of the black-and-white bedrooms are small and in serious need of remastering, we love this hotel's terrific location, relaxed atmosphere and friendly bar with a crackling fire in winter. The attic room is the best and brightest.

23 Rooms: *Cable TV, telephone, modular jacks, hairdryer (on request), bar, mini-fitness center.*

Hôtel Langlois

63 Rue Saint Lazare (9th). Tel. *01.48.74.78.24.* Fax *01.49.95.04.43. www.ersu.net/langlois.* Rate *€78-€98 single/double. Suite €130. AE, DC, MC, V.* M *Trinité*

Stone-fronted Hôtel Langlois exudes the sort of old fashioned elegance that has all but disappeared. From the ornate wood-and-stone lobby to the spectacular old-fashioned lift, everything radiates a romantic atmosphere of a time gone by. That includes the spacious bedrooms, some of which have incredible marble fireplaces, 19th-century paintings and sculptures, and mahogany woodwork. Happily even the rates are retro and only the bathrooms are of this decade. The time warp even extends to the elderly uniformed waitress in the high ceilinged breakfast room. The single, large suite—which includes two bedrooms, a kitchenette and views of Montmartre—must be one of Paris's best buys. The hotel is situated on a street near the Grands Boulevards, close to several important Métro lines.

27 Rooms: *Cable TV, telephone, hairdryer, minibar, internet access in the lobby.*

Hôtel Ermitage

24 Rue Lamarck (18th). Tel. *01.42.64.79.22.* Fax *01.42.64.10.33.* Rate *€70-€84 single/double. No Cards* M *Lamarck Caulaincourt*

Tucked away on a quiet street behind Sacré-Coeur, the intimate Ermitage exudes the genuine charm of a homey B&B. It is at once far enough away from the maddening crowds, yet close enough to the cafés and restaurants of Montmartre to make it feel like you've found something special. Marked only by a discreet sign, the entrance is as low-key as the hotel itself, which feels like an over-decorated private home. Think gold-and-cream floral wallpaper, a clutter of antiques, and deep red carpeting overlaid with rugs. Guestrooms are large and light, though baths are somewhat size-challenged. Accommodations on the upper floor have great views of Paris, while the ones below open onto a garden. "Charm" also means there are no televisions, and credit cards are not accepted.

12 Rooms: *Tele-phone, hairdryer, wheelchair access.*

Hôtel du Globe

15 Rue des Quatres-Vents (6th). Tel. *01.43.26.35.50.* Fax *01.46.33.62.69.* Rate *€70-€105 single/double. MC, V.* M *Odéon*

We give high marks to the Globe for its distinctive individuality and very good price-to-quality ratio. The 17th-century former abbey contains a suit of armor in the tiny lounge, and uniquely styled guestrooms that speak of attention to details. Accommodations can be small, but each feels somewhat special. The best have antique furniture, and four poster beds draped with crochet spreads. The worst have showers and toilets behind painted folding doors, which doesn't afford the privacy we demand. Breakfast in bed is mandatory; there is no breakfast area, so the morning meal is delivered to each room.

15 Rooms: *TV, telephone, hairdryer (on request).*

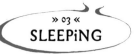

Hôtel Esmeralda

4 Rue Saint-Julien-le-Pauvre (5th). **Tel.** *01.43.54.19.20.* **Fax** *01.40.51.00.68.* **Rate** *€50-€85 single/double. No cards.* M *Saint-Michel*

When price and location are more important than clean and comfortable, you can do no better than this classic budget hotel situated directly across from Notre-Dame. With its monumental wooden staircase and smattering of antiques, the Esmeralda exudes all the eclectic charm of an old curiosity shop. Its quirky rooms offer little in the way of creature comforts except good plumbing. But some do have beamed ceilings, and all of Paris is at your doorstep.

19 Rooms: *Telephone.*

Hôtel Jeanne d'Arc

3 Rue de Jarente (4th). Tel. *01.48.87.62.11.* Fax *01.48.87.37.31. www.hoteljeannedarc.com.* Rate *€57-€99 single/double. MC, V.* M *Saint-Paul/Bastille*

Upon entering the Jeanne d'Arc, guests are immediately confronted—some would say assaulted—by a riotously modern mirror studded with colored glass, zinc flags and flashing lights. Other like-minded eclectica is strewn about this 17th century Marais building, though decoration in guestrooms feels completely indifferent. In a city where space is at a premium, this hotel offers good value for money, with well-sized bedrooms and bathrooms that can be downright commodious. Because rates strike us as somewhat of a bargain, we feel this hotel is one of the city's hidden jewels. Ask for one of the rooms containing a couch; or for attic accommodations with their great views.

36 Rooms: *Cable TV, telephone, hairdryer (on request).*

Hôtel Mondia

23 Rue du Grand-Prieuré (11th). Tel. *01.47.00. 93.44.* Fax *01.43.38.66.14. www.hotel-mondia.com.* Rate *€51-€64 single/double. AE, DC, MC, V.* M *Oberkampf*

If you're looking for a genuine bargain without compromising on perks like cable TV, hairdryers and direct dial phones, Mondia is for you. This budget find enjoys a positive self-image, evidenced in a charming, stained-glass breakfast room and hard-working, friendly staff. Guestrooms are small and won't win any prizes for their frumpy decor, but everything is in place and spotlessly clean. The hotel's Place de la République location isn't great, but the Bastille and the Marais are both within walking distance; and at less than 400F (€61.20) per night we don't want to receive any letters of complaint.

23 Rooms: *Cable TV, telephone, modular jacks, hairdryer, wheelchair access.*

Hôtel Prima Lepic

29 Rue Lepic (18th). **Tel.** *01.46.06.44.64.* **Fax** *01.46.06.66.11.* *www.hotel-paris-lepic.com.* **Rate** *€78-€123 single/double. MC, V.* **M** *Blanche/Abbesses*

The Rue Lepic remains one of the most unspoiled streets this district that runs from the gaudy sex shops of Pigalle to the over-touristed heights of Montmartre. The rooms have been recently renovated, each decorated differently in light and airy florals and paisley prints. Beds and baths are strictly basic, but they are well-sized, and those on the top floor benefit from a fair degree of natural light. The long walk up to Sacré-Coeur is excellent and, by night, it's just a short stroll for a "date" on Pigalle.

38 Rooms: *TV, telephone, hairdryer, babysitting, internet access.*

Hôtel Sainte-Marie

6 Rue de la Ville-Neuve (2nd). **Tel.** *01.42.33.21.61.* **Fax** *01.42.33.29.24.* **Rate** *€38-€71 single/double. AE, MC, V.* **M** *Bonne-Nouvelle*

On a quiet street near the Grands Boulevards, the Sainte-Marie provides decent accommodations at rock-bottom prices. Rooms are very small, aggressively utilitarian and relatively bright, as long as you avoid the ones overlooking the courtyard. There are no bathtubs, only showers. Importantly, the *patronne* is charming and the breakfast room is bright and agreeable, two elements that are increasingly difficult to find in this price range.

19 Rooms: *Cable TV, telephone.*

Hôtel de Nesle

7 Rue de Nesle (6th). Tel. *01.43.54.62.41.* Fax *01.43.54.31.88. www.hoteldenesle.com.* Rate *€50-€100 single/double. MC.* M *Odéon*

Not only is the Nesle an unabashed throwback to the 1960s, it's also one of the few budget hotels in Paris that could be described as fun. Each spotless guestroom is individually themed and painted with a unique mural that suggests someplace exotic, like Casablanca or Cairo. But don't get us wrong, this is simple stuff. Only about half the rooms have private showers and none have their own toilet; WCs are located on each floor. But where else could you spot a pet goose wandering about the terrace, or breakfast next to a long-haired intellectual just back from a Tibetan retreat, who introduces you to an elderly American novelist who's been saving for his ticket home since 1970?

This place defines eccentric. Oh, and one other thing: they don't go for anything as bourgeois as reservations. Cool.

20 Rooms.

hOStELS

MIJE le Fauconnier

11 Rue Fauconnier (4th). Tel. *01.42.74.23.45.* Fax *01.40.27.81.64. www.mije.com.* Rate *€24-€26 per bed in a multishare.* M *Pont-Marie*

MIJE stands for "*Maisons Internationales de la Jeunesse et des Etudiants,*" or as we'd say in English, "youth hostel." There are three MIJE hostels in the Marais, all characterful places. But this one is the real winner in terms of atmosphere and architecture. Accommodations are the usual hostel standard, but the reception and public areas are worthy of a grand hotel. The more people who share a room, the cheaper it works out. And, with a whiff of Gallic morality, nobody over thirty will be paired off with an unknown roommate.

Le Village

20 Rue d'Orsel (18th). Tel. *01.42.64.22.02.* Fax *01.42.64.22.04. www.villagehostel.fr.* Rate *€46–€50 double, €20–€21.50 per bed in a multishare.* M *Anvers*

It's all about location at this recently remodeled hostel at the base of the Sacré-Coeur basilica. Rooms are a bit tight, but all are equipped with private bathrooms. The internationalists who bed down here are a relatively sedate bunch. And there's a kitchen available for guests' use.

Auberge de Jeunesse d'Artagnan

80 Rue Vitruve (20th). Tel. *01.40.32.34.56.* Fax *01.40.32.34.55. www.fuaj.org/aj/paris-dartagnan/.* Rate *€19 per bed in a multishare.* M *Porte de Bagnolet*

Hostel meets entertainment center at this fully-loaded place near Père-Lachaise Cemetery. In addition to shared guestrooms with 3-4 beds each, the hostel includes a movie theater, pool table, video games, Internet access (you have to buy a special card at the front desk), a full bar/night club, and even a rock-climbing wall. It's open nonstop, except for a short period from 2-4pm for cleaning.

No 04

PARiS' GREAtEST HiTS

SiGhtSEEiNG

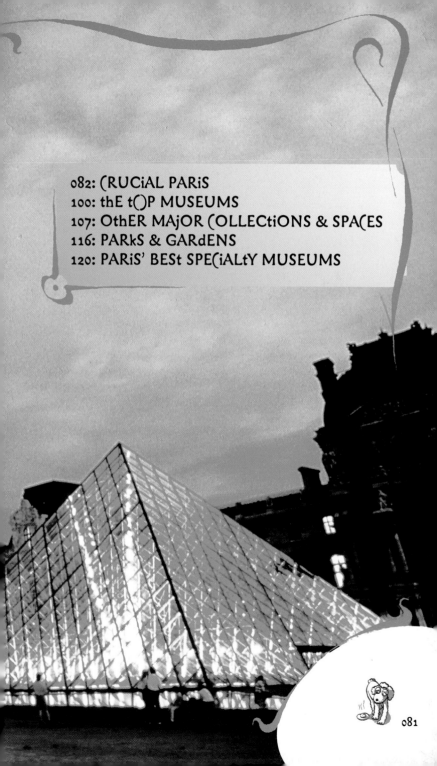

Arc de Triomphe

Place Charles-de-Gaulle (8th). Tel. 01.55.37.73.77. Open Apr-Sept, daily 10am-11pm; Oct-Mar, daily 10am-1030pm. Closed May 1, Dec 25, Jan 1, and mornings May 8, July 14, Nov 11. Last admission 30 minutes before closing. Admission €7 adults, €4.50 for youths under 25. M Charles-de-Gaulle-Etoile

The Arc de Triomphe, that ginormous marble monument to the Napoléonic French ego, owes its international reputation to its monumental proportions, dignified classicism and ground-zero location at the top of the Champs-Elysées. Commissioned by Napoléon Bonaparte in 1806, just two years after he was crowned Emperor, this heap of stone built on a heap of glory (to paraphrase Victor Hugo) was slapped down smack in the middle of the most important intersection in the city, at the hub of twelve avenues that radiate from the monument like slices of a pie.

Opened to the public in 1835, the monument was inspired by ancient Rome's Arch of Constantine. But at 164 feet (50m) high and 148 feet (45m) wide, it's twice as large as the original, making it the second-largest arch of its kind in the world (kooky North Korea built one that's just a smidgen bigger). The original plan called for a giant stone elephant on this spot too; that was one of Napoleon's personal symbols. But Waterloo put an end to that folly, along with the Little Emperor's personal brand of "European Union."

From the Champs-Elysées, an underground passage delivers you to the Arc's two massive toes. If the weather is clear it's worth the trudge up the stairs to the observation terrace for terrific views across Paris.

Back on the ground, pay your respects at the Tomb of the Unknown Soldier, which is surrounded by plaques engraved with the names of former generals and the battles in which they fell. Each evening at 6pm the Eternal Flame is tended to by rotating branches of the French military. The best show is put on by the *Garde Républicaine*—dashing, saber-wielding cavaliers dressed in leather riding boots, white breeches and silver helmets topped with horse tails. *Quelle Allure!* It's no wonder Frenchmen continue to be gloriously spellbound by Napoléon's *Belle France*.

La Grande Arche de la Défense

La Défense. Tel. 01.49.07.27.57. Open June 20-Sept 20, daily 10am-8pm; Sept 21-June 19, Mon-Fri 10am-7pm, Sat-Sun 10am-8pm (last ascent one hour before closing). Admission €7 adults, €5.50 students and youths 6-17 years old, under 6 free. M La Défense

If you've never been out to see France's take on Manhattan, it's well worth the short Métro ride to La Défense, the corporate ghetto just west of central Paris. Said to be the largest concentration of tall buildings in Europe, this contemporary complex consists of office buildings, hotels, apartments, shops and restaurants. What makes it unique is the fact that the whole concrete slab on which this mini city is built is a car-free zone; roads, parking and subway links are all underground.

Begun in 1958 to ease pressure on development within Paris, La Défense required the relocation of over 25,000 people and the removal of some 700 businesses. The somewhat chilly result smacks of one great skateboard pad, complete with immense blank walls that cry out for graffiti.

The biggest towers began to sprout in the 1970s, commissioned by industrial giants like Fiat and Elf. These were followed by more stylish structures like PB6, a chic glass curve designed by IM Pei and Partners. Copious outdoor art includes several colorful sculptures by Joan Miró, and the last work by Alexander Calder–an immense red "stabile" situated outside Les Quatre Temps shopping mall. The esplanade is a popular shopping ground for young suburbanites; its vast architectural proportions are truly awesome.

The main attraction for the casual visitor is the futuristic **Grande Arche.** Completed in 1989, it was designed by Johann Otto von Spreckelsen, a relatively obscure architect whose previous achievements were limited to a few churches in his native Denmark. An office tower in the shape of an enormous open cube, the Arche echoes in modern language the shape of the Arc de Triomphe, with which it is visibly aligned. Mired in financial controversy since Day One, the building is at once a symbol of urban success and an impressive tourist attraction, with its high-speed lifts whisking visitors to great views over the city. From the top you can easily see that the cube completes a long series of monuments that extends from the Louvre in the center of Paris, up the Boulevard Champs-Elysées and through the Arc de Triomphe to a small monument commemorating the defense of Paris during the Franco-Prussian War (1870-1871). It is that last small statue, now dwarfed by the skyscrapers surrounding it, for which La Défense is named.

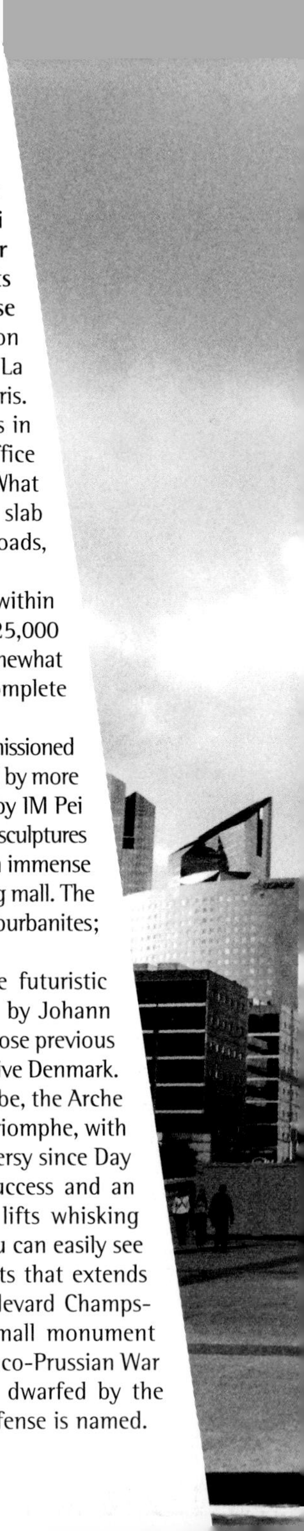

The Eiffel Tower

Champs de Mars (7th). Tel. 01.44.11.23.23.
Open Mid Jun-Aug, daily 9am-midnight; Sept-Mid June, daily 930am-11pm. Admission €3.70, €7 and €10.20 adults; €2.30, €3.90 and €5.50) children under 12 to take the elevator to the first, second and third stories, respectively; €3.30 to climb the stairs to the first and second stories; under 3 free. M Ecole Militaire/Bir-Hakeim

Going to the top of the Eiffel Tower may sound like a tourist trap, and the international United Colors of Benetton crowd can be stifling, but the *Tour Eiffel* is actually one of Paris' most thrilling attractions. The throng worsens as the weather improves but, at dusk, when the lights of the city are twinkling below, the view is as wonderful and awesome as any we've ever experienced.

Built for the 1889 World's Fair, this 7,000-ton marvel of wrought-iron was almost disassembled in 1909 because so many prominent Parisians considered it to be an eye-sore. But demolition was averted when the tower's defenders promoted the structure as the ultimate radio-transmitting utility pole, a role it still serves to this day.

Old hydraulic "inclinators" (or 700 steps) take visitors up to the tower's first level, which is just above the city's rooftops. Orientation tables point out the sights while various signboards offer tidbits about famous former visitors, including Adolf Hitler. There's a souvenir store and even a post office which cancels postage with the mark *Tour Eiffel.*

On the second level, reached by elevator or 1,652 steps, you can get a good feel for the layout of the city. There are more schlock-souvenir sellers (a miniature ET anyone?), a lackluster buffet and the Jules Verne, a celebrated Michelin two-star restaurant (*see* Chapter 8/The Restaurant Scene).

At about 900 feet (274 meters), the third level is more than twice as high as the second and it's well worth the extra euros to see this summit. On the clearest days you can make out the cathedral at Chartres, 47 miles (75km) away. Closer to home, stretched out below you, the city simmers, bubbles and pulsates to the beat of light industry, torrid passions, passionate strikes and placid student life. And if that doesn't make you giddy, climb a few more steps where you'll find wax figures of Gustave Alexandre Eiffel and Thomas Edison chilling-out in the mile-high apartment that was once the famous French civil engineer's private quarters.

Notre-Dame de Paris

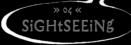

6 Place du Parvis-Notre-Dame (4th). Tel. 01.42.34.56.10. Cathedral open daily 8am-645pm. Towers and Crypt open July-August, Mon-Thurs 9am-730pm, Fri-Sun 9am-11pm; April-June and September 930am-730pm; Winter, daily 10am-530pm. Crypt closed Mondays. Services Sun 930am. Church admission free; Tower admission €5.50 adults, €4.50 youths 18-25, under 18 free; Crypt admission €3.30 adults, €1.60 under 27 and €2.20 over 60. M Cité

More than seven hundred years after its cornerstone was laid, the Cathedral of Notre Dame (Our Lady) continues to be one of the world's best advertisements for Roman-Catholicism. Its architecture is so exuberant that even oppressive tour-bus crowds can't dampen the spectacle.

Before entering, take time to admire the famous facade, which became a model for cathedrals throughout Europe in the Middle Ages. The ornate rose window is considered a masterpiece of Gothic engineering for its large glass surface area, supported by a seemingly delicate web of carved stone tracery. It is surrounded by intensely elaborate images in fresco and stone that join in a brilliant, writhing mass of biblical scenes, and allegories of vices, virtues, sciences and crafts. The central portal depicts the Last Judgment. Twenty-eight statues above the three richly carved doors were decapitated during the Revolution by Jacobeans who mistook these Kings of Judea for representations of French kings. These heads are copies; the originals have been removed to the Musée National Du Moyen Age (see below).

Begun in 1163 by Bishop Maurice de Sully, Notre Dame was the first great cathedral in Paris. It heralded an experimentation in Gothic architecture that raised ceilings, voided walls and reduced the size of the internal supports. The side chapels, which completely encircle the nave and choir, were later additions, built in the late 13th and early 14th centuries. The cathedral lost most of its medieval glass and original fittings during the 18th century, and the entire building was massively restored during the 19th.

Over the years, Notre-Dame has witnessed many important events, including the coronation of Emperor Napoléon Bonaparte and the Empress Joséphine (1804), an assassination attempt on Charles de Gaulle (1944), and the funeral of socialist President François Mitterand (1996).

The enormous crypt is worth checking out to see an archeological record going back sixteen centuries. Beneath the cathedral's forecourt are the remains of streets and ruins from churches that stood on this site from as early as the Third Century. Interactive exhibits (in French only) trace the evolution of Paris from its earliest days, with architectural breakthroughs like cisterns and vaulting.

If you can stand the crowds, it's absolutely worth taking the cramped corkscrew staircases to the top of the church's towers for great views over Paris and close-ups of the phantasmic gargoyles. A guide often lets visitors use a bronze wand to tap a tune on the 14-ton (13,000-kg) church bell and listen to its magic "bongggg." Arrive early to beat the lines; the tower entrance is on Rue du Cloître-Notre-Dame.

There are free guided tours in English on Wednesday and Thursday at noon, Saturday at 230pm, and daily throughout August at 230pm. Free organ concerts are held each Sunday at 530pm.

Sainte-Chapelle

4 Blvd. du Palais (1st). Tel. 01.53.73.78.52. Open daily 930am-6pm, Nov through Feb until 5pm. Admission €5.50 adults, €3.50 youths 18-25, under 18 free; €8 combined ticket with Conciergerie. M Cité

Sainte-Chapelle is a 13th-century architectural tour-de-force with a set of stained-glass windows to die for. This spacious palace chapel, built by Louis IX on the Île de la Cité, is one of the most amazing churches anywhere. The structure as a whole is an outstanding example of Gothic building. But it's the glass that keeps the crowds coming.

The art of colored glass reached its zenith just about the time this church was consecrated, in 1248. During Louis IX's long reign—from 1226 to 1270—Gothic architecture entered the Rayonnant phase, named for the radiating spokes of the enormous rose windows that are one of the most prominent features of the style. Having conquered the problem of height, architects concerned themselves with expanding window areas and reducing the masonry in order to make buildings appear less weighty.

At the same time, decorative statues took on more naturalistic forms that included courtly affectations and a more delicate spirituality. This is particularly noticeable in the more manneristic and maternal cult statues of the Virgin Mary who, from this time onward, is depicted playfully balancing the Christ child on her hip. This image, which made its first appearance on the lower portal of the Sainte-Chapelle, was disseminated in infinite variations throughout Europe in the ensuing centuries.

Sainte-Chapelle was built next door to the former royal palace to house the Crown of Thorns and a fragment of the Holy Cross, phony relics that the pious Louis IX was duped into buying for what can only be described as a king's ransom.

But, back to the windows that make Sainte-Chapelle so special. Rising from just above the ground to the arches of the vaults, they are so immense that the whole interior seems to be made entirely of glass. Go on a sunny day, when the 1,134 biblical scenes shine brightest; or at sunset, when the gigantic rose window, which depicts the Apocalypse, alights like fire.

Basilique du Sacré-Coeur

37 Rue Chevalier de la Barre (18th). Tel. 01.53.41.89.00. Church open daily 6am-11pm; dome open daily 915am-530pm. Admission to the crypte and dome €5. M Abbesses

The toylike Basilique du Sacré-Coeur (Sacred Heart) is a whimsical feat of Roman-Byzantine architecture and one of the best-known sites in the city. Perched atop the Butte Montmartre—the highest hill in Paris—the trademark wedding cake facade looks more like a mosque than a Catholic church. The basilica is built from local stone that cleans itself automatically by releasing white calcite whenever it gets wet; each time it rains the church grows brighter.

Sacré-Coeur was constructed after the Franco-Prussian War (1870-71) as an act of penitence for the sins of the Communards. Ever since 1885, there has been someone on duty here—nonstop—praying for the sins of the Commune. The local believers who paid for the building were also interested in bolstering their religion in the face of anti-Catholic backlash under the new republican regime. The preposterous result is something of an embarrassment. Or at least it should be. From the get-go, local opposition feared that building the church would forever alter Montmartre's village-like character. And indeed it has, as millions of tour-bus trekkers traipse through annually. "It isn't possible that God, if he exists, would agree to live there" said Adolphe Willette, architect of the Moulin-Rouge. He is now immortalized with a square at the foot of Sacré-Coeur.

Sacré-Coeur's interior is cavernous and gloomy. You can climb to the basilica's summit, but better views can be had elsewhere. And you can descend into the dank crypt, but the cellar museum is a snooze. Still, Sacré-Coeur is worth visiting once in your life—for the view over Paris from the Butte, the tourist circus on the stairs, and just to say you saw it.

Mass is held here Mon-Fri at 1115am, 3pm (Fri only) 630pm and 10pm; Sat at 1115am, 10pm; and Sun 11am, 6pm, 10pm.

To reach Sacré-Coeur you can either walk up the steep steps or take the *Funiculaire* from Square Willette. It runs daily from about 6am-1230am and is the same price as a single short Métro ride.

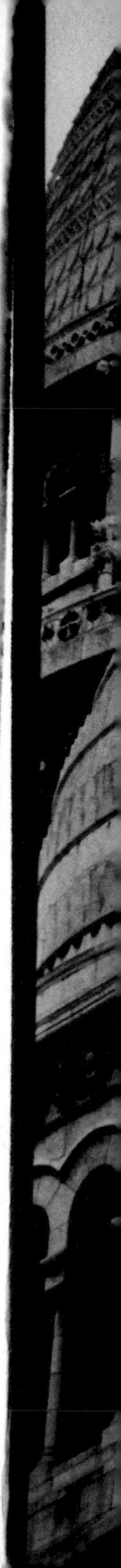

Le Cimetière Père-Lachaise

16 Rue du Repos (20th). Tel. 01.55.25.82.10. Open Mon-Sat 8am-530pm, Sun 9am-530pm. Admission free. M Père-Lachaise/Phillipe Auguste

Paris' most prestigious bone yard is home some of the world's coolest dead people. Celebs buried here include writers Gertrude Stein, Honoré de Balzac and Marcel Proust; dancer Isadora Duncan; singer Edith Piaf; composers Chopin and Bellini; painters Pisarro, Modigliani and Léger; members of the Rothschild dynasty and countless other princes, presidents and generic rich people.

The Doors' Jim Morrison is buried here too, having dropped dead from an overdose in a suitably squalid hotel room nearby. Fans still turn up *en masse*—banging bongos, sipping wine and sucking joints—but the infamous graffiti on the surrounding graves was recently cleaned, and a full-time guard aims to keep it that way.

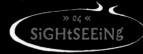

The grave of Oscar Wilde is a monolith carved with a puffy-faced Egyptian sphinx. The Irish dramatist and wit came to Paris upon his release from two years of hard labor in England. Penniless, he suffered with meningitis in the bowels of St-Germain-des-Prés.

There are hundreds of other interesting tombs, including a kitsch temple for the Russian princess and mining heiress Elisabeth Demidov, and a statue of poet George Rodenbach rising from his grave, rose in hand. The tomb of Romantic painter Théodore Géricault incorporates a frieze of his masterpiece "Le Radeau de la Méduse." And the life-size statue of Victor Noir, a young journalist assassinated by Prince Pierre Bonaparte, depicts the writer at his moment of death with the bulge in his pants giving new meaning to "rigor mortis." Visitors have taken to rubbing this "mourning wood" for luck, making it the best-polished monument in the cemetery.

Named after Louis XIV's confessor, Father Père Lachaise, the cemetery was begun in the late 1700s on a hillside overlooking the city. Today this cemetery is Paris' largest, and is so popular with visitors it's almost comical. The huge, wooded burial ground is built with twisting lanes marked with white-and-blue enamel street signs. And hundreds of feral cats call this marble-town home. Many shops surrounding the cemetery sell detailed maps to the star's graves. You can also usually pick up a less-detailed map (*un plan*) free from the guard booth at the cemetery's main entrance on Rue de la Roquette.

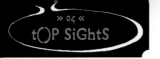

Hôtel des Invalides

Place des Invalides (7th). Tel. 01.44.42.37.72. Museum open Oct-Mar 10am-5pm daily, April-Sept 10am-6pm daily; Dome and tomb open same hours and until 645pm June 15-Sept 15. Closed hols. Admission €7 adults, €5.50 youths 18-25, under 18 free. M Invalides/Latour-Maubourg/Varenne

First and foremost, Hôtel des Invalides is an awesome masterpiece of 17th-century classical French architecture. Everything about it was designed to impress, from its overpowering size and commanding city-center location, to its blazing dome radiating with almost 30 pounds (13.6 kilos) of gold leaf.

Louis XIV built this Mother of all Old-Age Homes in the 1670s for the thousands of veterans who suffered injuries while fighting for France. Back in the day, *les Invalides* (French for "disabled") housed up to 3000 men, with the State picking up the tab for most everything, right down to the dry-cleaning. Today only a few dozen aging warriors remain.

A long formal esplanade leads from the River Seine to the main building. In the center of the complex is the church of Saint-Louis, also known as the Soldiers Church. Its royal chapel, the Dôme des Invalides, is considered to be a masterpiece of French Baroque design. When the classical composer Hector Berlioz premiered his *Requiem* here, the orchestra included a battery of artillery men in the courtyard.

The eastern wing of the palace is now given over to the **Musée de l'Armée**, a military museum containing one of the world's richest collections of killing implements, tools of war, armor, flags and assorted other combat paraphernalia from the Stone Age to WW2.

Needless to say all that war stuff is not our bag, baby. But there is some interesting Napoleon-related gear including the Emperor's battle tent, a reconstruction of the room in which he died (supposedly of stomach cancer), and a famous portrait by Jean-Auguste-Dominique Ingres.

The best excuse for visiting Hôtel des Invalides is to see **Napoleon's tomb**, an appropriately grandiose red- and green-rock crypt containing six coffins—one inside the other, nesting-doll style. Brought here 19 years after his death in exile on the island of St. Helena, Napoléon lies under the massive Dôme, surrounded by twelve apostle-like carved figures representing the Emperor's military victories.

The Paris Sewers (Les Egoûts de Paris)

At Pont de l'Alma (7th). Tel. 01.53.68.27.81. Open Oct-Apr, Sat-Wed 11am-4pm; May-Sept, Sat-Wed 11am-5pm. Closed last 3 weeks in Jan. Admission €3.80 adults, €3.05 children 5-10, under 5 free. M Pont de l'Alma

The French are a very proud people. So proud, in fact, that they even put their urban septic tanks on display for the world to see. And see you should, because we know of no other major city that offers regularly scheduled public tours of their stenching sewers. Parisians have been showing off their waste waters since 1867, when underground excursions took place in luxurious boats—which white-clad sewermen pushed from behind.

Sewer construction began in 1825 and these clammy channels became an integral part of Haussmann's majestic architectural plan for Paris. Today there are over 1250 miles (2000 Km) of underground piping. Each channel is marked with a replica of the street sign above it. The underground journey is a lowbrow thrill that proves once and for all that French bowels stink just the same as everyone else's. The entrance is located in front of 93 Quai d'Orsay.

The Panthéon

Place du Panthéon (5th). Tel. 01.44. 32.18.00. Open Apr-Sept, daily 10am-630pm; Oct-Mar, daily 10am-615pm. Admission €7 adults, €4.50 youths 18-25, under 18 free. M Cardinal Lemoine

The enormous neoclassical Panthéon is basically a secular mausoleum containing the remains of France's most revered compatriots. Clad with more marble than the bathrooms at the Ritz, the Panthéon's enormous cellar is the final resting place of such luminaries as Voltaire, Rousseau, Hugo, and Zola. The odd politician is here too, along with plenty of other well-connected mortals you've never heard of. Until 1995, when the ashes of Marie Curie (a.k.a. Marya Sklodowska) were moved here, the famous inscription above the Panthéon's ornamental front "To The Fatherland's Great Men, In Gratitude" had to be taken literally, as none of the distinguished personalities who lay buried here were women (not counting the lucky wife of chemist and politician Marcellin Berthelot). Born in Warsaw, Madam Curie moved to Paris at age 24 where she studied both physics and mathematics, then went on to win two Nobel prizes for the discovery of natural radioactivity and for determining the atomic weight of radium. She died of leukemia in 1934.

Designed in 1764 as the Church of Sainte Geneviève, the patron saint of Paris, the Panthéon was converted into the nation's burial vault less than 30 years later, during the French Revolution. The building itself is an architectural flop that began to fall into disrepair even before it was completed. Repairs have been underway for more than a decade and will still be when you visit.

The main attraction above ground is the great interior of the Panthéon itself, and the dome from which Foucault hung his pendulum to prove the rotation of the Earth. There's really not much in the sterile crypt, but it's worth a quick visit only to see how lonely and cold death can be.

The Catacombs

1 Place Denfert-Rochereau (14th). Tel. 01.43.22.47.63. Open Tues 11am-4pm, Wed-Sun 9am-4pm. Closed hols. Admission €5 adults, €3.30 students, under 14 free.
M Denfert-Rochereau

Strictly speaking, catacombs are where bodies are buried. The Paris Catacombs are actually an ossuary—a dank, winding labyrinth where bones are stocked and stacked–sixty feet beneath the paving stones of Montparnasse.

Fear of disease from rotting corpses lead to the transferring of human remains from the former *Cimetiere des Innocents* near the Beaubourg to these ancient abandoned quarries; the rocks from which were used to build Paris. Most of the grisly work was performed on cold winter nights between 1785 and 1787. The transfer of skeletons from other cemeteries continued until the 1870s.

There are about 190 miles (300km) of tunnels under the city. Many of these subterranean caves are now the permanent home to the remains of five million Parisians. Their bones are sorted by type and neatly stacked.

The Catacombs have hosted novelty parties for members of the nobility, and served as the headquarters of the French Resistance during World War II. Today they're a tourist attraction.

The entrance is located in a pavilion that was once known, ironically, as Place d'Enfer—"Place of Hell." A long spiral staircase corkscrews down to the bowels of Paris into a warren of limestone tunnels that are as holed as Emmenthal cheese. The tour is an abbreviated hour-long trip that allows you to poke in and out of the galleries, and come face-to-face with countless anonymous skulls as fat drops of slimy water fall on your head. Grills block all the secondary tunnels so you can't get lost like Philibert Aspairt, a doorman at nearby Val-de-Grâce hospital whose skeleton was found in a remote tunnel 11 years after he went missing—identifiable thanks to a ring of keys by his side.

When you exit, through a plain metal door on a nondescript side street, a guard might check you haven't pocketed a souvenir skull.

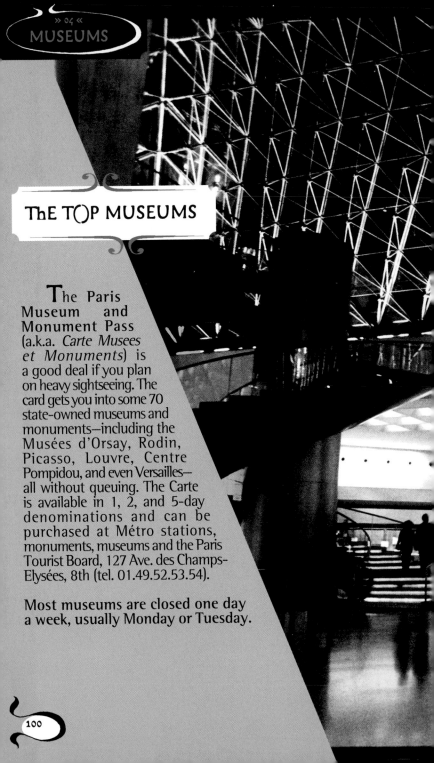

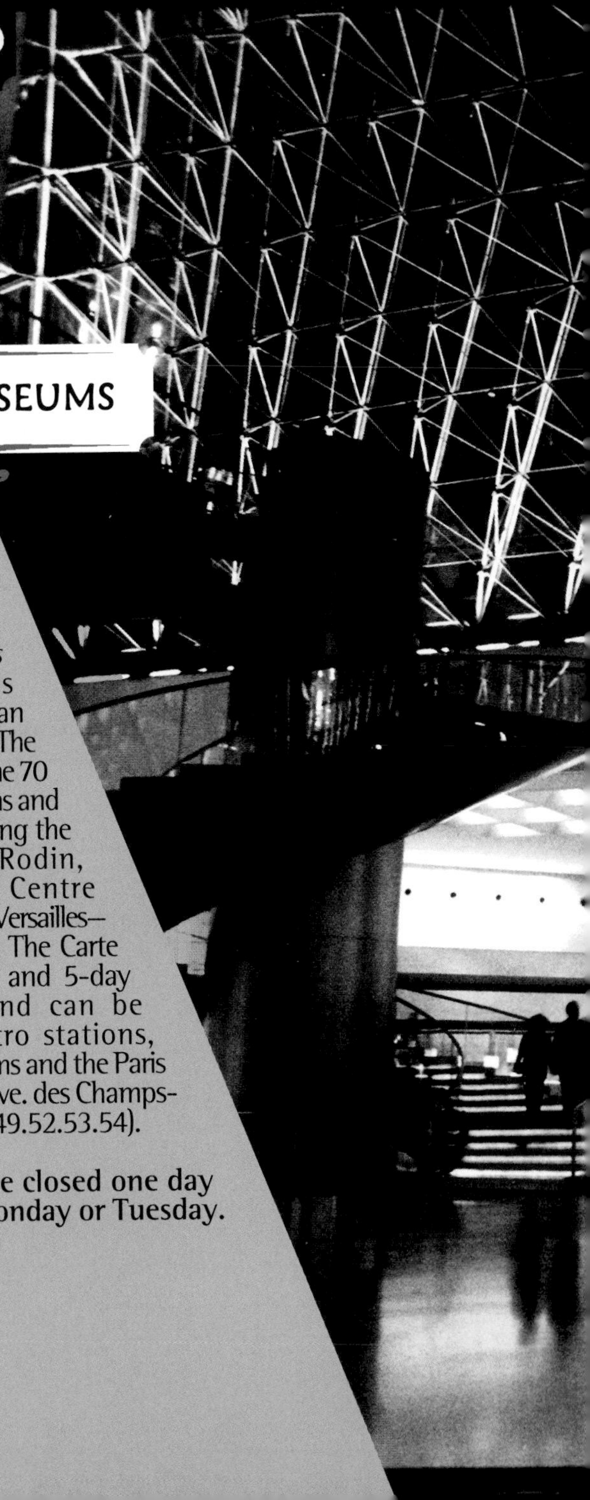

ThE T()P MUSEUMS

The Paris Museum and Monument Pass (a.k.a. *Carte Musees et Monuments*) is a good deal if you plan on heavy sightseeing. The card gets you into some 70 state-owned museums and monuments—including the Musées d'Orsay, Rodin, Picasso, Louvre, Centre Pompidou, and even Versailles—all without queuing. The Carte is available in 1, 2, and 5-day denominations and can be purchased at Métro stations, monuments, museums and the Paris Tourist Board, 127 Ave. des Champs-Elysées, 8th (tel. 01.49.52.53.54).

Most museums are closed one day a week, usually Monday or Tuesday.

RICHELIEU

Musée du Louvre

Main entrance under the pyramid. Tel. 01.40.20.51.51 (recording); 01.40.20.53.17 (live). Open Mon 9am-945pm (most popular collections only), Wed 9am-945pm, Thurs-Sun 9am-6pm. Closed Tues and major hols. Admission €7.50 until 3pm, €5 thereafter and all day Sun; free first Sun of each month and daily for under 18s and art youths with ID. Temporary exposition at Hall Napoléon €7, (combined ticket €11.50, €9.50 after 3pm and Sundays). M Palais Royal

The Mother of All Art Museums, occupying the former residence of the kings of France, is a marvel of monumental architecture that began in 1546 and has seen major additions in every century since.

Opened In 1793, the Louvre was the first public museum in Europe. Its original collection centered on a group of Italian Renaissance paintings, including several by Leonardo da Vinci, and works acquired from the estate of England's King Charles I, after he was beheaded. The Louvre's riches grew dramatically from the spoils of Empire seized by Napoléon during his European and Egyptian campaigns. Subsequent purchases, gifts and archaeological finds have expanded the holdings so that, today, the museum's vast collections occupy 225 galleries in three main wings (Sully, Richelieu and Denon) and are some of the world's most complete; a one-stop shop for Egyptian tombs, ancient Roman coins, meditating marble Buddhas, Renaissance masters paintings, African ceremonial masks, muscular Greek torsos, Asian ceramics, Tiffany windows, European arms and armor... the list seems endless.

The museum's seven curatorial departments move from strength to strength, from famed collections of Oriental antiquities to the Crown Diamonds of France. But it's the Department of Paintings for which the museum is most famous, and widely considered the most important of its kind in the world. All the various European schools from the Middle Ages to the early 19th century are represented, in both quality and quantity. Look for the best examples of northern masters like Rubens, Vermeer and Rembrandt, to top Italian Renaissance works by Botticelli and Raphael. Only the 20th Century galleries lag but, then again, modern and contemporary art have separate museums all to themselves.

Getting the most from the Louvre requires a good floor plan (available free at the entrance), and a decent sense of direction.

The oldest works—from pre-classical Greece and the Middle Ages of Northern Europe—are displayed below street level. In the cellar of the Sully wing you can see parts of the Medieval Louvre and wander amidst towers, draw-bridges, moats and dungeons.

Highlights on the ground floor include Egyptian antiquities in the Sully wing, where you'll find a beautiful and diverse collection that includes statues, sarcophagi, masques, papyrus scrolls, jewelry and hieroglyphics. We love the animal head-deities and the shriveled up mummies.

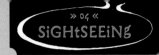

The Greek, Etruscan and Roman antiquities, on the ground and first floors (Sully and Denon wings), include a plethora of historical marble nudes, including the *Sleeping Hermaphrodite* (woman behind, man in front), and two of the most famous sculptures of the ancient world: *Victory of Samothrace* and the armless *Aphrodite*, a.k.a. *Vénus de Milo*. Does the winged *Victory of Samothrace* remind you of anything? Look for her on the hood of your Rolls-Royce the next time you open the garage.

Also on the first floor of the Denon wing are spectacular, large-format French paintings, most of which teem with hundreds of personalities. The most celebrated of these is Théodore Géricault's *The Raft of the Medusa*. Turn the corner to find what seems like miles of classical Italian painting from the 13th through 18th centuries, and a little painting called *Mona Lisa*.

On the opposite side of the museum, in the Richelieu wing, are the apartments of Napoléon III—entire rooms decorated in the preferred style of a 19th century French king (sort of high-class, *fin de siécle* bordello).

Upstairs, on the second floor of the Richelieu wing, are two dozen rooms of Flemish and Dutch paintings, the largest of which is given over entirely to Peter Paul Rubens. This massive collection of the painter's famous plump breasts, billowing clouds and floating cherubs were created for Rubens' patron, Queen Marie de Médicis.

Decent English-language audio tours cover the highlights with succinct descriptions. Handphone sets are available at the entrance to each wing for about €5.

Serious students should begin their museum journey in the massive bookstore (located beneath the pyramid), where several excellent, in-depth museum guides are sold.

Regulars to the Louvre usually dodge the long lines by entering the museum by the back door; through the *Carrousel-du-Louvre* shopping mall, which has direct access from the Tuileries métro. Visit on Mondays and Wednesdays after 5pm to avoid the heaviest crowds.

You can also avoid lines by buying tickets in advance at any Fnac store (the nearest one is in the Les Halles shopping mall), or the through the museum's website (www.louvre.fr).

Tickets are valid for an entire day with reentry privileges, so you can take time out and avoid having an art-attack. The chic **Café Marly**, with its terrace overlooking the Pyramid, is one of the best places in Paris to unwind (*see* Chapter 8/Cafés).

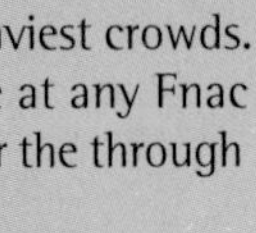

Centre Georges Pompidou
Musée National d'Art Moderne—Beaubourg

Place Georges Pompidou (4th). Tel. 01.44.78.12.33. Centre Pompidou open Wed-Mon 11am-10pm (last admission 9pm, open Thurs until 11pm), museum open Wed-Mon 11am-9pm (last admission 8pm). Closed Tues and some hols. Admission to the Centre Pompidou free. Admission to the museum and expositions €10 adults, €8 youths 13-25, under 13 free; free first Sun of each month. M Rambuteau/Hôtel-de-Ville

Reopened in 2000 following a two year nip-and-tuck, the Beaubourg (as the Centre Georges Pompidou is known to locals) remains one of Paris' most lovable oddities. What some see as an icon of pipes-and-glass post-modernism, others compare to an ugly oil refinery. Designed by Richard Rogers and Renzo Piano, this post-modern temple to contemporary art is a high-tech "inside-out" building with all its brightly-colored "guts" (elevators, water pipes, electrical conduits and the like) on the outside. There can be no debate that the unorthodox architecture has helped make the Beaubourg a bona fide landmark, and one of the most-visited places in Paris.

The museum's fantastic art collection includes definitive examples from all the principal schools and "isms" of 20th-century art (fauvism, cubism, surrealism), including stunning work by Braque, Balthus, Bacon and Basquiat–just to name a few of the "B's." All the stars are here, from cubists Pablo Picasso and Georges Braque to abstract expressionists and pop artists like Jackson Pollock and Andy Warhol.

The exhibition space is ample, offering plenty of room for both art and visitors. The best strategy is to begin on the top floor and work your way down. There's usually a temporary show or two offered, for which an extra admission is often charged.

The Centre Pompidou also houses a center for industrial design, an institute for electronic music, and a concert hall dedicated primarily to modern music.

The museum is ridiculously crowded on weekends. It's worst during the week before 3pm, when school groups are clogging the buildings arteries.

Georges restaurant, overlooking the roofs and spires of Paris, is a terrifically trendy place to wine or dine (*see* Chapter 8/The Restaurant Scene).

The excellent ground-level museum store carries lots of cool contemporary design objects including furniture, culinary objects, clothing and accessories, toys, games and even office supplies.

Musée d'Orsay

1 Rue de la Légion d'Honneur (7th). Tel. 01.40.49.48.14. Tues-Wed and Fri-Sat 10am-6pm, Thurs 10am-945pm, Sun 9am-6pm. Closed Mon. Opens from 9am from mid-June through Sept. Admission €7 adults, €5 youths 18-25 and everyone on Sun. Under 18 free. Additional €1.50 to see temporary exhibitions. M Solférino

The Musée d'Orsay is a knockout, delivering a one-two punch of sensational modern art in an equally spectacular one-of-a-kind setting. The museum's extensive holdings–paintings, sculptures, photographs, and other works of art–reads like a summery of the creative hits from 1848 to 1914. The collection is arranged chronologically in three main galleries.

On the ground floor are early works, ranging from French neoclassical paintings through early impressionism and the Barbizon School. Highlights include *La Source*, by Jean-Auguste-Dominique Ingres, and *Arrangement in Black and Grey No. 1: The Artist's Mother*, better known as *Whistler's Mother*, by the American painter James Abbott McNeill Whistler.

Naturalism, and the symbolist movement are represented on the mezzanine level, which also features a large collection of art nouveau furniture and objets d'art by the likes of Charles Rennie Mackintosh and Lalique.

The top floor, dedicated to later impressionist and post-impressionist works, is the Orsay's *pièce de résistance*. Paul Gauguin, Camille Jacob Pissarro, Georges Seurat, Henri de Toulouse-Lautrec and most every other well-known turn-of-the-century artist is represented, often by his or her very best work. While other museums thrill to have single canvases by the likes of Paul Cézanne or Vincent Van Gogh, the Orsay offers entire rooms filled with their masterpieces. Many icons of modern and contemporary art are always on display, including *Racing at Longchamps* by Edgar Degas, *Self-Portrait* by Vincent Van Gogh, *Le Moulin de la Gallette* by Pierre Auguste Renoir, *Le Déjeuner Sur l'Herbe* by Edouard Manet, and Monet's five paintings of Rouen Cathedral.

The luminous iron-and-glass train station in which the museum makes its home was built to receive visitors to the Paris Expo in 1900. It was beautifully converted for art's sake in 1987. The station's two massive clocks have also been restored. One provides the backdrop for the top floor **Café des Hauteurs**, in which you can enjoy reasonably-priced drinks and lunches.

Of course, when it comes to crowds, the Orsay's comparison to a working train station is unavoidable. For the most elbow room, go in the early morning or Thursday after 5pm. Pick up a free floorplan upon entering and take some comfort in the fact that tickets are valid all day, so you can leave the building for a breather and reenter as you please. Audioguides in English are about €5.

OThER MAjOR COLLECTiONS & SPACES

Le Musée National Du Moyen Age des Thermes de Cluny

6 Place Paul-Painlevé (5th). Tel. 01.53.73.78.00. Open Wed-Mon 915am-545pm. Closed Tues. Admission €5.50 adults, €4 youths 18-25 and Sun. for everyone, free first Sun and under 18. M Saint Michel

This historical double bill celebrates the Middle Ages and the remains of Roman-era thermal baths that once stood on this site. The 15th-century museum building, a Gothic mansion that was once home to the enormously wealthy abbot of Cluny, features courtyard gargoyles, stained-glass windows, and a multitude of spires, balustrades and arcades. The museum is best known for its tapestries, each of which weaves an intricate story. *Mille Fleurs* (Thousand Flowers) depicts aristocratic life with all its distractions, including hunting, courting, embroidering and bathing. *Lady with the Unicorn*, the most famous of the lot, is a series of six perceptive panels, each of which represents one of the senses. Middle Age furnishings, suits of armor, jewelry and stained glass are also displayed, as is Paris's oldest sculpture, *Boatman's Pillar*, made between AD 17 and AD 37. In one room are the enormous contents of a house that a lord might have taken with him when traveling around the countryside or fighting abroad.

Unfortunately, the only bit that remains from the Roman bathhouse is the Frigidarium, where the citizens of Lutèce (as ancient Paris was called) hung out some twenty centuries ago.

Guided tours in English are scheduled Saturdays at 1130am and Sundays at 10am. They last 90 minutes and cost about €6 for adults and €4.50 for children under 18 (includes museum entrance).

Le Musée des Arts Décoratifs

Palais du Louvre, 107 Rue de Rivoli (1st). Tel. 01.44.55.57.50. Open Tues-Sun 11am-6pm. Admission €7 adults, €5.50 youths 18-25, under 18 free. M Palais Royal

The Louvre Museum shares its royal palace with the maximalist Museum of Decorative Arts, an orgy of interior design from the Middle Ages through the early 20th Century. The 100-plus rooms of this remarkable museum are filled with furniture, jewelry, objets d'art and paintings. Charles VIIIs Gothic bedroom is faithfully reconstructed, complete with furnishings and tapestries. Another room is typical of those found in French homes during the Renaissance. There's plenty of religious art, Flemish tapestries and Venetian glass, and well as fine examples of art nouveau and art deco.

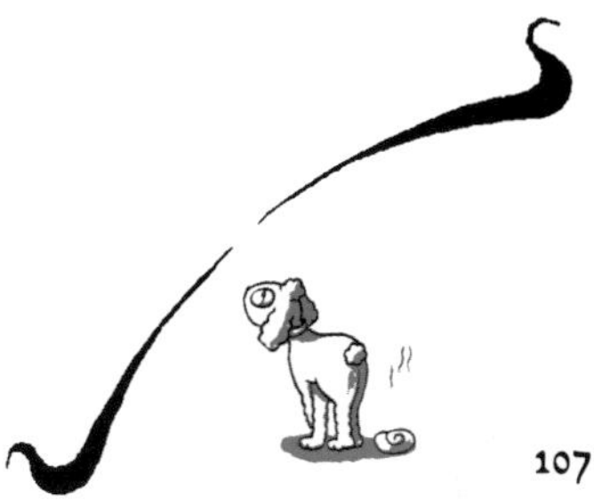

Musée Picasso

Hôtel Salé, 5 Rue Thorigny (3rd). Tel. 01.42.71.25.21. Open Wed-Mon 930am-530pm Oct-Mar, 930am-6pm April-Sept. Admission €5.50 adults (Sun €4), €4 youths 18-25, free first Sun of each month and for under 18s. M St-Paul/Chemin Vert. Pablo Picasso used to describe himself as "the world's leading collector of Picassos," as he kept the majority of his work to himself. When he died, in 1973, the master's huge personal *oeuvre* was donated to the country and the Musée Picasso was born. If you didn't know it before, this collection makes clear how amazingly prolific Picasso was, and in a wide variety of media. There are over 3500 sketches, drawings, engravings, collages, illustrated books, ceramic works, paintings, and a large collection of sculptures. The museum offers a complete overview of the artist's 80 years of work, and offers the opportunity to follow Picasso's career in its entirety. The exhibition begins upstairs with early paintings that include his famous Harlequins, and moves chronologically—painting and sculpture together—through the artist's Blue and Pink periods and cubist and neoclassical phases, to his late-in-life grotesques and predominantly black final canvases.

The museum itself is a particularly magnificent, 17th-century *hôtel particulier* in the Marais. Known as *Hôtel Salé*, it is named after its 17th-century owner, Pierre Aubert de Fontenay, a *nouveau riche* businessman who made his fortune collecting salt taxes.

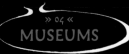

Musée Rodin

Hôtel Biron, 77 Rue de Varenne (7th). Tel. 01.44.18.61.10. Open Tues-Sun 930am-545pm. Admission €5 adults, €3 youths 18-25, under 18 free; gardens only €1 M Varenne

The elegant Hôtel Biron once housed the studios of a number of artists, including Auguste Rodin, who died here in 1917. Today the entire 18th century mansion is a museum dedicated to the world's best-known modern sculptor. Hundreds of white-marble statues fill the building, and the artist's bronzes dot the exquisite gardens outside. All the hits are here, including *The Age of Bronze*, *The Thinker*, *Burghers of Calais*, and *Le Baiser*, a kiss so ardent you can practically taste it.

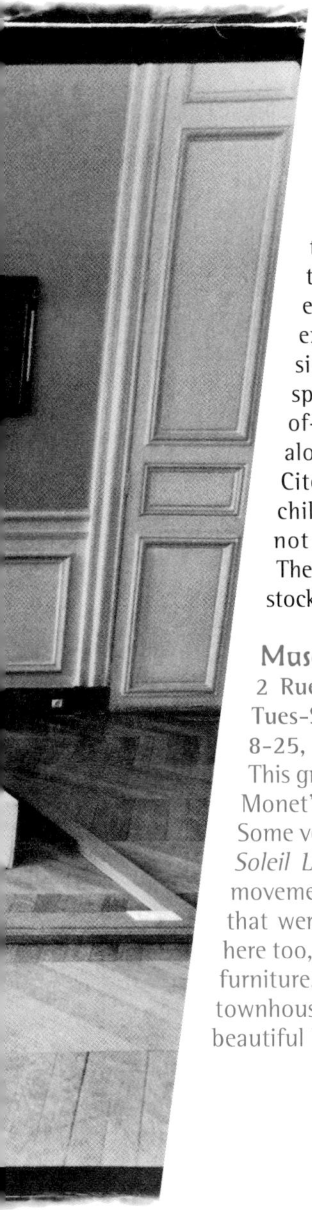

The City of Science and Industry—Parc de La Villette

30 Ave. Corentin-Cariou (19th). Tel. 01.40. 05.80.00. Open Tues-Sun 930am-545pm April-Sept. (garden closes at 645pm), 930am-445pm Oct-Mar (garden closes at 5pm). Admission €7.5 adults, €5.50 youths 8-25,. M Porte-de-la-Villette

More than a museum, this salute to science is something of a technological Disneyland in which people, especially young people, are invited to experience and discover science on a very personal level. The City of Science and Industry aims to help non-scientists understand natural phenomena through hundreds of hands-on exhibits with twisting dials, flashing screens, and big sound effects. A characteristic recent exhibit, "Frogs," explained the idiosyncrasies of the creatures via sights, sounds and science. Other exhibits focus on space technology, computers and astronomy. A top-of-the-line planetarium is one of the main attractions, along with an aquarium, an Omnimax cinema and the Cité des Enfants, which has hands-on exhibits for children ages 3-5. A great museum that's definitely not just for kids.

There are several restaurants, and an excellent gift shop stocked with cool gadgets.

Musée Marmottan Claude Monet

2 Rue Louis Boilly (16th). Tel. 01.44.96.50.33. Open Tues-Sun 10am-6pm. Admission €6.50 adults, €4 youths 8-25, under 8 free. M La Muette

This great little museum was created in 1971, after Claude Monet's son donated 65 paintings created by his father. Some very important works are here, including *Impression, Soleil Levant* the painting from which the Impressionist movement took its name. Works by other Impressionists that were once part of Monet's private collection are here too, along with some Renaissance-era art and furniture. It's all in an elegant 19th-century townhouse near the Bois de Boulogne, on beautiful Ranelagh Park.

Musée National d'Histoire Naturelle

57 Rue Cuvier (5th). Tel. 01.40.79.30.00. Open daily 10am-6pm, until 10pm on Thurs. Admission to individual galleries ranges from €5-€9, reduced rates for youths 18-25. M Jussieu/Gare d'Austerlitz

Established by Louis XIII in 1635, Paris's premiere nature museum has been brought out of the Stone Age with a magnificent facelift that has rendered it one of the world's most user-friendly warehouses of history. Situated in several separate pavilions within the Jardin des Plantes botanical garden, the museum's *piece de résistance* is **La Grande Galerie de l'Evolution**, in a majestic building at the far end of the park. Like the Forum Shops in Las Vegas, lighting here is accelerated to replicate the passage of a single day in a matter of moments. Meanwhile, the drama of Evolution is played out in three acts on a trio of floors: humanity's relationship to the world, the mechanics of evolution, and bio-diversity of the animal world. Terrific interactive exhibits, excellent lighting and contemporary displays make a visit here both fun and educational for almost everybody. The tableaux featuring a parade of animals of the African savannah will even appeal to Creationists, as the beasts look like they're getting set to board Noah's Ark.

Across the park, the **Gallerie de Minéralogie** wows with its permanent exhibition "Cristaux Géants," a unique collection of boulder-size crystals that are in their own way an endangered species. The usual fossils, insects and skeletons are found nearby, along with the **Galerie de Paléontologie** which draws school kids *en masse* with its raptor and T-Rex skeletons.

Le Musée Carnavalet

Hôtel Carnavalet, 23 Rue de Sévigné (3rd). Tel. 01.44.59.58.58. Open Tues-Sun 10am-6pm. Free admission to the permanent collections. Temporary expositions €5.50 adults, €2.50 youths 14-26, free for those under 14. M St-Paul/Chemin Vert

This museum of the history of Paris is one of our favorite museums in the city. Situated inside one of the finest mansions in the Marais, the Carnavalet is a comprehensive repository of the city's past, from pre-Roman times to the present day. A tour of the building is something of a crash-course in art history, with many different disciplines—applied arts, painting and furnishing—brought together to weave a single story. Displays are set chronologically with rooms devoted to Renaissance collections, the Revolution and French literature. As is to be expected, there's plenty Napoléona too, including the ornate cradle he presented to the city upon the birth of his son.

Le Musée Maillol

61 Rue de Grenelle (7th). Tel. 01.42.22.59.58. Open Wed-Mon 11am-6pm. Closed Tues and hols. Admission €7 adults, €5.50 students, under 16 free. M Rue du Bac

This remarkable little museum devoted to the French-Catalan sculptor Aristide Maillol is a compact gem of a place that shouldn't be missed. The museum gathers the collections of Dina Vierny, Maillol's favorite muse and model. The assortment is astonishing. Aside from Maillol's work, the holdings include great art and sculpture by Redon, Duchamp, Bonnard, Renoir, Maurice Denis, Picasso, Ingres, Degas, Foujita, Kandinsky, Cézanne and many others.

In addition to displaying one of the best small collections of art in Paris, the museum itself is one of the prettiest anywhere, set in one of the city's most chic neighborhoods. There's a pleasant cafe and a good gift shop. And the fact that this museum is unknown to most tourists only adds to its charm.

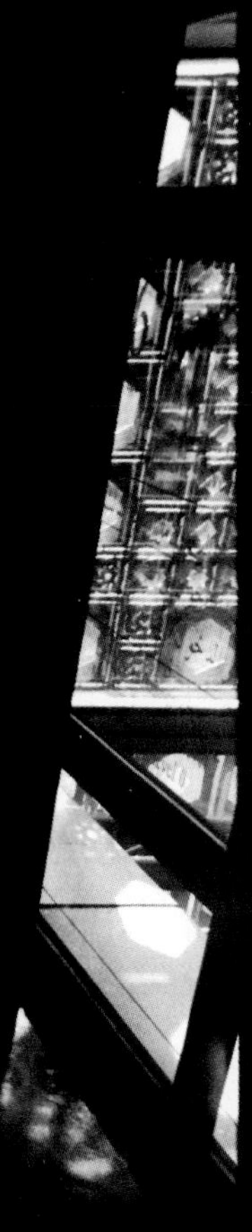

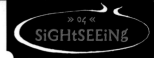

Institut du Monde Arabe

1 Rue des Fossés Saint Bernard (5th). Tel. 01.40.51.38.38. Open Tues-Sun 10am-6pm. Admission €4 adults, €3 youths 12-25, under 12 free; Prices for temporary exhibitions vary. M Jussieu/Maubert-Mutualité

The Arab World Institute is not just a showplace of Middle-Eastern art. It's a lively cultural center—comprising a museum, library, cinema, shop and a tea room—all wrapped in one of Paris' most interesting buildings. Designed in the 1980s, the striking glass-and-steel facade is built with photo-sensitive windows; mechanized metal panels which act like the aperture of a camera to regulate the flow of light into the building. At the same time, the windows cast shadows that are reminiscent of the lattice screens from Moorish palaces. The permanent collection includes art from ancient times to the current day, with regular temporary shows filling in the gaps. Don't miss the rooftop terrace, from where there are fabulous views over Paris.

PARkS & GARdENS

Paris has an infamously low ratio of green space per inhabitant. As in London, the largest open areas in this city were originally protected from development by their status as royal preserves. Chief among these is the **Bois de Boulogne**, a huge wooded area just west of the center that's mirrored on the city's eastern side by the **Bois de Vincennes**, which also contains a botanical garden, some museums and the city's main zoo (*see* Chapter 5/Digging Deeper).

In addition to the parks listed below, you'll find benches and grass on the **Champs de Mars** (by the Eiffel Tour), on the **Esplanade des Invalides** (in front of the Hôtel des Invalides), and in the **Jardin du Palais Royal** (just north of the Louvre; *see* Chapter 5/Digging Deeper).

Luxembourg Gardens

Boulevard Saint-Michel/Rue de Vaugirard/Rue Guynemer/Rue Auguste-Comte (6th). Open daily sunrise-sunset.
M Notre-Dame-des-Champs/Luxembourg/St-Michel

Studded with centuries-old trees, winding paths, statues, lawns and reflecting pools, the Jardins du Luxembourg top our list as the shadiest, coziest, sexiest green space in the capital. And it's always great for people-watching. Look at the middle-aged joggers, the old men reading *Le Monde*, the youngsters sunbaking, the lovers who stroll, and the ones who stop to smell the flowers. Look at the boys who play chess, and their fathers playing *les boules*. Look at the couples playing tennis, students debating politics or philosophy, tourists trying to pick up Swedish au pairs, who are pushing prams full of fresh French babyflesh. See the legislators hurry into the Senate, and those who leave it exhausted. There are artists sketching statues, workers who keep the bees, and ladies who lean forward to read the names of all the different varieties of fruit trees in the Conservatory—*belle d'été, racine rouge, la nationale*. This is the lung of Paris.

Jardin des Tuileries

Between the Louvre, the Seine, Rue de Rivoli and Place de la Concorde (1st).
M Concorde/Tuileries

With its ground-zero location, the Tuileries are perfectly situated for a rest in the sun between hard-core central-Paris sightseeing. The gardens are laid-out in elaborately formal French style, with symmetrical pools, terraces and museums—the **Jeu de Paume** and the **Orangerie**. The Tuileries is the original back garden of a palace that once stood on this site, and is named for an even older "tileworks" that was located here. During the time of the French Revolution, King Louis XVI and his family were forced to abandon the Palace of Versailles and take up residence in the Tuileries. Four years later, in 1793, the king was tried and executed. The palace was burned down during the Commune of 1871, but the gardens remain as a public park. Twice yearly—Christmas and summer, a colossal Ferris wheel is erected at the western end of the park offering great views over the city center.

Jardin des Plantes & Le Ménagerie

57 Rue Cuvier (5th).
Tel. 01.40.79.30.00.
Garden open daily sunrise to sunset; Greenhouses open Wed-Mon 1pm-6pm (summer) and 1pm-5pm (winter); Menagerie open daily 9am-5pm (winter) 9-6pm (summer).
Garden admission free; greenhouses €3; menagerie €6 adults, €3.50 children 4-18.
M Jussieu/Gare d'Austerlitz

Began in the 1600s as a medicinal herb garden, the Jardin des Plantes has blossomed into a large series of outdoor gardens and greenhouses thriving with "exotic" plants, including France's first cocoa tree and tobacco plants, which were originally introduced into the country by Jean Nicot (of nicotine fame) in 1561.

Le Ménagerie, on the north side of the park, is a small zoo housing forlorn-looking wolves a small wild horse, and lot of baby animals. Most guides will gleefully tell you that during the Prussian Siege of Paris in 1871, the animals of the Ménagerie were eaten by starving Parisians.

Our favorite part is the Microzoo, which focuses on the acariens and bacteria that inhabit our bodies, carpets and clothes.

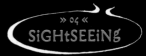

Bois de Boulogne

M Porte Maillot/Porte Dauphine/Porte d'Auteuil

An enormous forested park located on the up-market western side of the city, this is where Paris comes to bicycle, jog, ride horses, go birding and trail walk. Originally a private hunting ground for the kings of France, the bois includes a several small fishing ponds and two big lakes, the larger of which (called, paradoxically, *Lac Inférieur*) is great for canoeing. Boats are available for rent. You can paddle (or take a little barge) to a small island in the center that's perfect for picnicking.

Bikes can be hired near the lake, and in front of the **Jardin d'Acclimatation** (*see* Chapter 6/Biking). Then take to the numerous well-trodden nature paths.

A walk to the Bois from the Arc de Triomphe takes you along **Avenue Foch**, a swanky street that's home to some of the most expensive apartments in the capital.

Top destinations in the park include the **Pré-Catelan**, an oasis of harmony with lawns, flower beds and playgrounds located west of the lake; and the **Bagatelle**, a magnificent rose garden with a small château that was built by the brother of King Louis XVI. It's said that Count d'Artois bet his-sister-in-law, Marie-Antoinette, 100,000 pounds that he could have the palace built before she returned from a stay in Fontainebleau. He won. It was completed in just 67 days. The roses bloom in late May.

The **Jardin d'Acclimatation**, at the northern end of the park, comes complete with a miniature farm and Enchanted River boat rides.

A good map of the Bois, is available from the **Paris Tourist Board**, 127 Ave. des Champs-Elysées, 8th (tel. 01.49.52.53.54), will help you get the most out of your walk through the woods.

Parc des Buttes Chaumont

Entrances on Rue de Crimée, Rue Manin, Rue Botzaris (19th).

M Buttes Chaumont/Botzaris/Laumière

Situated in the northeastern corner of the city, Parc des Buttes Chaumont is the Dolly Parton of Paris parks. Everything is fake here, but that's part of the charm. It's also one of the biggest and prettiest parks in the capital. Verdant, rambling and hilly, the park includes a cavernous grotto with artificial stalactites, an impressive full-size waterfall, and a mini-mountain set in the center of an human-made lake, from which there is a great view of Montmartre. There aren't many tourists here; just locals walking with their dogs, children playing and lovers strolling.

PARIS' BEST SPECIALTY MUSEUMS

Musée de l'Air et de l'Espace
Aéroport du Bourget. Tel. 01.49.92.71.71. Bus 350 from Gare de L'Est or Gare du Nord
Hangars and tarmacs full of French planes, helicopters and rockets.

Institut Français d'Architecture
6 Rue de Tournon (6th) Tel. 01.46.33.90.36. M Odéon
Temporary exhibitions of contemporary architecture.

Pavillon de l'Arsenal
21 Blvd. Morland (4th) Tel. 01.42.76.33.97. M Sully-Morland
A giant floor model of Paris plus terrific exhibits on city architecture.

Le Musée d'Art et d'Histoire du Judaïsme
Hôtel de Saint-Aignan, 71 Rue du Temple (3rd). Tel. 01.53.01.86.60. M Rambuteau/Hôtel-de-Ville
Impressive Jewish museum in one of the most prestigious *hôtel particuliers* in the Marais.

Musée des Arts et Métiers
292 Rue St-Martin (3rd) Tel. 01.53.01.82.00. M Arts et Métiers
Technological museum celebrating homegrown science and sweat.

Musée d'Art Moderne de la Ville de Paris
11 Ave. de Président Wilson (16th). Tel. 01. 53.67.40.00. M Iéna/Alma-Marceau
Blockbuster modern art shown behind a Brutalist facade.

Musée d'Art Naïf Max Fourny
Halle St. Pierre, 1 Rue Ronsard (18th). Tel. 01.42.58.72.89. M Anvers
Sublime naïve art in an equally joyful steel-and-glass building.

Musée d'Arts et Traditions Populaires
6 Ave. du Mahatma Gandhi (16th). Tel. 01.44.17.60.00. M Sablons
Documentation of the lives, customs, tools and even the clogs of French peasants.

Le Musée de l'Assistance Publique
47 Quai Tournelle (5th). Tel. 01.46. 33.01.43. M Maubert-Mutualité
Paupers, madmen, idlers, orphans—fascinating account of the down-and-out through the ages.

Maison de Balzac
47 Rue Raynouard (16th). Tel. 01.55.74.41.80. M Passy
The author Honoré's former home, packed with memorabilia, first editions and more.

Bibliothèque Forney
Hôtel de Sens, 1 Rue du Figuier (4th). Tel. 01.42.78.14.60. M Pont-Marie
Applied and graphic arts in the oldest mansion in the Marais.

Musée Bourdelle

16 Rue Antoine Bourdelle (15th).
Tel. 01.49.54.73.73.
M Montparnasse-Bienvenue
Studio where Rodin's assistant lived and worked, complete with hundreds of sculptures.

Musée Bouilhet-Christofle

112 Rue Ambroise Croizat, Saint Denis . Tel. 01.49.33.43.00.
M Saint Denis Porte de Paris
Fantastic art nouveau and deco pieces by the celebrated silversmith.

Atelier Brancusi

Centre Pompidou, Place Beaubourg (4th). Tel. 01.44. 78.12.33.
M Hôtel-de-Ville/Rambuteau
Faithfully reconstructed studio where sculptor Constantin Brancusi lived and worked.

Musée Bricard

1 Rue de la Perle (3rd).
Tel. 01.42.77.79.62.
M St. Paul/Chemin Vert
Elegant Marais museum entirely dedicated to locks and locksmithing.

Musée du Cabinet des Médailles

Bibliothèque Nationale Richelieu, 58 Rue de Richelieu (2nd).
Tel. 01.47.03.83.30. M Bourse
Medals, coins and miniatures, plus Charlemagne's chess set, King Dagobert's throne, and more.

La Fondation Cartier Pour l'Art Contemporain

261 Blvd. Raspail (14th).
Tel. 01.42.18.56.51. M Raspail
Cartier jewelers' excellent collection of contemporary art, in a swanky, ultra-modern showplace.

Musée Cernuschi

7 Ave. Velasquez (8th).
Tel. 01.45.63.50.75.
M Villiers/Monceau
Buddhas, Bodhisatvas and Chinese arts from the 5th Century through the T'ang Dynasty.

Chapelle St-Louis de la Salpêtrière

47 Blvd. de l'Hôpital (13th).
Tel. 01.42.16.04.24.
M Gare d'Austerlitz
17th-century chapel known for sensational, ultra-contemporary art installations.

Musée de la Chasse et de la Nature

l'Hôtel Guénégaud, 60 Rue des Archives (3rd). Tel. 01.53.01.92.40.
M Temple
Taxidermical tour-de-force with some Rubens' and Rembrandts thrown in for good measure.

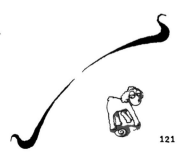

Cité De La Musique Museum
Parc de la Villette, 221 Ave. Jean-Jaurès. (19th) Tel. 01.44.84.45.00.
M Porte de Pantin
Exceptional collection of Western musical instruments through the ages.

Musée Cognacq-Jay
Hôtel Donon, 8 Rue Elzévir (3rd). Tel. 01.40.27.07.21. M St. Paul
Treasure trove of 18th-century art and furniture in an awesomely charming *hôtel particulier.*

Musée de la Contrefaçon
16 Rue de la Faisanderie (16th).
Tel. 01.56.26.14.00.
M Porte Dauphine
The same Hermés and Chanel counterfeits you might see at the local flea market. Cool.

Musée du Cristal Baccarat
30 bis, Rue de Paradis (10th).
Tel. 01.47.70.64.30. M Poissonnière
The celebrated glassmakers' HQ includes a small museum of homemade crystal.

Musée de la Curiosité
11 Rue St-Paul (4th).
Tel. 01.42.77.45.62.
M St-Paul/Sully Morland
Museum of magic with Vegas-style illusions and plenty of smoke and mirrors.

Ecole Nationale Supérieure des Beaux-Arts Gallery
13 Quai Malaquais (6th).
Tel. 01.47.03.50.00.
M St-Germain-des-Prés
Top student shows and rotating exhibitions from the school's extensive collections.

Musée Edith Piaf
5 Rue Crespin du Gast, 11th.
Tel. 01.43.55.52.72.
M Ménilmontant
Two-room tribute to the "little sparrow" open by appointment.

Musée Eugène Delacroix
6 Rue de Furstenberg (6th).
Tel. 01.44.41.86.50.
M St-Germain-des-Près/ Mabillon
The artist's former studio and apartment filled with self-portraits, watercolors and drawings.

Musée de l'Eventail

Atelier Hoguet,
2 Blvd. de Strasbourg (10th).
Tel. 01.42.08.90.20.
M Strasbourg-St. Denis
Private collection of fans, from 18th-century ivory wands to handhelds by Karl Lagerfeld.

Maison Européenne de la Photographie

5 Rue de Fourcy (4th).
Tel. 01.44.78.75.00.
M St-Paul/Pont-Marie
Beautifully restored Marais mansion filled with contemporary photography.

Musée de l'Erotisme

72 Blvd. de Clichy, 18th.
Tel. 01.42.58.28.73. M Blanche
Ancient sacred phalluses, fertility idols, Kama Sutra drawings, homo-erotic Aztec sculpture....

Musée de l'Histoire de la France
l'Hôtel de Soubise,
60 Rue des Francs-Bourgeois (3rd).
Tel. 01.40.27.61.78.
M Rambuteau/Hôtel-de-Ville
Over-the-top décor and self-important historical documents, including Napoléon's will.

Musée de la Franc-Maçonnerie
16 Rue Cadet (9th).
Tel. 01.45.23.20.92. M Cadet
Record of Freemasonry since medieval times, but the secrets remain intact.

Musée Gustave Moreau
14 Rue de La Rochefoucauld (9th).
Tel. 01.48.74.38.50. M Trinité
Former home and studio of the symbolist painter, crammed with over 8000 works.

Musée Grevin
10 Blvd. Montmartre (9th).
Tel. 01.47.70.85.05.
M Grands Boulevards
Paris' wax museum is a French cultural icon and international tourist trap rolled into one.

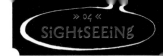

Musée d'Histoire de la Médecine
Université René Descartes, 12 Rue de l'Ecole de Médecine (6th).
Tel. 01.40.46.16.93. M Odéon
Medical tools and techniques from ancient Egypt through 1960s France.

Musée de l'Homme
Palais du Chaillot,
17 Place du Trocadéro (16th).
Tel. 01.44.05.72.00. M Trocadéro
The history of humankind laid bare in the city's primary ethnographic museum.

Musée Jacquemart-André
158 Blvd. Haussmann (8th).
Tel. 01.45.62.11.59.
M St-Philippe du Roule/Miromesnil
Sumptuous mansion with rich furnishings, Gobelins tapestries, frescoes, paintings and more.

Musée National de la Légion d'Honneur
2 Rue de Bellechasse (7th).
Tel. 01.40.62.84.25. M Solférino
Almost a millennium's worth of chivalric decorations, and the best collection of Napoléona.

Musée Guimet (Musée National des Arts Asiatiques)
6 Place d'Ièna (16th).
Tel. 01.56.52.53.00. M Ièna
An annex of the Louvre with excellent collections of pan-Asian art.

Musée Hebert
Hotel de Montmorency-Bours, 85 Rue du Cherche-Midi (6th).
Tel. 01.42.22.23.82.
M Vaneau/St-Placide
Paintings, watercolors and drawings by late 19th-century artist Ernest Hébert.

Mémorial du Maréchal Leclerc—Musée Jean Moulin
Jardin Atlantique, 23 Allée de la 2eme D.B. (15th). Tel. 01.40.64.39.44.
M *Montparnasse-Bienvenue*
Propaganda-packed homage to the wartime general and Resistance leader.

Musée de la Mode et du Costume
Pallais Galliera, 10 Ave. Pierre 1er de Serbie (16th). Tel. 01.56.52.86.00.
M *Iéna*
Two centuries of dresses from all the big couturiers, in a magnificent Renaissance-style palace.

Musée de la Mode et du Textile
In the Rohan Wing of the Louvre, 107 Rue de Rivoli (1st). Tel. 01.44.55.57.50.
M *Palais Royal-Musée du Louvre*
Clothing, costumes and accessories from the 18th Century to the present day.

Musée de la Monnaie
11 Quai de Conti (6th). Tel. 01.40.46.55.35. M *Pont-Neuf*
Paris' old mint turned tribute to coins and medals of realms past.

Musée des Monuments Français
Palais de Chaillot, 1 Place du Trocadéro (16th). Tel. 01.44.05.39.10. M *Trocadéro*
Monumental architecture told in models, molds and murals; it's like France in miniature.

Musée de Montmartre
12 Rue Cortot (18th). Tel. 01.46.06.61.11.
M *Lamarck-Caulaincourt*
Homage to Montmartre's heydays at the epicenter of bohemian artistic life.

Musée du Montparnasse
21 Ave. du Maine (15th). Tel. 01.42. 22.91.96.
M *Montparnasse-Bienvenue*
Montparnasse through the eyes of Marie Vasilieff, friend of Braque, Picasso, Matisse and Modigliani.

Musée National des Arts d'Afrique et d'Océanie
293 Ave. Daumesnil (12th). Tel. 01.44.74.84.80. M *Porte Dorée*
Deco building full of world art, plus tropical aquaria with live crocodiles and piranhas.

Musée National de la Céramique
Place de la Manufacture, 92310 Sèvres. Tel. 01.41.14.04.20.
M *Pont de Sèvres*
Factory/showroom/museum that's ground-zero for Sèvres porcelain.

Musée National Jean-Jaques Henner
43 Ave. de Villiers (17th). Tel. 01.47.63.42.73.
M *Malesherbes*
The paintings of the Alsatian artist whom Rodin admired and Degas detested.

Galerie Nationale du Jeu De Paume
Jardin des Tuileries, Place de la Concorde (1st). Tel. 01.47.03.12.50
M *Concorde*
Napoléon IIIs tennis court now plays host to top temporary art exhibits.

Musée National de la Marine
Palais de Chaillot, 17 Place du Trocadéro (16th). Tel. 01.56.65.69.69. M Trocadéro
Boats, floats and a former Emperor's canoe.

Centre National de la Photographie
11 Rue Berryer (8th). Tel. 01.53.76.12.32. M George V
French photography in a terrific Rothschild mansion.

Musée Nissim de Camondo
63 Rue de Monceau (8th). Tel. 01.53.89.06.40. M Villiers or Monceau
A fantastic townhouse decked out in top-of-the-line 18th-century style.

Musée de l'Opéra
Place de L'Opéra, main entrance to the Opéra (9th). Tel. 01.47.42.07.02. M Opéra
Everything you ever wanted to know about Parisian opera but were afraid to ask....*

Musée de l'Orangerie
Jardin des Tuileries, Place de la Concorde (1st). Tel. 01.42.97.48.16. M Tuileries
Paintings from the post-Impressionists to the *entre-deux-guerres.*

Musée de l'Ordre de la Libération
51 bis, Blvd. de La Tour Maubourg (7th). Tel. 01.47.05.04.10. M Latour-Maubourg
The official French spin on five years of Resistance and deportations.

Musée des Parfumeries-Fragonard
9 Rue Scribe (9th). Tel. 01.47.42.04.56. M Opéra
Scents from the perfume house Fragonard. Displays on manufacture, nosing and bottles.

Musée Pasteur
Institut Pasteur, 25 Rue du Dr. Roux (15th). Tel. 01.45.68.82.83. M Pasteur
Pasteur's former flat contains personal objects, memorabilia and the famous chemist's tomb.

Musée de la Publicité
Palais du Louvre, 107 Rue de Rivoli (1st). Tel. 01.44.55.57.50. M Palais Royal
Poster and advertising museum with an emphasis on graphic arts.

La Mission du Patrimonie Photographique
Hôtel de Sully, 62 Rue St-Antoine (4th). Tel. 01.42.74.47.75. M Bastille/St-Paul
Temporary exhibitions of historical photographs.

Musée de la Poste
34 Blvd. de Vaugirard (15th). Tel. 01.42.79.23.45. M Montparnasse-Bienvenue
Old stamps and the letters they rode on. But you won't learn why French mail is always late.

Musée de la Poupée
Impasse Berthaud (3rd). Tel. 01.42.72.73.11 M Rambuteau
Museum of late 19th-century dolls with originals from the world's top manufacturers.

Musée de la Préfecture de Police
4, rue de la Montagne Sainte-Geneviève (5th).
Tel. 01.44.41.52.50.
M Maubert-Mutualité
Museum for wannabe cops and those interested in pursuing a life of crime.

Petit Palais
1 Ave. Dutuit (8th).
Tel. 01.45.51.19.31.
M Champs-Elysées-Clemenceau
Eclectic mix of European furniture, Egyptian art, Renaissance gewgaws, Oriental gimcracks...

Musée de Radio-France
116 Ave. du Président-Kennedy (16th).
Tel. 01.56.40.15.16. M Ranelagh
Guided studio tour plus the history of French radio and TV. By appointment.

Musée de la Vie Romantique
16 Rue Chaptal (9th).
Tel. 01.48.74.95.38. M Pigalle
19th Century painter's studio, now an ode to Romantics Frédéric Chopin, George Sand and others.

Salvador Dali Museum —Espace Montmartre
11 Rue Poulbot (18th).
Tel. 01.42.64.40.10. M Abbesses
300 illustrations and 30 sculptures by the surrealist master. No paintings though.

Musée du Service de Santé des Armées
Val de Grâce,
Place Alphonse Laveran (5th).
Tel. 01.40.51.40.00. M Gobelins
Military medicine through the ages, in a beautiful Baroque building.

Maison de Victor Hugo
Hôtel de Rohan-Guémené,
6 Place des Vosges (4th).
Tel. 01.42.72.10.16.
M Bastille/St-Paul/Chemin Vert
Memorabilia and personal effects of the great author, who lived here for fourteen years.

Le Musée Du Vin Et Caveau des Echansons
5 Square Charles Dickens (16th).
Tel. 01.45.25.63.26. M Passy
All about French wine, by region. Tastings and sales as well.

Musée Zadkine
100 bis, Rue d'Assas (6th).
Tel 01.55.42.77.20.
M Port-Royal
The Russian sculptor's studio-cum-shrine with 300-plus cubist and abstract works.

Nº 05

DiGGINg dEEPER

EXPLORING

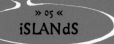

ThE iSLANdS

Despite their ground-zero location, the pair of islands that loiter in the Seine between the river's left and right banks remain in something of a time warp as life here feels somewhat removed from the chaos of the city at large.

Paris started life on the **Île de la Cité**, and the remains of an entire Gothic village surly lingers beneath today's pavement. Spanned by the **Pont-Neuf**, the capital's oldest (and most incongruously named) bridge, there is now something of a bleak quality to the island. Baron Haussmann killed it when he destroyed the island's maze of medieval streets in order to give the exalted Notre-Dame Cathedral some breathing room. The

result, however, is that the great church is now choked by the coachload, as windshield tourists are systematically deposited for the their compulsory 22-minute tours.

The nearby **Concièrgerie, Sainte-Chapelle and Palais de Justice** are all part of the medieval palace complex that once occupied the lion's share of the island. Like Notre-Dame, Sainte-Chapelle remains one of Paris' top sights, and is covered extensively in Chapter 4. The Concièrgerie, the seat of the Parisian judicial system, is less compelling, but history buffs might want to drop in for a glimpse of the 14th-century palace of Capetian kings, to check out mementos from the French Revolution, and to see the cells of Robespierre, Danton, Marie Antoinette and other unfortunates who were imprisoned here before having their heads handed to them.

Parisians usually find themselves on the Île de la Cité for a less tempting prospect, as it's also home to the **Préfecture de Police.** At some time or another, a situation is bound to arise which calls for a day-killing, and ultimately fruitless, battle with French bureaucracy. But if things don't come up roses inside the official buildings, the flowers are always in bloom just outside, on Place Louis-Lépine, home to the best flower and plant market Paris (open Mon-Sat 8am-4pm). There is lots of atmosphere and plenty of colorful characters, perhaps even more so on Sundays, when the Place transforms into a chirping bird market.

Place Dauphine, squeezed between the Concièrgerie and the Pont-Neuf, is also worth a stroll. Shaded by tall buildings, the plaza can be a bit

depressing in winter. But on warm nights, when summer lovers are romancing the stones, one can understand why the triangular and centrally-located Dauphine has been dubbed "the vagina of Paris."

At the opposite end of the island, on its far eastern tip, is a testimonial of quite another sort. Surrounded by bucolic gardens is the chilling, subterranean **Mémorial de la Déportation**, a moving monument to French Jews who were rounded-up and deported to Nazi concentration camps. The fact that the governmentos on the other side of the island were responsible for organizing those trips to the slaughterhouses should be lost on no one.

The **Île St-Louis** lies just across a tiny pedestrian bridge which connects it to the Île de la Cité. Built with narrow streets and beautiful tree-lined *quais*, it is not surprisingly a prime residential area. The historical houses and palaces here are some of the city's finest, making a stroll around these parts an eye-popping adventure. Poke into any open door for a glimpse of the interior courtyards which grace the island. With no Métro station and little commercial activity, the island has maintained a semblance of calm and seclusion that belies its heady central location. Having said that, a stroll down Rue St-Louis, the main drag that slices the island lengthwise, will take you past some wonderful galleries, nice hotels, quirky old-fashioned grocers, interesting restaurants and gaudy souvenir shops. **Berthillon**, one of the world's top ice cream makers, is here too (*see* Chapter 8/Tea Rooms & Desserts). On Sundays throngs of loyalists and wannabes queue patiently for scoops. But, by nightfall, the island once again reverts to its lonely essence, shaded in romantic gloom.

Conciergerie

*1 Quai de l'Horloge (1st). Tel. 01.53.73.78.50. **Open** May-Aug, daily 930am-6pm; Sept-April, daily 10am-5pm.*

QUARTiER LAtIN & ST-GERMAIN-dES-PRÉS

Before French became the *lingua franca*, Latin was the language of the learned, which is what gave the **Latin Quarter** its name. This is, after all, home to the venerable Sorbonne, one of the Continent's best and most prestigious universities. Only until very recently, the Quarter was synonymous with students. But in recent years this district, along with adjacent **St-Germain-des-Prés**, has been undergoing radical change. Where there once was a cluster of bookshops and student hangouts, there is now Vuitton, Armani, Cartier and plenty worse. The intellectual side of Paris is losing touch with its roots, and that's a cause for concern to many long-time local residents. Homegrown chanteuse Juliette Greco heads up a "Save St-Germain" campaign. But surely it's impossible to turn back the tide when it's encroaching on one of the most sought after and attractive areas in Paris.

Once again, money talks as "Gianni come-lately's" buy into luxuriously remodeled 17th-century garrets that are within a gold-card's toss to some of the city's most endearing shops, restaurants and cafés. And who can blame them?

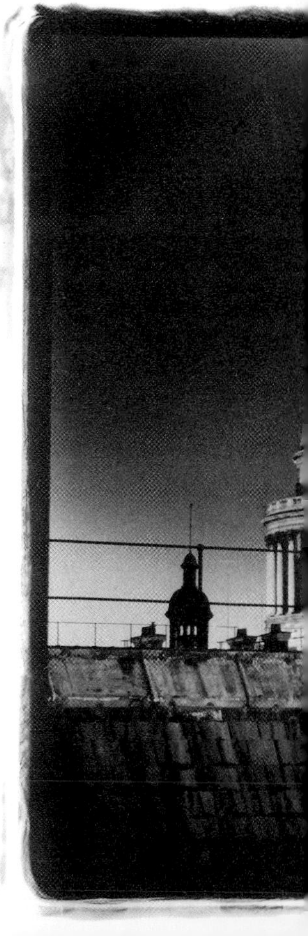

But the new **St-Germain-des-Prés**, which is often just called "St-Germain," has plenty of its past intact, including that mother of all expat English-language bookshops, **Shakespeare and Company**. Sylvia Beach's original bookstore, on Rue Dupuytren, was the soul of the 1920s English-language literary circle of Paris. It won international fame as the publisher of James Joyce's Ulysses, which Beach released in February, 1922 in a limited edition of 1000 copies (*see* Chapter 7/Shopping).

The literary cafés **Flore** and the **Deux Magots** also live on (*see* Chapter 8/Cafés). While the background noise has changed from the scraping sound of pencils on paper to the incessant ringing of cell phones, these institutions continue to reflect the essence of Left Bank life for the chattering classes. The subject has changed from the latest fashionable novel to the novel fashions of late, but the passion remains the same.

Hard by the river, at the foot of Boulevard St-Michel, is the St-Michel fountain which depicts Saint Michael slaying his dragons. Near the convergence of the 1st, 4th, 5th, and 6th arrondissements, Place St-Michel is a favorite student hangout and a kind of hub from where you can head off in different directions to explore the various eighths of these Quarters.

The maze of streets around the Place St-Michel throbs with the energy of tourists, drop-outs, international students, vagabonds, and just about everyone else. The drunkest and most unaware of the lot mill around while munching on nasty *sandwiches grecs*—the ubiquitous Parisian budget fast-food that exits just as hastily.

A few blocks up the Boulevard St-Michel you come to the junction with the Boulevard St-Germain, a busy crossroads since Roman times, when the **Cluny Baths** were built here. Today only remains remain, along with a relatively recent garden (*see* Chapter 4/Other Major Collections).

Further up the Boulevard St-Michel is the copula-topped Sorbonne, the center of scholarship and sedition since the 13th century. Today this birthplace of organized French education (and the 1968 student uprising) is only part of a vast university that's been decentralized and spread throughout the city. Divided and conquered, the students also seem to have lost their revolutionary zeal.

Hovering over the **Sorbonne**, admonishing students like both a carrot and a stick, is the domed **Panthéon**, the illustrious national

mausoleum in which dust of France's great the good are installed for time immemorial (*see* Chapter 4/The Top Sights).

You have to dogleg around the Panthéon to reach the far more convivial **Rue Mouffetard**, an ancient market street that still bustles with authenticity. Rue Mouffetard and the streets which surround it are burgeoning with mediocre budget restaurants and cafés serving the enormous population of local students and visiting parents.

To the east, stuck between the Rue Monge and the Rue de Navarre is the **Arènes de Lutèce**, a beautiful and peaceful hidden garden that contains the remains of the **Amphitheater of Lutèce.** Built during the Gallo-Roman period at the end of the First Century, the theater could hold 17,000 spectators on its terraces.

It all fell into to obscurity until 1869, when it was rediscovered by the General Omnibus company during construction on the site.

Back down to the Cluny Baths, head west on the Boulevard St-Germain to Place de l'Odéon, where the Quarter's most commercial "west end" cinemas are found. A bit further along, the Boulevard is dominated by the **Église de St-Germain-des-Prés**, the oldest church in Paris which lends the neighborhood its name. It's worth popping in here to see the tomb of 17th-century mathematician and philosopher René Descartes, then walk south to the newer, bigger, and far more pompous **Église de Saint-Sulpice**, which is decorated with frescoes by Delacroix. *Heliodorus Driven from the Temple* and *Jacob's Wrestling with the Angel* were the artist's last two great works.

From the Église de Saint-Germain-des-Prés, walk down Rue Bonaparte (towards the river), and you'll come to the **Ecole Nationale Superieure des Beaux-Arts** (on your left), Paris' most famous fine arts school. Inside is an exhibit space in which something good is usually going on, ranging from paintings and sculptures, to installations and video.

Continue to the Seine and step up onto the car-free (care-free?) **Pont des Arts**, for picture-postcard river views of Paris, then stroll along the quais where picturesque bookstalls flip their lids to reveal enthralling collections of maps, postcards and books with tattered covers.

The streets between the Pont des Arts and Boulivard St-Germain (Rue de Seine, Rue Bonaparte, and Rue des Beaux Arts) are full with **art galleries** that could easily take up an afternoon of exploring.

Heading east from the Cluny Baths on the Boulevard St-Germain you come to the busy Place Maubert, and the tangle of medieval streets around the Rue de Bièvre (where the late President Mitterand lived). At the far and of the Boulevard sits the **Institut du Monde Arabe**, a great, newish building by Jean Nouvel dedicated to Arabic art and culture (see Chapter 4/Major Collections).

The **Mosquée de Paris**, nearby, is a splendid, tiled creation containing an exotic 1920s hammam (*see* Chapter 6/Spas) and tea room (*see* Chapter 8/Tea Rooms & Desserts). It's also an important site for many of France's five million Muslims.

The **Luxembourg Gardens** is one of the city's most popular and beloved parks (*see* Chapter 4/Parks & Gardens). The Gardens were once the private yard of the **Palais du Luxembourg**, seat of the French senate since 1799. Completed in 1620 by architect Salomon de Brosse, Luxembourg Palace forecasted the style of monumental, formalized baroque architecture that would subdue all of France.

Le Musée National
Du Moyen Age des Thermes de Cluny
6 Place Paul-Painlevé (5th). Tel. 01.53.73.78.00. Open Wed-Mon 915am-545pm. Closed Tues.

The Sorbonne
17 Rue de la Sorbonne (6th). Courtyards open Mon-Fri 9am-430pm.

The Panthéon
Place du Panthéon (5th). Open Apr-Sept, daily 10am-630pm; Oct-Mar, daily 10am-615pm.

Arènes de Lutèce
Entrances on Rue Monge, Rue de Navarre and Rue des Arènes. Open daily 10am-dusk. Admission free.

Église St-Sulpice
Place St-Sulpice (6th)
Tel. 01.46.33.21.78. Open daily 8am-730pm

Ecole Nationale
Superieure des Beaux-Arts
13 Quai Malaquais (6th).
Tel. 01.47.03.50.00. Usually open Tues-Sun 1-7pm.

Institut du Monde Arabe
1 Rue des Fossés Saint Bernard (5th). Tel. 01.40.51.38.38. Open Tues-Sun 10am-6pm.

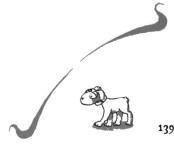

MONtPARNASSE

Montparnasse is best known as a has-been artists' quarter; where the likes of Picasso and Leger moved to escape the rising rents in Montmartre on the other side of the city. Plenty of writers lived here too, including Ernest Hemingway, F. Scott Fitzgerald and Henry Miller, who gushed about his sexual escapades in the neighborhood in his books *Tropic of Cancer* and *Tropic of Capricorn*. Ditto goes for Anaïs Nin and her biographical novel, *Henry & June*.

Today, the area feels a whole lot less artistic and literary. And the porn parlors on Rue de la Gâité notwithstanding, a lot less sexy too. Montparnasse has grown into a relatively staid residential and commercial district that languishes somewhere between the low-end and the high brow.

Having said that, art does come down into the streets every Sunday when both beginners and experts sell their photographs, sculpture, jewelry, painting and more. The **Art Market** is held on Boulivard Edgar Quinet, between Rue du Départ and Rue de la Gaîté, from 10am-7pm.

Each evening the **Boulevard du Montparnasse** hums with activity, primarily due to its classic brassieres and cafés like **La Coupole, Le Select, and Closerie des Lilas**, all of which were regular haunts of the 1920s "gauche caviar," the Left Bank literary elite (*see* Chapter 8/Dining). And the **Place du Dix huit Juin 1940** (at the intersections of Rue de Rennes, Boulevard du Montparnasse and Rue du Départ) is home to one of the highest concentrations of movie screens in the city.

There are some good daytime sightseeing activities too, including the **Cimetière Montparnasse**, where you can wander amongst the tombs of many of France's top artists and intellectuals, including Charles Baudelaire, Constantin Brancusi, Serge Gainsbourg, Simone de Beauvoir and Jean-Paul Sartre.

Just east of the cemetery is the **La Fondation Cartier Pour l'Art Contemporain**, a swanky, ultra-modern art gallery with rotating exhibits of some of the most avant art found anywhere. It's owned by the jewelers.

The monstrous **Montparnasse Tower** office building that soars above the Left Bank has been one of the most maligned structures in the city from the get-go. It's been said that the only place in the neighborhood where it doesn't ruin the view is from the observation terrace on the building's 59th floor. This is undoubtedly one of the great views over Paris, but we hate to give the building's few supporters any ammunition by paying to go up top.

Cimetière de Montparnasse
3 Blvd. Edgar-Quinet (14th). Tel. 01.44.10.86.50. Open 16 Mar-5 Nov, Mon-Fri 8am-6pm, Sat-Sun 9am-6pm; 6 Nov-15 Mar, Mon-Fri 8am-530pm, Sat-Sun 9am-530pm.

La Fondation Cartier Pour l'Art Contemporain
261 Blvd. Raspail (14th). Tel. 01.42.18.56.51. Open Tues-Wed & Fri-Sun noon-8pm, Thurs noon-10pm. Closed Mon. Admission €5 adults, €3.50 students, free for youths under 10.

Tour Maine Montparnasse
33 Ave du Maine. Tel. 01.45.38.52.56. Open summer 930am-1130pm, winter 930am-1030pm (until 11pm Fri-Sat). Admission €8.

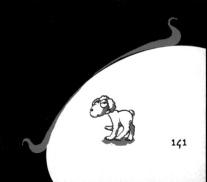

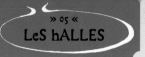

LES hALLES & CHÂtELET

The dismantling and destruction of the legendary **Les Halles wholesale food market** in the late 1960s has to rank with the greatest architectural catastrophes of the 20th Century. Especially when you consider the horrible, subterranean **Forum des Halles** shopping mall that replaced it. The 800-year-old market was transferred to the south of the city to ease congestion in the center, and for years after, all that was left here was a gigantic hole in the ground. After much metropolitan angst, shrugging of shoulders, and shady government dealings, a "prestigious" underground mall was built. The poorly designed shopping center rapidly frayed at the edges, then rotted to the core, becoming the city's *de facto* Boys and Girls Club for disenfranchised, drug-addled youth. All this is a long-winded way of saying that the Forum des Halles is not a great place to shop.

Not everything was destroyed, however. Designed by Jean Goujon in 1549, the magnificent Renaissance **Fontaine des Innocents**, adjacent to the mall, is a terrific touchstone to history, and a popular place to meet friends and hang out. The Fountain sits in the Square des Innocents, once Paris' largest cemetery, before the remains were removed to The Catacombs in an effort to control plague epidemics (*see* Chapter 4/The Top Sights).

Since the destruction of the Les Halles market, the focus of the neighborhood has shifted east, toward the **Centre Georges Pompidou** (a.k.a. Beaubourg), one of the world's greatest museums of modern and contemporary art (*see* Chapter 4/The Top Sights). Savor this unusual structure and the medieval streets that flank it by taking a stroll completely around the building. Portraitists, mimes, jewelry sellers, jugglers, pick-pockets, punk rockers, fire-eaters, pigeons and pedestrians... the square in front of the Beaubourg hums with all the color and diversity of a Third World souk.

The **Stravinsky Fountain**, facing the Centre's southern side, is a whimsical pond full of fun metal machines and little multi-colored, water-spouting mobiles that dance on the water's surface. Created by Swiss artists Niki de Saint-Phalle and Jean Tinguely, each sculpture represents a composition by the great Russian composer.

Further east still is the **Hôtel de Ville**, a spectacular Renaissance-style city hall that was built in the late 19th century by Italian architect Il Boccadoro. The interior, which is only open to independent visitors on the first Monday of each month, is as sumptuous as you'd imagine, built with opulent reception halls, gilded sconces, ornate woods, and triumphant murals.

Église St-Eustache, the church on the north side of Forum des Halles, is the second largest in Paris. It's notable for its stained-glass windows and terrific acoustics that make it a favorite for choral and organ recitals. The French playwright Molière was baptized here in 1622, and Franz Liszt's Grand Mass premiered here in 1866.

The **Rue Saint-Denis**, which runs north from Les Halles, is convenient for its erotic video shops with private cabins in which you can do the

"five-finger shuffle." A late evening stroll here is an education of sorts. For a more refined walk, head a bit further north into the 2nd arrondissement, to the pedestrianized market streets around **Rue Montorgueil Petits**, an ancient and characterful area that's home to the newly-restored **Tour de Jean Sans Peur** (20 Rue Etienne-Marcel), a 15th-century townhouse that remains a fascinating relic of an earlier age.

South of the Forum des Halles mall is **La Samaritaine** department store. This multi-building complex beside the Seine is an art nouveau gem and bona fide institution. Shoppingwise, this store is not as tony as Les Galleries or Printemps, but architecturally, it trumps them both. The best thing about La Samaritaine is the view from the roof, which is not only one of the best in Paris, it's also free. Take the elevator to the top floor, then climb two flights of stairs, past the terrace café, to the observation deck. The 360-degree view puts the Pont-Neuf at your feet, and the Invalides dome and the Notre Dame gargoyles at eye-level. A 1920's enamel frieze identifies the landmarks.

East along the Quai, by the **Pont au Change** (which is named for the medieval money-changers that operated there), is the flamboyant Gothic **Tour St-Jacques**. Standing in a small park that's closed to the public, this bell tower is all that's left of the church of St-Jacques la Boucherie. It is now used as a weather station.

Église St-Eustache
Rue du Jour (1st).
Tel. 01.40.26. 47.99.
Open Mon-Sat 9am-7pm, Sun 815am-1230pm and 230pm-7pm.

La Samaritaine
19 Rue de la Monnaie (1st).
Tel. 01.40.41.20.20. Open Mon-Wed & Fri-Sat 930am-7pm, Thurs 930am-10pm.
M *Pont Neuf*

RU
BÉAR

LE MARAiS

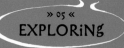

The Marais is many things to many people. It's a quiet neighborhood for some lucky rich people and a funky shopping district for everyone from name-brand wearers to the fashion unconscious. It's a museum-packed quarter with a maze of narrow streets that has become something like the SoHo of Paris. It swarms with tourists, some of whom certainly go home with "Marais, Paris" T-shirts. It's gay HQ and ground-zero for Jews. It's packed with intimate cafés and budget falafel joints. And it's one of our favorite stomping grounds anywhere.

Once swamped by the River Seine, the Marais is named for the marshland that was here until it was drained in the 12th century. Jews were some of the first inhabitants, followed by aristocrats and kings. After the French Revolution the district fell into disrepair. It was considered to be a bad neighborhood until the mid-1960s when the Marais was designated a protected historical district. How we wish we bought real estate then. These days the Marais is the hippest place to live on the Right Bank. There are still plenty of kosher butchers and bakers mixed in with the ever-increasing number of pricey boutiques and tapas bars.

While the Marais is undeniably beautiful, some detractors complain about the Disneyfication of the district, and that it has become something of a lifeless museum to its past. And while the edge has certainly moved elsewhere—primarily to Oberkampf and Ménilmontant—there are still lots of great galleries, streets and scenes here that are worthy of days of exploration.

The quieter, upscale residential area of the Marais is centered around the spectacular red brick **Place des Vosges**, which is widely considered to be one of the prettiest squares in Paris. Its center, which was once a popular dueling ground, is now a park, filled with slides, sandboxes and swings for children. The perimeter is ringed with sumptuous arcades that seem as though they were tailor built for romantic strolls.

In the southeast corner of the square you can visit **Maison de Victor Hugo**, where the great French author lived and worked for 14 years. It's filled with memorabilia and his personal effects, including several first editions.

While exploring the Marais you will see many *hôtels particuliers*, former aristocratic residences that are now home to some top museums and institutions. Most have spectacular carved doorways and quiet private courtyards, and are renovated back to top condition. Two of the finest mansions in the area contain two of the best museums: the **Hôtel Carnavalet**, houses the museum of the history of Paris, and **Hôtel Salé**, is home to the **Musée Picasso** (*see* Chapter 4/Top Museums). Don't miss the elegant **Hôtel de Sully** and the **Hôtel de Soubise**, which forms part of the **Musée de l'Histoire de la France**. Inside you'll find over-the-top décor and self-important historical documents that include Napoléon's will.

West of Place des Vosges is the Jewish heart of the Marais, centered around the **Rue des Rosiers.** Here Hassids rub shoulders with gay gym queens, making for an interesting cultural juxtaposition of falafels and poppers.

Goldenberg's (7 Rue Rosiers; tel. 01.48.87.20.16), the most famous nosherie in the neighborhood, is an old-school deli in the French mold that mixes smoked fish and hanging meats with caviars, vodkas and *foie gras*. The bullet holes in the windows are from a racist attack that ended with the tragic death of a policeman.

The center of gay life is just a few streets around the nearby **Rue Sainte Croix de la Brettonerie.** It's a lively area, but small compared with San Francisco's Castro or New York City's Chelsea.

Maison de Victor Hugo
Hotel de Rohan-Guéménée, 6 Place des Vosges (4th). Tel. 01.42.72.10.16. Open Tues-Sun 10am-6pm. Free admission to the permanent collection.

Hotel de Sully
62 Rue Saint Antoine. **Courtyards open** *daily 9am-630pm daily.* **Admission** *free.*

Musée de l'Histoire de la France
l'Hotel de Soubise, 60 Rue des Francs-Bourgeois (3rd). **Tel.** *01.40.27.61.78.* **Open** *Tues-Sun 11am-5pm.* **Admission** *€5.*

BOULANGERIE

BASTiLLE

There was a time, not too long ago, when the Bastille was an a bastion of furniture makers and craft workshops. But rising real estate prices have turned this traditionally working-class neighborhood into one of the trendiest places to live. Like St-Germain and the Marais before it, the former workshops have been transformed into fashionable living lofts, while ground-floor spaces have become cafés and bars. Around the **Place de la Bastille** the change has been so thorough that this has become the liveliest spot for nightlife in the city. **Rue de Lappe**, and the streets that surround it, probably have the highest concentration of bars in Paris (*see* Chapter 9/Nightlife).

The centerpiece of Place de la Bastille is the **July Column**, which commemorates those who died during the July 1830 Revolution. Some of the revolutionaries' remains are buried below.

Each year, on July 14th, the square packs with Bastille Day celebrants who come to drink, dance and generally make louts of themselves; which is only quantitatively different than the way it is here almost every other night of the year.

Boulevard Richard Lenoir runs from the Place de la Bastille to the northern reaches of the neighborhood, where it teams up with the **Canal Saint-Martin**, the most charming and romantic section of Paris' vast system of canals. Threaded with picturesque humpback bridges, the canal supports three sightseeing companies, making this an original alternative to the touristy Bateaux Mouches that ply the Seine: **Canauxrama** (tel. 01.42.39.15.00), and **Paris Canal** (tel. 01.42.40.96.97).

The completion of the infamously-designed **Bastille Opera House** on the south side of the Place de la Bastille capped the neighborhood's transformation into a haven for the cell phone set. Because of a nasty little problem in which the Opera's facade tiles tend to fall off, the building's main doors have been permanently shut. Its central staircase has been colonized by the city's youth, who hang out here as a prelude to a big night on the town.

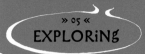

The **Promenade Plantée**, an elevated garden pathway between the Bastille and the Bois de Vincennes is one of our favorite spots for strolling, blading and biking. This 19th century elevated train viaduct runs among flowers for several miles, above the smog and traffic. The **Viaduc des Arts**, beneath it, is a showcase for arts and crafts filled with almost 50 galleries and exhibition spaces. Look for it southeast of Place de la Bastille, behind the Opera House.

OBERKAMPF, MÉNILMONTANT & BELLEVILLE

The hip new East End is spreading to Oberkampf and Belleville, as these neighborhoods fall to the latest generation of "hipocrits." The trend began on the Rue Oberkampf (which French author Jean Genet once provocatively called "the most beautiful street in Paris"), and is gradually spreading North. It started with down-and-out artists. It always does. Budget bars and restaurants followed, becoming darlings or the artier wing of the Bastille crowd.

Café Charbon is often credited with being the first kid on the block to reestablish the primacy of **Rue Oberkampf**, the main drag of cool Parisian nightlife. A huge variety of bars and cafés soon followed, along with lots of restaurants serving strong punch and salsa. World music, *chanson Française*, jazz, funk, electronic music... there's something for everyone. Because the east end of Paris is still a working-class area, prices remain reasonable. And unlike in the Bastille, where velvet rope policies have cropped up, the only reason you'll be turned away here is because there are too many people (*see* Chapter 9/Nightlife).

The dynamism continues to unfold right up the hill to the previously poor areas of Ménilmontant and Belleville, which are built with an eclectic mix of 1960s apartment buildings, ancient workshops and newly-restored worker's cottages. The area is just as eclectic ethnically, with a jumble of everybody that's especially heavy with North Africans, Chinese and home-grown French. A neighborhood with a long rebellious streak, it's the last place the barricades came down during the Paris Commune of 1871. And the following century, residents thwarted government plans to tear down their shabby tenements.

Before being annexed to the capital in 1860, Ménilmontant was part of the hamlet of Belleville. It is situated on some of the highest hills of Paris and is built with steep little streets that have kept their village character.

The heart of Belleville is the intersection of the boulevard and rue of the same name, and where the 10th, 11th, 19th and 20th *arrondissements* meet. Edith Piaf spent her youth in this gutsy area, and used to claim that she was born on **Rue de Belleville**, literally on the street. This bit of history is now commemorated with the **Musée Edith Piaf**, a private mini-museum celebrating the life and times of the diminutive "little sparrow."

Nearby, the **Parc de Belleville** has been re-landscaped and provides another wonderful, and tourist-free, vantage point over the city.

Musée Edith Piaf
5 Rue Crespin du Gast, 11th.
Tel. *01.43.55.52.72.*
Open *by appointment.*

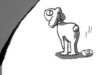

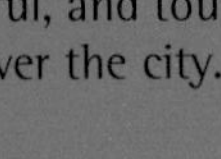

ThE LOUVRE & PALAiS-ROYAL

Located in the geographical center of the city, the Louvre was originally built as a palace for the kings of France. Construction began in 1546, and the building has undergone major additions in every century since. The most ambitious project of the 20th Century was the remaking of the main entrance, the innovative **glass pyramid** designed by Chinese-American architect Ieoh Ming Pei. From John Hancock Tower (Boston, 1976) and the Jacob K. Javits Convention Center (New York City, 1986) to the Rock and Roll Hall of Fame (Cleveland, 1995) and the San Francisco Main Public Library and Civic Center (1996), Pei's firm has been responsible for some of the most important construction projects of the late-20th century.

From **Cour Napoleon**, in the main courtyard of the Louvre, you can take in a series of landmarks in a single glance: IM Pei's glass pyramid, the Obelisk at the Place de la Concorde, the Tuilieries gardens, the Champs-Elysées and the Arc-de-Triomphe in the background. On a clear day you can even see the Grande Arche at La Defense in the far distance.

After the French Revolution, the sprawling, monumental Louvre was transformed into one of the most important art museums in the world, containing encyclopedic collections spanning the history of human consciousness. See Chapter 4/The Top Museums for complete information.

The **Palais-Royal**, just across the road from the Louvre, was built in 1630 as a private home for Cardinal Richelieu. It's now the address for the Ministry of Culture and Conseil d'Etat. In the 18th century the Palais began to house numerous coffee houses and restaurants, some of which are still there today. Check out the spectacular decoration of the **Grand Véfour** restaurant, which has just won its third Michelin star. Behind the Palais is the **Jardin du Palais Royal**, a calm aristocratic square. Courting couples and upmarket nannies perambulate under the shady chestnut trees while looking in the elegant shops and galleries that line the arcades. Only the infamous black and white columns of modern sculptor Daniel Buren disfigure the central courtyard, depending on your attitude to conceptual art of course.

The southeast corner of the square is home to the **Comédie Française**, a bastion of classical French theater. But Racine and Molière present a challenge even to Anglophones who think their French is good (*see* Chapter 9/Stage).

The rest of the neighborhood north is taken up with the business side of Paris life,

dominated by the impressive looking **Bourse** or **Stock Exchange.**

Nearby, the stylish oval **Place des Victoires** is dedicated to serious fashion houses. And restaurants in the area make for an intriguing mix of Kenzo shoppers and insider dealers, all enjoying the legendary Parisian long lunch.

The arcaded **Rue de Rivoli** begins near the Bastille and runs along the length of the Louvre and the Tuileries to the Place de la Concorde. It's a seriously long street that was built for military parades. Today, it's a parade of cars. If you feel the need to buy a T-shirt with "Paris" scripted in gold sequins, then this where you will find it. And the numerous bureaux de change here offer Paris' poorest exchange rates.

From the Rue de Rivoli, Rue de Castiglione leads north to **Place Vendôme**, the most beautiful Louis XIV square in the city. The column in the center is a replica of one that was erected to celebrate Napoléon's victories, but was pulled down during the 19th-century Commune uprising. Today there is little revolutionary spirit to be found here, as the Place is known for its stunning collection of the world's most expensive jewelers and perfumeries, and the ritzy **Ritz Hotel**, where Princess Diana enjoyed her last supper. The staff at this top hotel is famous for its ironclad discretion. And the basement bar is famous for its cocktails. "When I dream of afterlife in heaven," Ernest Hemingway supposedly said, "the action always takes place at The Paris Ritz" (*see* Chapter 9/Nightlife).

After passing the Tuileries, Rue de Rivoli empties into the **Place de la Concorde**, an enormous open plan square that remains Paris' largest and busiest. It would be a great boon to be able to cross into the center for a look at the Obelisk (which comes from Egypt's Temple of Luxor) and the newly-restored fountains without being mown down by a passing taxi. If you've got the cash, the best view of the square is had from the Hôtel de Crillon's marble-clad **Les Ambassadeurs** restaurant (*see* Chapter 8/Top Food).

Palais-Royal
main entrance Place du Palais-Royal, other entrances in Rue de Montpensier, Rue de Beaujolais, Rue de Valois (1st). **Gardens open** *daily dawn-dusk.* **Admission** *free.*

Grand Véfour
17 Rue de Beaujolais (1st).
Tel. *01.42.96.56.27.*

La Bourse
Palais Brongniart, Place de la Bourse. **Tel.** *01.49.27.55.50.* **Guided tours** *Mon-Fri 1.15-4pm.* **Admission** *€5.*

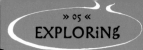

Hyped as "the most beautiful avenue in the world," the **Champs-Elysées** is far more popular with tourists than the locals.

The landscaped lower part of the avenue, beginning at the Place de la Concorde, sports a few stylish restaurants and is a pleasant place to stroll and look at the occasional temporary art exhibition under the trees.

The 18th-century **Palais de l'Elysée** which noses into the park's northern side, is the official residence of the French President. The palace is not open to the public but can be glimpsed through the guarded iron gates at 55 Rue du Faubourg St-Honore.

Close to the Rond Point des Champs-Elysées, where the Avenue changes character from grassy promenade to paved mega-street, you'll find the **Petit Palais** and the **Grand Palais**, two enormous glass-and-iron exhibition spaces that were built for the Universal Exhibition of 1900. These extravagantly ornamental, but increasingly dilapidated, *belle époque* buildings host some of the most prestigious art exhibitions in the capital. The Grand Palais also houses the **Palais de la Decouverte**, a scientific cultural center that includes an excellent planetarium. Much of the building is off-limits to the public because it's falling apart. After bits of the central atrium started crashing down on people, the Grand Palais began one of those long-term, nothing-much-happening restoration projects. In the meantime, however, both museums continue to feature important large-scale exhibitions.

The **Avenue Montaigne**, which branches off to the southwest, is a major high-end shopping street showcasing its own glamorous take on *haute couture* (*see* Chapter 7/Shopping). The vintage 1913 **Théâtre des Champs Elysées**, on the same street is the most attractive theater in Paris (*see* Chapter 9/Nightlilfe).

The shop-lined section of the Champs runs from Avenue Montaigne to the Arc de Triomphe, and this is where the controversy begins, as large, impersonal chain stores rub shoulders with tacky tourist cafés–and worse. The Avenue was once lined with chic boutiques, terrific bistros and grand hotels that gave the neighborhood its identity. The rot set in at the beginning of the 1970s when shopping malls and fast-food transplants were the beneficiaries of frenetic real-estate speculation. In the last few years there has been a genuine attempt to skillfully restyle the area with wide sidewalks, new trees, and smart new traffic lights. A branch of the top patisserie Ladurée moved in, along with Sephora, Louis Vuitton, Zara, and a new Café Costes, all of which are steps in the right direction. But it remains to be seen whether Parisians will reclaim the grand avenue as their own. At present the only places you are likely to find natives at play are at the chic restaurant Fouquets, and across the road, at the top nightclub Le Queen.

See Chapter 4/Top Sights for information on the **Arc de Triomphe**.

Musée du Petit Palais
1, Ave Dutuit, 8th. Tel. 01.40.05.56.78

Grand Palais
3 Ave du Gen. Eisenhower, 8th. Tel. 01.44.13.17.30. Open Wed 10am-10pm, Thurs-Mon 10am-8pm. Admission €7-€11.

LES gRANdS bOULEVARdS

The area which surrounds the Palais Garnier Opéra is known as the Grands Boulevards. A product of Baron Haussmann's comprehensive redesign of Paris in the mid-19th Century, these wide boulevards are big on monumental architecture and department stores, but small on personal Parisian charm. This is one of the rare areas in the city where few people live; the overall feeling here is of a dead-by-night business district.

The **Paris Opéra** was designed by Charles Garnier, and completed in 1875. The construction of this *belle époque* wedding cake flattened an entire neighborhood. Home to the Paris Opéra Ballet, it's a masterpiece of Second Empire craftsmanship that has recently been restored to its ornate, neo-baroque grandeur. The Opéra is decorated both inside and out with sculpture, fresco, and colored marble. There's a ceiling mural by Marc Chagall, and a 7-ton chandelier that inspired the most dramatic scene in Andrew Lloyd Webber's *Phantom of the Opera*. The docent-led tour the building is excellent but, unfortunately, does not include the legendary lake in the basement. If you do persuade the guide to take you the building's bowels, however, you'll find a stone vaulted cellar filled with murky water; a 9-foot-deep cistern that was dug when the builders ran into a troublesome tributary of the Seine.

The **Musée Jacquemart André** on Boulevard Haussmann neatly encapsulates the grand Haussmanian style of architecture and contains one of the best collections of pictures in Paris, including works by Italian and Dutch masters as well as a newly restored fresco by Tiepolo. Take advantage of the stylish tearoom attached to the museum before heading off for the **Galleries Lafayettes** or **Printemps** (*see* Chapter 7/Shopping).

Leave the main streets to the cars, as the most atmospheric sights are the neighborhood's many passages; covered shopping malls that were before their time. The most elegant of these are the tiled **Passage Véro Dodat** and the neo-classical **Passage Vivienne.** Wander down the **Passage des Panoramas** and admire the shop front of the printers Stern. Or cross the road and take the **Passage Jouffroy**, where you'll find the lifeless waxworks, the **Musée Grévin**, along with lots of shops selling everything from cinema posters to antique canes. **Passage Brady** is often called the "Indian" passage because its packed with restaurants and shops from the Sub-Continent.

This leads you towards the 9th arrondissement, and past the enormous auction house **Drouot**, where bargains are still to be had for the courageous hunter (*see* Chapter 7/Shopping).

The area around the church **Notre-Dame-de-Lorette** was once famous for its pretty girls and artistic atmosphere, and is now a quiet, but charming residential area. This section of city is called Nouvelles Athènes,

RESTAURANT
OORI
TANDOORI
Tél. 01.48.00.08.85
Charbon de Bois
8.00.08.85
YASMIN
RESTAURANT INDIEN
PLATS A EMPORTER
TANDOORI
45 23 04 25
YASMIN
RESTAURANT
RESTAURANT
YASMIN
Spécialités Indienn
CURRY (Poulet-Agneau-Poisson)
CURRY DE VIANDE HACHEE
EPINARDS ou LENTILLES ou LEGUMES
• avec riz Basmathi ou Nan Nature
ENTREES
Chicken Tandoori + Pakora
Shamee Kebab + Samosa : Legume - Viande
Sheek Kebab
Mouton Tikka - Chicken Tikka
Nan Nature - Nan Fromage

for its plethora of neoclassical architecture.

The neighborhood is also rich in memories of Georges Sand and Frédéric Chopin. Don't miss the housing estate, just off the Rue Taitbout, where the couple had apartments within earshot of each other. The **Musée de la Vie Romantique** houses a collection of mementos of the writer's life in a perfect artist's studio setting.

Nearby is a row of impressive villas, one of which was the home of symbolist painter Gustave Moreau. Now the **Musée Gustave Moreau,** it retains its original studio atmosphere and contains the finest collection of the artist's work to be found anywhere in the world.

Boulivard des Capucines connects the Opéra Garnier with **Place de la Madeleine**, an enormous square that surrounds the enormous **Madeleine Church**, which was built to look like the Greek Parthenon, complete with 52 Corinthian columns. The pompous Napoléonic architecture of this Grecian-temple/church wins few fans. But its square is surrounded by some of the best food shops in the city (Fauchon, Hédiard, and La Maison des Truffes) and locals take to the steps of the Madeleine on warm spring mornings, often with croissant in hand.

Opéra Garnier
Place de l'Opera (9th). Tel. 01.40.01.25.14. Open daily 10am-430pm; English tours Sat 1230pm. Admission €6 for unguided tour, €10 for guided tour.

Musée Jacquemart-André
158 Blvd. Haussmann (8th). Tel. 01.45.62.11.59. Open Tues-Sun 10am-6pm. Admission €8.

Galerie Véro-Dodat
Between the Les Halles food market and the Palais Royal. Closed evenings and Sundays.

Galerie Vivienne
Between Palais Royal and the Bibliothèque Nationale.

Passage des Panoramas
Between Boulevard Montmartre and Rue Saint Marc.

Passage Jouffroy
A continuation of the Passage des Panoramas, above.

Musée Grévin
10 Blvd. Montmartre (9th). Tel. 01.47.70.85.05. Open Mon-Fri 10am-530pm, Sat-Sun 10am-6pm. Admission €15 adults, €9 youths 6-14.

Passage Brady
Between Rue du Faubourg St-Martin and Rue du Faubourg St-Denis.

Musée de la Vie Romantique
16 Rue Chaptal (9th). Tel. 01.48.74.95.38. Open Tues-Sun 10am-6pm. Free admission to the permanent collection.

Musée Gustave Moreau
14 Rue de La Rochefoucauld (9th). Tel. 01.48.74.38.50. Open Mon, Wed 11am-515pm, Thurs-Sun 10am-1245pm and 2-515pm. Admission €3.50

Le Madeleine
Place de la Madeleine. Tel. 01.44.51.69.00. Open Sun-Fri 730am-7pm, Sat 9am-7pm. Admission free.

The 7th Arrondissement

The swanky 7th is both governmental and residential, home to many of the city's richest institutions and residents. Appropriately, some of the richest art collections are here too. The point where the 6th meets the 7th around the Rue de Lille, Rue du Bac and Rue de l'Université, is known as the **Carré**, where upmarket antique shops and galleries vie for your attention. Just opposite the **Musée d'Orsay** (*see* Chapter 5/Top Museums) is the **Musée National de la Légion d'Honneur**, housing a millennium's worth of chivalric decorations, and France's best collection of Napoléona in an elegant, yet rarely-visited building.

Across the road is Napoléon's final resting place, under the cupola of the **Hôtel des Invalides** (*see* Chapter 4/Top Sights).

Otherwise the area between Les Invalides and the 6th is a mass of former aristocratic mansions, most of which have been converted into embassies or official government buildings. Apart from occasional open days, the magnificent courtyards and private gardens are hidden behind imposingly closed double doors. The best street to walk down to get a feel of the area is the **Rue de Varenne**. At no. 51 you can peep in at the exclusive **Cité Varenne** and at no. 57 you can spy the **Hôtel Matignon**, home to the French

prime minister, who has only a short stroll to the Parliament, the Assemblée Nationale in the Palais Bourbon.

The 18th-century facade on the back side of the **Assemblée Nationale** exhibits the building's original facing. The 19th-century Greek-temple-like Seine frontage was added to echo the Madeleine on the Right Bank.

Rue de Bourgogne, which connects the Assemblée Nationale with Rue de Varenne, shows 7th life at its most classical. Buttoned-up restaurants, quiet flower shops, and uptight delicatessens populate this area, while looking with longing across the river to their more formal Right Bank neighbors.

You might not ascend the Eiffel Tower, but you should at least look at it from the **Parc du Champs de Mars**, below. This rectangular green is perfect for picnicking, and is a great place to take a rest from touring the tony neighborhood just to it's north.

The building opposite the city's most famous monument, at the far end of the Champ de Mars, is the **Ecole Militaire**, a still-functioning military academy with spectacular façades.

Just behind the Ecole is the **UNESCO** headquarters, worth a detour for the modern sculptures by Picasso, Calder, Giacometti and others that decorate the foyers and gardens.

Musée National
de la Légion d'Honneur
2 Rue de Bellechasse (7th). **Tel.** *01.40.62.84.25.*
Open *Tues-Sun 11am-5pm.* **Admission** *€5.*

Assemblée Nationale
33 Quai d'Orsay. Tel. 01.40.63.64.08. Guided tours Sat 10am, 2pm & 3pm, when there is no government business. ID required (arrive at least 20 minutes in advance).

UNESCO
Place de Fontenoy (7th). **Open** *Mon-Fri 9am-6pm.*

tHE 16Th ARRONDiSSEMENt

The 16th is the bourgeois heart of Paris. The merest mention of the *arrondissement* carries with it a message of moneyed middle class living. Perhaps for this reason, it is generally considered a rather dull embassy strewn area. Nonetheless there are some fine buildings by art nouveau architect Hector Guimard, and some terrific modernist houses by Le Corbusier, the most famous of which was designed for a Swiss art collector and is now home to the **Fondation Le Corbusier.**

Just across the river from the Eiffel Tower is the 1930s-era **Trocadéro** complex, which houses a couple of specialized museums (**Musée de la Marine** and **Musée de l'Homme**) and the **Théâtre du Chaillot.** And while the museums are of limited popular interest, the view of the Eiffel Tower and the fountains playing in the gardens below make the riverfront esplanade a wild favorite with visitors and locals alike. The terrace cafés are a good place to enjoy a drink before heading off for some heavy-duty sightseeing.

The **Musée d'Art Moderne de la Ville,** just down the road, has a great collection of Matisses and is often used for large scale one-off exhibitions of modern masters. The same building also houses a relatively new cinema museum. Nearby, the **Musée Guimet** houses the best collection of Asian art in the city.

Rue la Fontaine is the best place to see the work of art nouveau architect Hector Guimard, the man who is also responsible for the city's fanciful Métro entrances detailed in wrought iron, bronze, and glass. There are several buildings designed by him here, the most spectacular of which was his first, **Castel Béranger**. In this apartment house, completed in 1898, Guimard is responsible for every detail of the interior and exterior. His other houses are also notable for their sinuous curves and wrought-iron gates with vegetative and floral motifs.

Arriving at the **Place de l'Alma** you could well believe you had stumbled upon some obscure Eastern sect. Around the statue of a golden flame, a replica of the one on the **Statue of Liberty**, are gathered groups of tourists laying flowers and leaving poems. The

monument is, coincidentally, located almost on top of the infamous 13th column of the Tunnel de l'Alma, where Princess Diana and her lover Dodi Al Fayed had their fatal car crash on the 31st August 1997. A gift to the people of Paris from the *International Herald Tribune*, this "candle in the wind" has taken on new meaning. Plunging deeper into the 16th there is an attractive walk to be had around the **Maison de Balzac**. The author Honoré's former home is a reminder of a time when this area was still in the country and renowned for its mineral water sources. If you prefer wine to water then the nearby **Musée du Vin** has a tasting session at the end of your visit. The museum is situated in the ancient cellars of a monastery which previously covered this whole area, including the site of the cylindrical Radio France building, where broadcast buffs can find yet another museum.

Fondation Le Corbusier
Villa La Roche, 10 Square du Dr-Blanche. Tel. 01.42.88.41.53. Open Mon-Thurs 10am-1230pm & 130pm-6pm, Fri 10am-1230pm & 130pm-5pm. Closed Aug. Admission €3.20.

Musée National de la Marine
Palais de Chaillot, 17 Place du Trocadéro (16th). Tel. 01.56.65.69.69. Open Wed-Mon 10am-6pm. Admission €7.

Musée de l'Homme
Palais du Chaillot, 17 Place du Trocadéro (16th). Tel. 01.44.05.72.00. Open Wed-Sun 945am-515pm. Admission €5.

Musée d'Art Moderne de la Ville de Paris
11 Ave. de Président Wilson (16th). Tel. 01. 53.67.40.00. Open Tues-Fri 10am-6pm, Sat-Sun 10am-7pm. Free admission to the permanent collection, temporary expositions €5-€7.50.

Musée Guimet (Musée National des Arts Asiatiques)
6 Place d'Ièna (16th). Tel. 01.56.52.53.00. Open Wed-Mon 10am-6pm. Admission €7.

Maison de Balzac
47 Rue Raynouard (16th). Tel. 01.55.74.41.80. Open Tues-Sun 10am-6pm. Free admission to the permanent collection.

Le Musée Du Vin Et Caveau des Echansons
5 Square Charles Dickens (16th). Tel. 01.45.25.63.26. Open Tues-Sun 10am-6pm. Admission €6.50 (includes wine tasting).

MONTMARTRE

Touristed-out, but still picture-postcard pretty, Montmartre is a terrific place to explore. How should you approach it? Walking around is the way to go. Start at the bottom by the sex-shops and clip-joints of Pigalle. Then gain altitude and get lost in the tangle of small streets. Pass the Moulin Rouge, that famous old cabaret on Boulivard Clichy, and check out the last remaining windmills and the famous vineyard. Climb the staircases, and make your way across the push-and-shove of the Place du Tertre. Your goal is the oh-so-white Sacré-Coeur church on the summit. Montmartre is steep, but if you get tired of climbing it you can always lean against it.

The hill or butte of Montmartre has as its underbelly the legendary **Pigalle** on one side and the equally infamous **Goutte d'Or** on the other. Pigalle and the Moulin Rouge are part of most people's perception of seedy and sexy Paris. As you wander along the Avenue de Clichy, the sheer number of decaying sex shops and peep shows make for a pretty tawdry affair. Even the pharmacies look racy. And if the selling tactics seem aggressive, the sex shows themselves seem tamely retentive.

For real sleaze, the Goutte d'Or area, at the Barbès end of the 18th *arrondissement*, is the place to head. This area was once a real no-go district with low standard housing and a big drug problem. Now things have calmed down and property prices are rising. However the North African community still makes this an exotic area full of interesting shops. Not for the faint hearted it is nonetheless a side of Paris to be seen.

The hill became known as Mont des Martyrs, following the death of St-Denis, the first bishop of Paris, who was beheaded by Romans at the summit of the hill. According to legend, Denis then picked up his head, carried it to a fountain to wash it, then walked until he collapsed. That spot that is now commemorated by the **Basilique St-Denis**.

To climb up the hill is to experience a complete change of atmosphere. Rise above the sleaze-line and Montmartre's famous village atmosphere takes over. The former quarter of great turn-of-the-century artists is now polluted by coach loads of tourists who come in search of authentic *vie de Bohème*. There's a whole souvenir industry based on the ghosts of ex-inhabitants such as Lautrec, Van Gogh, Renoir, Modigliani, Picasso, Braque and Utrillo. The tacky little train ferrying around tourists in hope of discovering the next Cézanne is pitiful, as is the standard of caricatures and artwork offered in the undeniably picturesque **Place du Tertre**, a semi-hectare of terrace cafés (with only a few diners) plus some fringe of artists for "local color." The view over Paris is the most spectacular reason for the trip up. Even the wedding cake architecture of the Sacré-Coeur, completed in 1914, is not worthy of close

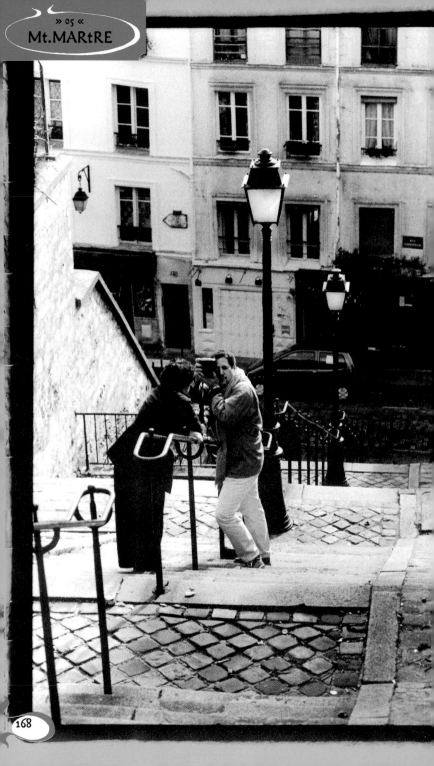

inspection, apart from the panoramic view from the dome. Far better to take a look in the charming Romanesque **Église St-Jean de Montmartre** just behind.

Systematically it's best to take the smaller streets in Montmartre where the occasional artist still lives in an attractive studio, though most of the bijou homes on the hill are taken up by the fit and successful of the city.

The **Musée de Montmartre** is an interesting exploration of life on the hill, when residents included Modigliani, Utrillo and Renoir. The latter painted the **Moulin de la Galette**, which, typically, is now a tourist restaurant. The **Salvador Dali Museum** shows some of the painter's later sculptures.

An interesting sight is the **Montmartre Vineyard**, which produces a small quantity of low quality, and high priced wine. Indeed, the grape-picking season is a fun time to experience the last remaining vestiges of old Montmartre life.

You can also visit the **Cimetière Montmartre**, a hillside gathering of graves of composers and authors, including Stendhal, Dumas, Offenbach and Zola.

Think about staging an early morning guerrilla raid, then escaping before the crowds become oppressive. That's the only way you'll catch any of the vibe that remains from a time, only a hundred years ago, when Montmartre was a village perched on a hillside just outside the city limits.

Musée de Montmartre
12 Rue Cortot (18th). Tel. 01.46.06.61.11.
Open Tues-Sun 10am-1230pm and 130-6pm
Admission €4.50.

Salvador Dali Museum—Espace Montmartre
11 Rue Poulbot (18th). Tel. 01.42.64.40.10.
Open daily 10am-630pm, July-Aug until 930pm.
Admission €7.

Cimetière Montmartre
20 Ave. Rachel (18th). Open Mon-Fri
8am-530pm, Sat-Sun 9am-530pm.
Admission free.

Nº 06

SPORTS, BEAUTY & FITNESS

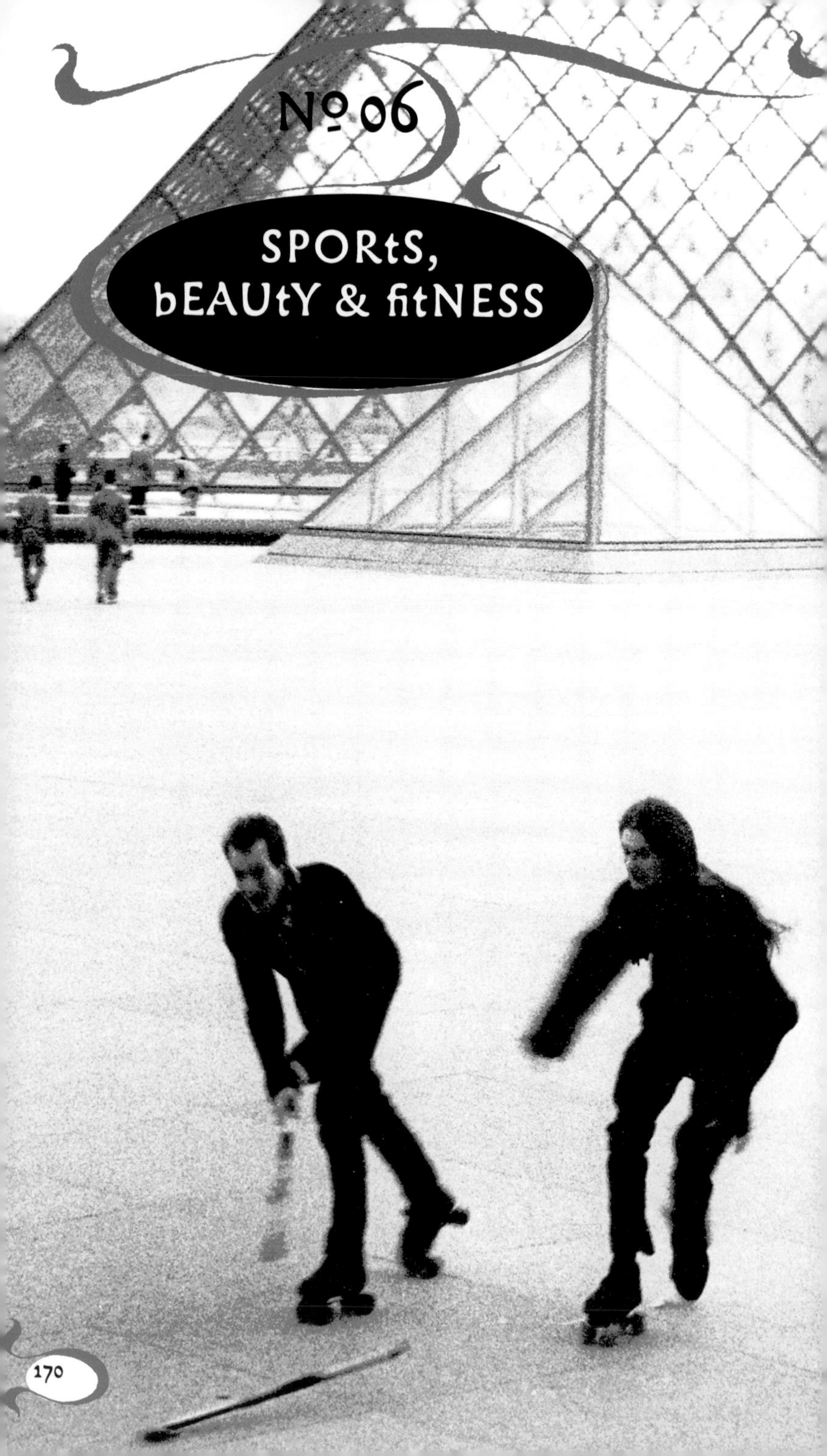

RECREATION & EXERCISE

If you have questions pertaining to swimming pools or other municipal recreational facilities, call **Allo Sports** (tel. 01.42.76.54.54), weekdays between 1030am and 430pm.

biCYCLiNG

Between the smog-belching automobiles and their Indy-style drivers, wheeling around the city can be downright hazardous to your health. Paris street cycling is not for the timid, but with a helmet and *cajones* you can play chicken with the Renaults and cover a lot of ground. We love dodging tourists on the Champs-Elysées, and zipping around the Marais for that real-live video game thrill. If a peddle in the park is more your speed, you'll love the miles of relatively flat, winding paths of Bois de Boulogne, Bois de Meudon or Bois de Vincennes. On Sundays between 10am and 4pm the quays along the Seine and Canal St-Martin are closed to cars.

Paris Vélo, 2 Rue du Fer à Moulin, 5th (tel. 01.43.37.59.22) is a tiny shop renting cool no-speed cruisers for about €14 per day. They're open Mon-Sat 10am-7pm (until 6pm Oct-May), Sun 10am-2pm and 5-7pm. M Censier Daubenton.

Bike 'n Roller, Esplanade des Invalides, 38 rue Fabert, 7th (tel. 01.45.50.38.27) rents bikes for €17 per day. Mon-Sat 10am-730pm, Sun 10am-7pm. M Invalides.

Weekends and holidays from March to October, the RATP "Roue Libre Cyclobus" rents bikes in the **Bois de Vincennes** on for €12 per day. Look for the Cyclobus parked outside the metro exit at Château de Vincennes. They rent bikes in the **Bois de Boulogne** from the Cyclobus outside metro exit Porte d'Auteuil. Open 9am-7pm. Tel. 01.48.15.28.88.

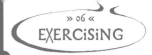

BOWLING

Bowling-Mouffetard

73 Rue Mouffetard (5th). Tel. 01.43.31.09.35. Open Mon-Fri 3pm-2am, Sat-Sun 10am-2am. Prices: €2.30 per game weekdays before 8pm, €5.50 at other times. Shoes €1.70. M Place Monge

Packed with long-haired students from the surrounding universities, and college graduates intent on recreational slumming, this modest eight-laner attracts kitsch-hunting low rollers almost every night of the week.

Bowling de Paris

Jardin d'Acclimatation, Bois de Boulogne (16th). Tel. 01.53.64.93.00. Open Sun-Thurs 9am-3am, Fri-Sat 9am-5am. Prices: €3-€6.55 per game. Shoes €1.85. M Les Sablons.

With two dozen lanes, numerous billiards tables, a comprehensive video arcade and even a swimming pool, Bowling de Paris is a one-stop shop for city slackers. To reach the front door you'll have to cough up an additional €2 for entrance into the Jardin d'Acclimatation. But at 3am who's complaining?

GOLF

The closest greens to downtown Paris is a nine-hole course located inside the Hippodrome de Saint-Cloud at the **Paris Country Club**, 1 Rue du Camp Canadien (Saint-Cloud). Tel. 01.47.71.39.22. Take the SNCF to Suresnes Longchamp. You don't have to be a member to use the driving range at the Golf du Bois de Boulogne, Hippodrome d'Auteuil, 16th (tel.44.30. 70.00). They charge €4 per half hour. Open daily from 8am-8pm. M Porte d'Auteuil.

GYMS

Although Parisians are famous for putting form ahead of function, there are surprisingly few fitness clubs in town. Still, chances are there will be *one* in your neighborhood. And most hotels have special deals with nearby clubs, if they don't have one of their own. When a question to the concierge is answered by a blank stare, we recommend the following high-tech spots where no membership is required:

Club Med Gym, 147bis Rue St-Honoré (1st). Tel. 01.40.20.03.03. Day pass €30. M Madeleine

Espace Vit'Halles, 48 Rue Rambuteau (3rd). Tel. 01.42.77.21.71. Day pass €20. M Rambuteau

Club Quartier Latin, 19 Rue de Pontoise (5th). Tel. 01.55.42.77.88. Day pass €14, students €11.50. M Maubert Mutualité

Club Med Gym, 28 Ave. Général-Leclerc (14th). Tel. 01.45.42.50.57. Day pass €30. M Mouton-Duvernet

Club Med Gym Waou, 11 Rue Chanez (16th). Tel. 01.46.51.88.18. Day pass €40. M Pte d'Auteuil

RUNNING/WALKING

Jogging is yet another American import that Parisians are avidly embracing and bemoaning at the same time. The most jogger friendly Parisian parks are the Champs de Mars gardens just behind the Eiffel Tower (M Iena), Parc Monceau (M Monceau) and the Jardin des Tuileries (M Tuileries/Concord/Louvre). On Sundays from March through October, it's hard to beat the roads on the banks of the Seine, which are reserved for pedestrians only between 9am and 5pm.

CLIMBING

Mur Mur

55 Rue Cartier Bresson (Pantin). Tel 01.48.46.11.00. Open Mon-Fri noon-11pm, Sat-Sun 930am-630pm. Admission €5.05-€12 (most expensive weekends and holidays). M Aubervilliers/ Pantin Quatre-Chemins

One of the largest and best indoor climbing spots in the world, Mur Mur boasts a spectacular 15,000 square feet of wall and almost 10,000 holds. There's even a special section of wall on which to practice ice climbing. Equipment can be rented on site.

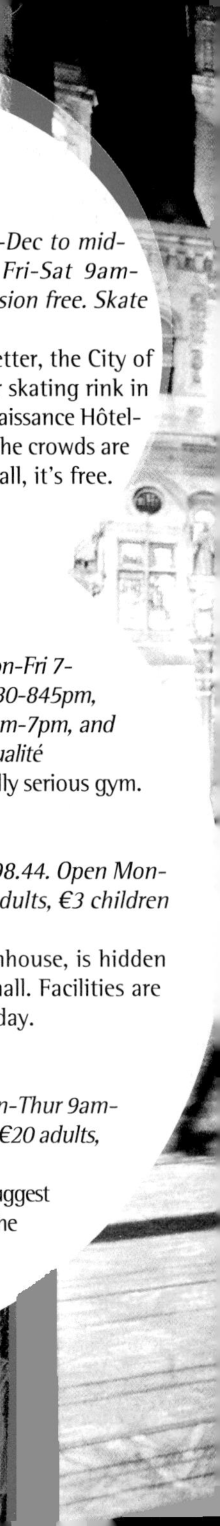

ICE SKATING

Hôtel-de-Ville Ice Rink

Hôtel de Ville (2nd). Open mid-Dec to mid-Feb, Mon-Thurs noon-10pm, Fri-Sat 9am-midnight, Sun 9am-10pm. Admission free. Skate rental €5. M Hôtel-de-Ville

Just like Rockefeller Center, but better, the City of Paris operates a fantastic open-air skating rink in front of the monumental neo-Renaissance Hôtel-de-Ville. The location is perfect, the crowds are surprisingly light, and best of all, it's free.

SWIMMING

Piscine Pontoise/Club Quartier Latin

9 Rue de Pontoise (5th). Tel. 01.55.42.77.88. Open Mon-Fri 7-830am, 1215-130pm and 9-1145pm also Mon-Tues 430-845pm, Wed 1215-845pm, Thurs 4-715pm, Fri 430-8pm, Sat 10am-7pm, and Sun 830am-7pm. Admission €2.90-€6.70. M Maubert Mutualité

A well-maintained Olympic-size pool connected to an equally serious gym.

Piscine Suzanne-Berlioux

Forum des Halles, 10 Place de la Rotonde (1st). Tel. 01.42.36.98.44. Open Mon-Fri 1130am-10pm, Sat-Sun 9am-630pm. Admission €3.80 adults, €3 children under 16. M Les Halles

This 50-meter pool, complete with its own tropical greenhouse, is hidden in the bowels of the monster Forum des Halles shopping mall. Facilities are clean, but very crowded both before and after each work day.

Aquaboulevard de Paris

4 Rue Louis Armand (15th). Tel. 01.40.6010.00. Open Mon-Thur 9am-11pm, Fri-Sat 9am-midnight, Sun 8am-8pm. Admission €20 adults, €10 for children under 12. M Balard

Aquaboulevard's "tropical" lagoon and wave pool suggest recreation more than workout. A fun place for the family.

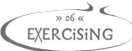

INLINE SKATING

Blading has taken Paris by storm. The city's wide boulevards are great for skating, as are the parks and river quays. The smooth sidewalks of Bastille are popular places to roll, along with the flat open spaces around the Trocadéro, Hôtel des Invalides and other historical sites. The **Promenade Plantée** (12th), a paved garden pathway above the **Viaduc des Arts** between the Bastille and the Bois de Vincennes is one of our favorite spots. This 19th century elevated train viaduct runs among flowers for several miles, above the smog and traffic.

The labyrinth of wide sidewalks and green spaces throughout the **Parc de la Villette** (19th) is another great roller spot.

Each Friday at 10pm an enormous roller brigade gathers at the Place Raoul Dautry (between the Tour and Gare Montparnasse, 14th; M Montparnasse) for a massive group skate through the city. As the group moves, police close the streets to cars providing unimpeded passage to the roller jockeys. As many as 28,000 people have shown up for these amazing and free events. The ride covers 15 miles in about three hours. For info contact **Pari-Roller** (tel. 01.45.87.47.44.; www.Pari-Roller.com). For a more laid-back group skate join the Sunday afternoon group at 230pm at 37 Blvd. Bourdon, 4th (near Place de la Bastille). For more info contact Rollers & Coquillages (tel.44.54.94.42; www.rollers-coquillages.org).

You can rent skates from **Bike 'n Roller**, Esplanade des Invalides, 38 rue Fabert, 7th (tel. 01.45.50.38.27) for €12 per day. They're open Mon-Sat 10am-730pm, Sun 10am-7pm. M Invalides.

There's a second location by the Eiffel Tower at 137 Rue St-Dominique, 7th (tel. 01.44.18.30.39) M Pont de l'Alma/Ecole Militaire.

Nomades, 37 Blvd. Bourdon, 4th (tel. 01.44.54.07.44), rents Rollerblades by the day, week and weekend. They're open Tues-Sun 11am-7pm M Bastille.

Skateboarders: May we suggest the Trocadéro (16th) and the Parvis de la Défense?

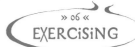

A SPA

La Mosquée de Paris Baths

39 Rue Geoffroy St-Hilaire (5th). Tel. 01.43.31.18.14. Hours for Women: Mon, Wed-Thurs and Sat 10am-9pm, Fri 2-9pm. Hours for Men: Tues 2-9pm, Sun 10am-9pm. Baths €15, Exfoliation €10, massage €10. M *Monge/Jussieu*

The exotic 1920s hammam attached to the city's main mosque is an off-beat favorite of fashion models and film types. The huge eucalyptus-scented steam room is built in chambers—the farther in you go, the hotter it gets. And the brawny, bald masseur is a deadringer for Mr. Clean. Guests loll around on marble slabs and floor mats sipping sweet mint tea between occasional trips into the steamer. The bravest order the Moroccan *gommage*, a brutal exfoliation in which your entire body is scraped with what looks like a pan scourer. From start to finish, it's an unforgettable ritual.

SPECTATOR SPORTS

Many world class sporting events are held in Paris. In late May and early June, the whole city seems to turn its head in unison to the strokes of the **French Open** tennis tournament. In July, all eyes are on the finish of the **Tour de France** bicycle race on the Champs Elysées. On the first Sunday in October, the rich and famous congregate at the Hippodrome de Longchamps (plebes watch on TV) for the **Prix de l'Arc de Triomphe** horse race. And a wide variety events are scheduled throughout the year at Paris' four main sporting venues: Stade de France, Parc des Princes, Bercy Omnisport Palace and Stade de Charlety.

To find out what's happening when you're in town, check the listings in the *Officiel de Spectacles* or *Pariscope*.

Tickets to most events can be ordered from Ticketnet (tel. 08.92.69.70.73; www.ticketnet.fr).

Stade de Charlety

99 Blvd. Kellermann (13th). Tel. *01.44. 16.60.60.* M *Cité Universitaire*

Situated on the city's southern edge, this stadium is the venue of choice for a wide variety of municipal events. You can also find international-caliber track and field events (the 1999 European Championships were held here) and the rare rugby match.

Bercy Omnisports Palace

8 Blvd. Bercy (12th). Tel. *01.40.02.60.60.* M *Bercy*

This indoor stadium, next to the massive Ministry of Taxation on the banks of the Seine, has the rather unique characteristic of being almost entirely covered with sod. It hosts the world-class Bercy Indoor Tennis Tournament, as well as martial arts competitions, boxing matches, volleyball tests and lots of big concerts.

Stade de France

La Plaine-St-Denis. Tel. *01.55.93.00.00.* M *Saint-Denis – Porte de Paris*

Built for the '98 World Cup, the Stade is an architectural jewel seating close to 80,000 spectators. Since the Cup, the stadium has been unable to lure a permanent resident team. Instead, the calendar is filled with an eclectic variety of events, from the Six Nations Rugby Tournament and track and field events to Monster Trucks on Ice.

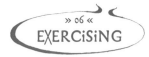

Parc des Princes

24 Rue du Cdt-Guilbaud (16th).
Tel. *08.25.07.50.78.*
M *Porte de Saint Cloud*

Parc des Princes holds a special place in the hearts of Parisians. It was the stage for the legendary triumphs of the "Platini Generation," when Michel Platini led the French national soccer team to the 1978 World Cup after decades of shame. Now that the national team plays at the Stade de France, this stadium is the place the see Paris's perennially disappointing Division 1 Saint-Germain team.

TENNIS

The **French Open** is the nation's premiere tennis event. And it's the only Grand Slam tournament played on clay. Founded in 1891, the glory days for French players were in the late 1920s and early '30s when they dominated the tournament. The year in which underdog René Lacoste (of alligator fame) beat US champion Bill Tilden for the title remains one of the most legendary moments in tennis. Stars from Ilie Nastase to Björn Borg have all lifted the silver cup above their heads, and Chris Evert won the tournament seven times.

The two-week-long championships usually begin the last week of May. It's usually easy enough to buy tickets at the gate for early rounds of play. But, needless to say, tickets for later rounds and the center court can be hard to come by. But with some perseverance, and a little bit of luck, you might be able to snag some.

A limited number of center court tickets are released each tournament day. Queues usually start to form around dawn, and if you arrive by 630am, there's a pretty good chance you'll happily be watching the Big Show later that afternoon. For information and tickets, contact **Roland-Garros/Fédération** Française de Tennis, 2 Ave. Gordon Bennett, 16th (tel. 01.47. 43.48.00). M Porte d'Auteuil.

HORSE RACING

When the trees began to bud, young Ernest Hemingway liked nothing better than to pack a box lunch, grab a bottle of red, and head to Vincennes with Hattie for a day at the races. Times have changed and the mythic adventures of the Lost Generation are a distant memory, but the excitement of the starting bell and charging thoroughbreds remains eternal. There are four race tracks in metropolitan Paris:

Hippodrome d'Auteuil

Porte d'Auteuil (16th). Tel. *01.40.71.47.47.* M *Porte d'Auteuil*
At Paris' steeplechase course, competitors chase an imaginary fox across a jump-studded track that's designed to suggest the French countryside.

Hippodrome de Longchamp

Route des Tribunes, Bois de Boulogne (16th). Tel. *01.44.30.75.00.* M *Porte d'Auteuil-Longchamp*
Opened in 1856, this august track is home to the tony Prix de l'Arc de Triomphe, France's answer to Ascot.

Hippodrome de Vincennes

in the Bois de Vincennes, 2 Route de la Ferme (12th). Tel. *01.49.77.17.17.* M *Château de Vincennes*
Extensive remodeling has lent truth to this course's claim to be the "world's most beautiful hippodrome for trotters."

Hippodrome du Val d'Or

1 Rue du Camp Canadien, Saint Cloud, Hauts-de-Seine. Tel. *01.47.71.69.26. From Gare St-Lazare: Train to St-Cloud-Val d'Or.*
Host of the annual "Grand Prix," Val d'Or is the city's largest track, located just a few minutes from central Paris.

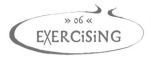

BICYCLING

If you're in town at the end of July, don't miss the finale of the **Tour de France** cycling race on the Champs Elysées. Perhaps one of the most punishing endurance events ever invented, the Tour requires more than a month of speed trials and includes killer climbs up the Alps. It's no wonder so many top cyclists have felt compelled to take performance-enhancing drugs.

RUNNING

The **Paris International Marathon**, usually held the first Sunday in April, draws over 25,000 runners from around the world. The race starts at 9am on the Champs Elysées. Entry info: tel. 01.41.33.15.68; www.parismarathon.com.

SOCCER/FOOTBALL

Winners of Euro 2000, Paris is a soccer town. The city's Division 1 Paris-Saint-Germain team plays at the Parc des Princes. If your timing is right, you can catch Zinadine Zidane, Laurent Blanc and the rest of *les Bleus*—the French national team—at the Stade de France. The football season runs from mid-August to early May and attracts fiercely loyal crowds. Thankfully tribal violence seems to be a thing of the past, but stands can still get rowdy. Think about splurging for seats. For tickets, contact the venues above, or **Ticketnet** (tel. 08.92.69.70.73; www.ticketnet.fr).

No 07

Shopping in the City

Buying

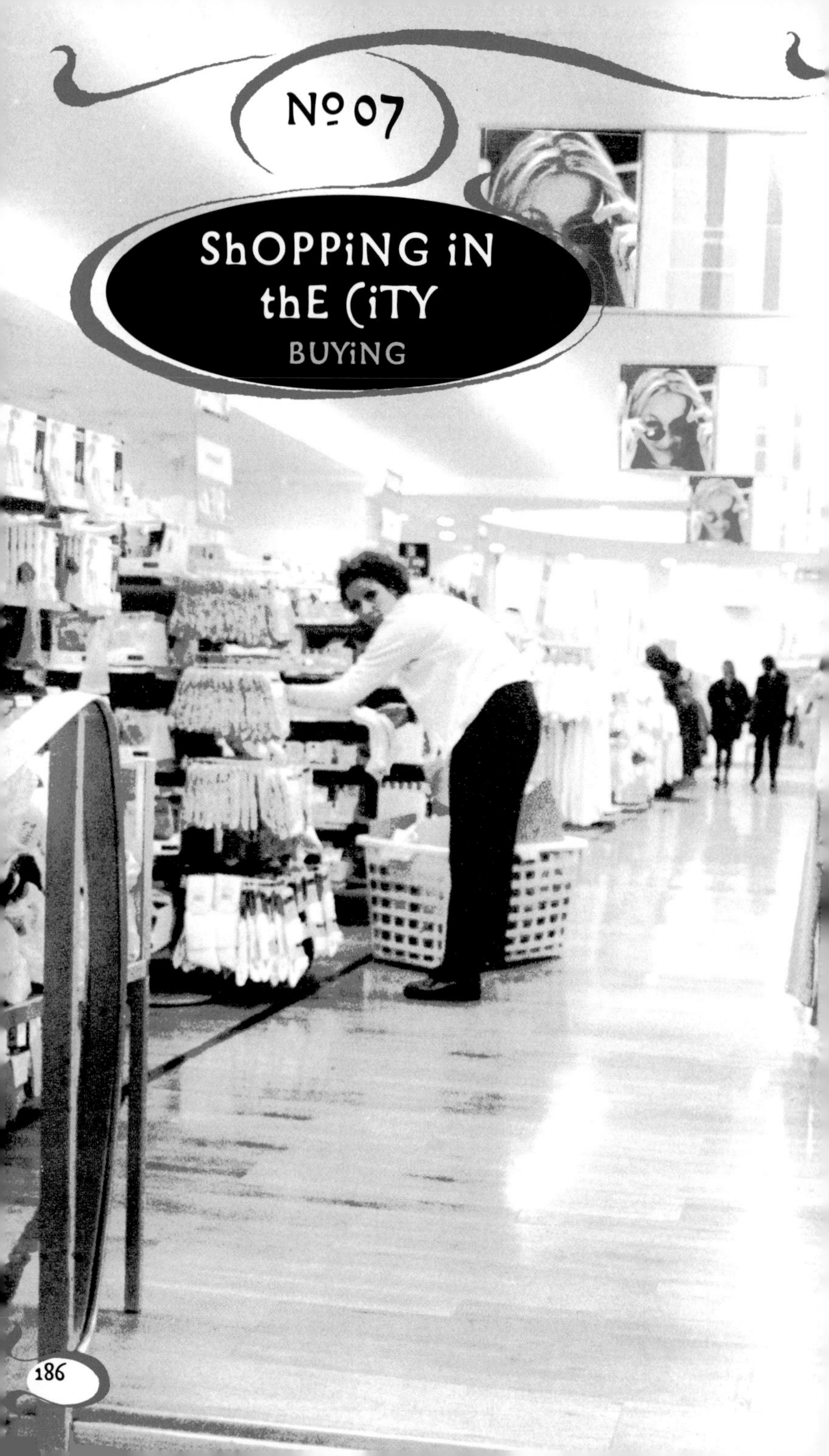

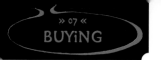

There was a time before you were born when shoppers had to actually travel to Paris to find the fashions they lusted for. You just couldn't get them anywhere else. For better or worse, globalization has changed all that. So, while there are plenty of great things to buy here—from art and antiques to clothes and comestibles—you can probably find many of the same items in London, San Francisco or New York, and often at lower prices.

But as every dedicated clothes-hound knows, shopping isn't just about saving money. It's a holistic, sensual experience that one just can't put a price on—especially if you're using someone else's credit card. Paris, of course, remains the world capital for clothing. And for the sheer pleasure of urban hunting-and-gathering, this city still leads the planet.

As in other major cities, one of the overarching trends in Paris are "lifestyle stores," boutiques, large and small, that offer their own distinctive take on everything from clothing and accessories to electronics, books, housewares and food.

With few notable exceptions, Paris has resisted the global trend toward urban "mallification," allowing shoppers to floss in and out of boutiques all day while strolling around some of the city's most beautiful little streets.

Sales

The government regulates all sales (*soldes*) in France; which are only allowed during the first three weeks of January (to liquidate stock after Christmas); for three weeks in July (to liquidate stock before the fall collections); and when a store is going out of business (*really* going out of business). Most retailers slash prices up to 50%.

Opening Hours

Shops are generally open Monday through Saturday from 930am to 7pm. Some smaller stores take Mondays off and many shut their doors for lunch. Almost everything is closed on Sunday (a policy that's supported by both the Catholic Church and the Communist Party), and lots of places are closed for the entire month of August.

VAT Refunds

Visitors from outside Euroland can reclaim 13–20% value-added tax (VAT) on most items, provided you spend more than €183 in a single store and stay in France for less than three months. Here's the drill: Pay the tax at the register, ask for a *détaxe* receipt, and present it to customs officials at the airport. Send the customs-stamped copy back to the store and they'll refund the tax, either by bank transfer, or via your credit card. The *détaxe* program doesn't apply to art or antiques.

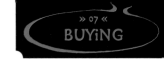

St-Germain-des-Prés

A spirited mix of high-fashion houses and simple shops put St-Germain at the intersection of irresistible and affordable. Formerly associated with intellectuals in black turtlenecks and smoky cafes, today this district is home to Vuitton, Dior, and Armani as well as scores of boutiques targeting young trendies. Cruise along Rue St-Sulpice and ply the length of Rue du Four, then continue along Rue de Grenelle, Rue du Cherche-Midi and Rue du Dragon for stylish shoes, bags and accessories.

Ave. Victor Hugo & The 16th

Lots of top shops have branches in this tony neighborhood, just across from the Eiffel Tower. Look for everything from clothing (Kookaï, Lolita Lempicka) to home deco, along with plenty of little lunch spots along the way.

The Champs-Elysées

While the Champs isn't as good as the good old days, it's come a long way since the late 1970s when fast food outlets, movie theaters and car showrooms brought to mind visions of a *belle époque* Times Square. Today this grand old avenue is recovering some of her youthful charm with class-act chains like Sephora, Fnac, and the Virgin Megastore. To get a whiff of the glory days, stick your nose into Guerlain at number 68.

The Golden Eighth & First

Paris shopping doesn't get any ritzier than the 8th Arrondissement. Top brands and *couture* houses are on the Avenue Montaigne and Rue du Faubourg-St-Honoré. Continue your stroll into Rue Royale and the streets around Place de la Madeleine, then dip into the 1st to Rue Étienne Marcel where you'll find some of the most exciting fashions in the city; and Place Vendôme, home to five of the world's best-known jewelers.

Les Halles & Environs

Once the belly of Paris, where the city converged to eat, drink and be very, Les Halles itself has deteriorated into a seedy park atop a beastly subterranean shopping mall. Nearby, however, you'll still find luxury goods on Rue de la Paix, and most of the city's principal department stores—including Galeries Lafayette and Printemps—have their flagship stores on Boulevard Haussmann. Just east is Place des Victoires and lots of boutique-filled 19th century passageways.

The Marais

Some of the trendiest shopping in Paris can be found in this quarter's hideaway shops. Its ancient streets now house as many designer fashion boutiques and modern art galleries as kosher butchers and falafel stands. Rue de Sévigné is a good bet for creative jewelry and gifts. Take a stroll down the Rue des Francs-Bourgeois and duck into the tiny medieval streets leading off of it.

The Bastille

This former blue collar neighborhood now teams with art galleries and interior design stores. Head east from the Place de la Bastille, along Avenue Daumesnil, and you'll find yourself under the Viaduc des Arts, a former railway bridge that now shelters an arcade of stores and workshops. Peek into the giant plate-glass windows to see craftsmen blowing glass, artisans painting porcelain, and women restoring antique lace.

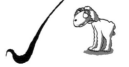

HiGH-ENd hOTLiST

Burberry's
8 Blvd. Malesherbes (8th).
Tel. *01.40.07.77.77.*
Open *Mon-Sat 10am-7pm.*
M *Madeleine*

Boucheron
26 Place Vendôme (1st).
Tel. *01.42.61.58.16.*
Open *Mon-Sat 1030am-7pm.*
M *Opéra*

Bulgari
45 Ave. Montaigne (8th).
Tel. *01.53.23.92.92.*
Open *Mon-Sat 10am-7pm.*
M *Franklin D. Roosevelt*

Céline
36 Ave. Montaigne (8th).
Tel. *01.56.89.07.91.*
Open *Mon-Sat 10am-7pm.*
M *Franklin D. Roosevelt*

Cerruti 1881
Women *42 Rue Grenelle (7th).*
Tel. *01.42.22.92.28.*
Open *Mon 11am-7pm,*
Tues-Sat 10am-7pm.
M *St-Sulpice.*
Men *27 Rue Royale (8th).*
Tel. *01.53.30.18.72.*
Open *Mon-Sat 10am-7pm.*
M *Concorde*

Chanel
31 Rue Cambon (1st).
Tel. *01.42.86.28.00.*
Open *Mon-Sat 10am-7pm.*
M *Madeleine*

Christian Dior
30 Ave. Montaigne (8th).
Tel. *01.40.73.54.00.*
Open *Mon-Sat 10am-7pm.*
M *Franklin D. Roosevelt*

Dolce & Gabbana
26 Ave. Montaigne (8th).
Tel. *01.47.20.42.43.*
Open *Mon-Sat 10am-730pm.*
M *Alma Marceau*

Fred
21 Place Vendôme (1st).
Tel. *01.42.86.60.60.*
Open *Mon-Sat 1030am-645pm.*
M *Opéra.*

Gianni Versace
62 Rue du Fbg-St-Honoré (8th).
Tel. *01.47.42.88.02.*
Open *Mon-Sat 10am-7pm.*
M *Opéra*

Giorgio Armani
6 Place Vendôme (1st).
Tel. *01.42.61.55.09.*
Open *Mon 11am-7pm,*
Tues-Sat 1030am-7pm.
M *Opéra*

Gucci
350 Rue St-Honoré (1st).
Tel. 01.42.96.83.27
Open Mon 11am-7pm,
Tues-Sat 10am-7pm.
M *Concorde*

Hermès
24 Rue de Fbg-St-Honoré (8th).
Tel. *01.40.17.47.17.*
Open *Mon 10am-1pm, 215-630pm,*
Tues-Sat 10am-630pm.
M *Madeleine*

Jil Sander
52 Ave. Montaigne (8th).
Tel. *01.44.95.06.70.*
Open *Mon-Sat 10am-7pm.*
M *Franklin D. Roosevelt*

Jean-Paul Gaultier
6 Rue Vivienne (2nd).
Tel. *01.42.86.05.05.*
Open *Mon-Fri 10am-7pm, Sat 11am-7pm.*
M *Bourse*

Louis Féraud
90 Rue du Fbg-St-Honoré (8th).
Tel. *0144.71.03.85.*
Open *Mon-Sat 10am-7pm.*
M *Opéra*

Max Mara
265 Rue St-Honoré (1st).
Tel. *01.40.20.04.58.*
Open *Mon-Sat 10am-7pm.*
M *Madeleine*

Nina Ricci
39 Ave Montaigne (8th).
Tel. *01.440.88.45.45.*
Open *Mon-Sat 10am-7pm.*
M *Alma Marceau*

Paco Rabanne
83 Rue des Saints-Pères (6th).
Tel. 01.45.48.82.26.
Open *Mon 11am-7pm, Tues-Sat 10am-7pm.*
M *Sèvres-Babylone*

Piaget
16 Place Vendôme (1st).
Tel. *01.55.35.32.80.*
Open *Mon and Sat 1030am-7pm, Tues-Fri 10am-7pm.*
M *Opéra*

Pierre Cardin
27 Ave de Marigny (8th).
Tel. *01.42.66.68.98.*
Open *Mon-Sat 10am-7pm.*
M *Miromesnil*

Salvatore Ferragamo
45 Ave. Montaigne (8th).
Tel. *01.47.23.36.37.*
Open *Mon-Sat 10am-7pm.*
M *Alma Marceau*

Prada
10 Ave. Montaigne (8th).
Tel. *01.53.23.99.40.*
Open *Mon-Sat 10am-7pm.*
M *Alma Marceau*
Branch *5 Rue de Grenelle, 6th*
Tel. *01.45.48.53.14.*
Open *Mon-Sat 10am-7pm.*
M *Sèvres-Babylone*

Thierry Mugler
45 Rue du Bac (7th).
Tel. *01.45.44.44.44.*
Open *Mon-Sat 10am-7pm.*
M *Rue du Bac*

Valentino
17 Ave. Montaigne (8th).
Tel. *01.47.23.64.61.*
Open *Mon-Sat 10am-8pm.*
M *Franklin D. Roosevelt*

Vuitton
101 Ave. des Champs-Elysées (8th).
Tel. *01.40.17.47.17.*
Open *Mon-Sat 10am-7pm.*
M *George V*

Van Cleef & Arpels
22 Place Vendôme (1st).
Tel. *01.53.45.45.45.*
Open *Mon-Sat 10am-7pm.*
M *Opéra*

Yves St-Laurent Rive Gauche
38 Rue du Fbg-St-Honoré (8th).
Tel. *01.42.65.74.59.*
Open *Mon 11am-7pm, Tues-Fri 1030am-7pm.*
M *Franklin D. Roosevelt*

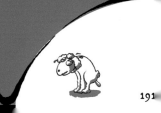

SHOPPING BY SUBJECT

CLOTHING—BASICS

Kookaï

2 Rue Gustave Courbet (16th). **Tel.** *01.47.55.18.00.* **Open** *Mon-Sat 1030am-730pm.* **M** *Trocadéro*

Like Agnès b. before it, and Zara after, Kookaï is where Parisian women pick up their fashion basics. This brand specializes in big-designer knock-offs, which means you can find trendy coats for about €150 and skirts, dresses and sweaters for around €45.

Branches: *Place Carré, Forum des Halles, 1st* (tel. *01.40. 26.59.11); 82 Rue Réaumur, 2nd* (tel. *01.45.08.93.69); 155 Rue de Rennes, 6th* (tel. *01.45.48.26.36).*

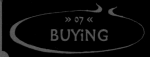

H&M

120 Rue de Rivoli (1st). **Tel.** *01.55.34.96.86.* **Open** *Mon-Sat 10am-8pm.* M *Châtelet*

This fast-expanding Swedish chain is the *au courant* reference for fashion victims with cash-flow issues. Go elbow-to-elbow with the locals for some of the world's best disposable fashion.

Branch: *1 Passage Havre, 9th (***Tel.** *01 55 32 87 97).*

Loft Design By

12 Rue du Faubourg-St-Honoré (8th).
Tel. *01.42.65.59.65.* **Open** *Mon-Sat 10am-7pm.*
M *Concorde/Madeleine*

France's best Gap clone (read: clean styling and medium prices), LDB is a better bet for men than women—especially those who like gray, beige and navy blue.

Branches: *12 Rue de Sévigné, 4th (*tel. *01.48.87.13.07); 56 Rue de Rennes, 6th (*tel. *01.45.44.88.99); 22 Ave. de la Grande Armée, 17th (*tel. *01.45.72.13.53); 175 Blvd. Pereire, 17th (***Tel.** *01.46.22.44.20).*

Mango

6 Blvd. des Capucines (9th). **Tel.** *01.53.30.82.70.* **Open** *Mon-Sat 10am-830pm.* M *Opéra*

Like the better-known Zara, Mango is one of the stores-of-the-moment for high-fashion-clone clothes at super low prices.

Zara

2 Rue Halévy (9th). **Tel.** *01.44.71.90.90.* **Open** *Mon-Sat 10am-730pm Mon-Sat.* M *Opéra*

In what seems like an overnight success, this invader from Spain has sprouted like mushrooms all over the city (and the world) to become THE destination for inexpensive, stylish basics. Look for shoes and skirts priced around €45, dresses for €60 and jackets around €85. Also casualwear, menswear and kids clothes.

Branches: *128 Rue de Rivoli, 1st (*tel. *01.44.82.64.00); 45 Rue de Rennes, 6th (*tel. *01.44.39.03.50); 59 Rue de Sèvres, 6th (tel. 01.45.44.61.60); 44 Ave. des Champs-Elysées, 8th (*tel. *01.45.61.52.80).*

Agnès b.
2, 3, 6, 19 Rue de Jour (1st). **Tel.** *01.45.08.56.56.* **Open** *Mon-Sat 10am-7pm.* M *Les Halles*
When she sold her first cardigan here in the 1970s, little did Agnès Bourgois dream that she was creating a fashion archetype as recognizable as Coco's suit. The Rue de Jour is something of an empire in microcosm, as it has become home to four Agnès b. boutiques for men, women, children and infants

A.P.C.
3 Rue de Fleurus (6th). Tel. 01. 42.22.12.77. **Open** *Mon-Sat 1030am-7pm.* M *Saint Placide*
Atelier de Production et de Creation has one of the best publicity machines in town, getting itself mentioned in French Elle at least once a month. After visiting this retail flagship, head over to their surplus store at 45 Rue Madame, 6th (tel. 01.45.48.43.71), where overstock from previous collections are sold at 40% to 70% off.

Balenciaga
10 Ave. George V (8th). **Tel.** *01.47. 20.21.11.* **Open** *Mon-Sat 10am-7pm.* M *Alma Marceau*
Thanks to the creations of Nicolas Ghesquière (formerly of Gaultier), Balenciaga's discreetly modern ready-to-wear has captured the hearts of the city's fashion mandarins. Everyone wanting to keep abreast of contemporary style is required to stop in for a look-see.

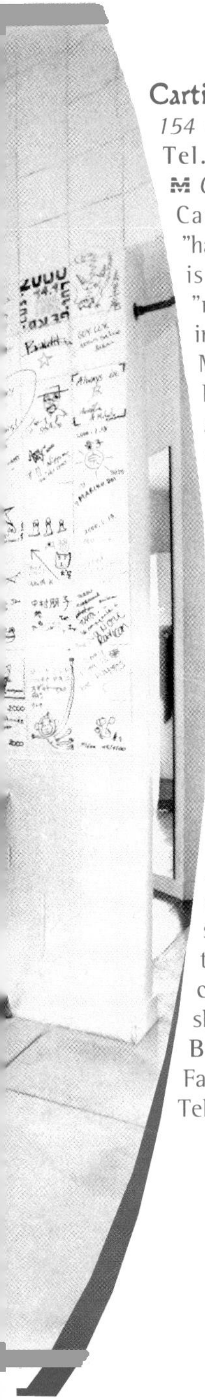

Cartier

154 Champs-Elysees (8th). **Tel.** *01.40.74.01.27.* M *Champs-Elysees.*

Cartier's brand-new "haute" jewelry emporium is the Champs' latest "must see." Designed by interior architect Bruno Moinard, who founded Ecart International with Andrée Putman, the store is fronted by a spectacular facade made of gold-veined black marble.

Chanel

31 Rue Cambon (1st). **Tel.** *01.42.86.28.00.* **Open** *Mon-Sat 10am-7pm.* M *Madeleine*

You know it: The little black dress, No. 5, and the supermodel chic of Karl Lagerfeld. A uniformed doorman greets highbrow shoppers as they enter this chi-chi shop of clothing, accessories, shoes and scents.

Branch: 21 rue du Faubourg St-Honoré, 8th. Tel. 01.53.05.98.95.

Chloé

54 Rue du Faubourg-St-Honoré (8th). **Tel.** *01.44.94.33.00.* **Open** *Mon-Sat 10am-7pm.* M *Concorde/Madeleine*

One of the sexiest *couture* houses of the moment.

Christian Dior

30 Ave. Montaigne (8th). **Tel.** *01.40.73.54.00.* **Open** *Mon-Sat 10am-7pm.* M *Franklin D. Roosevelt*

Built by American architect Peter Marino, this glitzy store is the perfect environment for John Galliano's outrageous creations. Dior himself would have been delighted by this juxtaposition of classy sophistication and youthful abandon. And if you want your daughter to be the belle of the nursery school, check out Baby Dior, next door.

Comme des Garçons

54 Rue du Faubourg-St-Honoré (8th). Tel. 01.53.30.27.27. Open Mon-Sat 11am-7pm. M *Saint Philippe du Roule*

Rei Kawakubo's unisex cuts are shaking off post-apocalyptic black and gray for a brighter, more playful look. Hidden in the inner courtyard, this boutique offers the complete range of Comme des Garçons clothing for men and women.

Christian Lacroix

73 Rue du Faubourg-St-Honoré (8th). **Tel.** *01.42.68.79.00.* **Open** *Mon-Sat 10am-7pm.* M *Saint Philippe du Roule*

Both colorful and baroquish, the clothes of Christian Lacroix are reminiscent of a brash and passionate love affair. Ready-to-wear, accessories, and jewelry are sold at 26 Ave. Montaigne (8th); jeans and the Bazaar line at 2–4 Place Saint Sulpice (6th).

Courrèges

40 Rue François 1er (8th). **Tel.** *01.53.67.30.00.* **Open** *Mon-Sat 10am-7pm.* M *Franklin D. Roosevelt*

Coqueline Courrèges' spiritual ready-to-wear includes fashions for men, women and children, along with the requisite ground floor café.

Emporio Armani

149 Blvd. St-Germain (6th). **Tel.** *01. 53.63.33.50.* **Open** *Mon-Sat 1030am-830pm.* M *St-Germain-des-Prés*

Armani's clean white cubist space features the designer's less-pricey lines and trademark crisp suits. In addition to the instantly-recognizable power clothes, there's an upstairs café, and a mezzanine-level CD shop that's perfectly positioned for lusting after the beautiful young salespeople below.

Branch: *6 Place Vendôme, 1st (tel. 01.42.61.02.34).*

Espace Jeunes Créateurs du Forum des Halles

Forum des Halles (1st), Porte Berger, level -1. **Tel.** *01.44.76.96.56.* **Open** *Mon-Sat 1130am-730pm.* M *Châtelet-Les Halles*

This is the only interesting place in the dreadful Forum des Halles mall. In a move to fill shops that would otherwise lie vacant, fifty young designers were lured into this huge retail space to sell their clothing, accessories and design objects. Most of the up-and-comers are unknowns; though some, including Xüly Bet, are emerging from the pack. There's always something fun to look at.

Givenchy

3 Ave. George V (8th). **Tel.** *01.44.31.50.23.* **Open** *Mon-Sat 10am-7pm.* M *George V*

Begun by Hubert de Givenchy in 1959, this classic boutique is now the showplace of Alexander McQueen's "Couture Givenchy." Softer lines and exciting, flowery eveningwear has won lots of fans. The new "Boutique" line is housed across the way, at 8 Ave. George V; and men's fashions are at Gentleman Givenchy, 56 Rue François 1er, 8th (tel. 01.40.76.00.21).

Hermès

24 Rue du Faubourg-St-Honoré (8th). **Tel.** *01.40.17.47.17.* **Open** *Mon 10am-1pm & 215-630pm, Tues-Sat 10am-630pm.* Ⓜ *Madeleine*

Begun as saddle and bridle makers to French aristocrats, Hermès is now best known for its trademark silk scarves, and Kelly bags (named for Grace Kelly, who appeared on the cover of Life Magazine dangling one on her arm). Of course there's fine china, towels and linens too.

Irié

8 Rue du Pré-aux-Clercs (7th). **Tel.** *01.42.61.18.28.* **Open** *Mon-Sat 1015am-7pm. Closed first three weeks in Aug.* Ⓜ *Rue du Bac*

Smashion mavens from the world over converge on this Japanese designer's marbleized, side-by-side boutiques. Irié's use of fake fur, sequins, hologram prints and plastic fabrics is beyond compare.

Isabel Marant

16 Rue de Charonne (11th). **Tel.** *01.49.29. 71.55.* **Open** *Mon-Sat 1030am-730pm.* Ⓜ *Bastille*

Isabel Marant travels the world in search of new fabrics. And her Paris shop is always full, a testament to the fact that the young designer's skirts, tops and sweaters make everyone look that much better. Prices are great too.

Branch: *1 Rue Jacob, 6th (tel. 01.43.26.04.12).*

Jean-Paul Gaultier

6 Rue Vivienne (2nd). **Tel.** *01.42. 86.05.05.* **Open** *Mon-Fri 10am-7pm, Sat 11am-7pm.* Ⓜ *Bourse*

The man who introduced the world to conical breasts presents his JPG line—mid-priced cyber/streetwear, jeans, sunglasses, fragrances, watches and shoes—in an industrialized space that's reminiscent of a dockfront warehouse. Hellooo sailor.

José Lévy à Paris

70 Rue Vieille du Temple (3rd). **Tel.** *01.48.04.39.16.* **Open** *Mon 1-8pm, Tues-Sat noon-8pm.* Ⓜ *Saint-Paul*

José Lévy is a man for all seasons. In addition to his own line, Lévy designs for Britain's hoity-toity Holland & Holland label, and the populist Monoprix department store. This flagship boutique offers men's and women's basics, all with impeccable flourishes that never fail to impress.

Kenzo

3 Place des Victoires (1st). **Tel.** *01.40. 39.72.03.* **Open** *Mon-Sat 10am-730pm.* Ⓜ *Bourse*

Along with the brand's trademark flower prints and bright-colored dresses, you'll find housewares, leather goods, shoes and fragrances.

Branches: Women/Home, *16 Blvd. Raspail, 7th (tel. 01.42.22.09.38);* Men, *17 Blvd. Raspail, 7th (tel. 01.45.49.33.75; 18 Ave. George V, 8th (tel. 01.47. 23.33.49); 23 Blvd. de la Madeleine, 8th (tel. 01. 42.61 .04.51).*

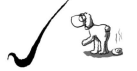

Lanvin

15 Rue du Faubourg-St-Honoré (8th). **Tel.** *01.44.71.33.33.* **Open** *Mon-Sat 10am-7pm.* M *Madeleine*

The his-and-hers Lanvin stores are a huge repositories of stylish ready-to-wear garments, wonderful accessory, fragrances and gifts. The hats by Gélot are definitely worth a look. And consider brunching at the reasonably-priced Lanvin Café Bleu.

Liwan

8 Rue St-Suplice (6th). **Tel.** *01.43.26.07.40.* **Open** *Mon 2-7pm, Tues-Sat 1030am-7pm.* M *St-Suplice*

Liwan sprawls over three levels of pantsuits, bathrobes and sandals from Lebanese designer Lina Audi. The Middle Eastern colors and cuts are popular with local trendsetters.

Lolita Lempicka

46 Ave. Victor Hugo (16th). **Tel.** *01.45.02.14.46.* **Open** *Mon-Sat 1030am-130pm & 230-7pm.* M *Rue de la Pompe*

Haute couture meets the Wicked Witch of the West at this store selling fairy tale fashions for women.

Louis Vuitton

101 Ave. des Champs-Elysées (8th). **Tel.** *01.53.57.24.00.* **Open** *Mon-Sat 10am-8pm.* M *George V*

Marc Jacobs' *prêt-à-porter* lines have been breathing new life into LV. And the company's trio of Parisian boutiques are true studies in elegance. The St-Germain store sells restored luggage from the Golden Age of travel.

Branches: 6 Place St-Germain-des-Prés, 6th (tel. 01.45.49.62.32); 54 Ave. Montaigne, 8th (tel. 01.45.62.47.00).

Martine Sitbon

13 Rue de Grenelle (7th). **Tel.** *01.44.39.84.44.* **Open** *Mon-Sat 1030am-7pm.* M *Rue de Bac*

Known as one of the first designers to tap the velvet goldmine, Sitbon has recently turned to the Jazz Age for inspiration. Situated in a former printing shop, this boutique was splendidly renovated by Stephan O'Reilly and manages to avoid the current obsession with minimalist design.

Paco Rabanne

83 Rue des Saints-Pères (6th). Tel. 01.45.48.82.26 Open Mon 11am-7pm, Tues-Sat 10am-7pm. M *Sèvres-Babylone*

Another architectural masterpiece, this beautiful store stocks the entire line of Paco's ready-to-wear clothes, accessories and fragrances.

Pierre Cardin

27 Ave Marigny (8th). **Tel.** *01.42.66.68.98. Mon-Sat 10am-7pm.* M *Miromesnil*

A defiant holdover from another era, this musty boutique has to be seen to be believed. And now that the '70s have re-infiltrated fashion, PC's ironic renaissance is due. Go with tongue firmly in cheek.

Sonia Rykiel

175 Blvd. St-Germain (6th). **Tel.** *01.49.54.60.60.* **Open** *Mon-Sat 10am-7pm.* M *St-Germain-des-Prés*

Clothes, accessories, tableware and cosmetics from the doyen of Left Bank fashion are beautifully displayed in this elegant, wood-paneled boutique. Floor-to-ceiling cubby holes are filled with brightly-colored sweaters and tops. And because this is the intellectual St-Germain, Madame Rykiel's favorite reading matter is displayed alongside her latest designs. Menswear is across the street at No. 194.

Branch: *70 Rue du Fbg-St-Honoré, 8th (tel. 01.42.65.20.81).*

Vanessa Bruno

25 Rue Saint Sulpice (6th). **Tel.** *01.43.54.41.04.* **Open** *Mon-Sat 1030am-7pm.* M *Saint-Sulpice*

Already huge in Japan (her bright, functional bags are everywhere), we predict that Vanessa Bruno is a designer you'll be hearing a lot more of in the near future. Upscale, modern sportswear is sold in an exciting purple-and-white space.

Yohji Yamamoto

3 Rue de Grenelle (6th). **Tel.** *01.42.84.28.87.* **Open** *Mon-Sat 1030am-7pm.* M *Sèvres Babylone/St-Sulpice*

The traditional kimono is the inspiration for Yamamoto's trendy, deconstructed jackets and long, asymmetrical coats. Y's is the designer's lower-priced bridge line.

Branches: Men, *47 Rue Étienne-Marcel, 1st (tel. 01.45.08.82.45).* Y's, *25 Rue du Louvre, 1st (tel. 01.42.21.42.93); 69 Rue des Saints Pères, 6th (tel. 01.45.48.22.56).*

Zucca

74 Rue Jean Jacques Rousseau (1st). Tel. 01.42.33.54.44. Open Mon-Sat 11am-730pm. M *Tuileries*

Suffused with light, this trendy boutique offers both men's and women's fashions at surprisingly accessible prices. Japanese influences are ubiquitous, inspiring the austere lines of shirts, skirts and blouses.

CLOhtiNG—BOUtiQUES

Absinthe

74 Rue Jean Jacques Rousseau (1st). **Tel.** *01.42.33.54.44.* **Open** *Mon-Sat 11am-730pm.* Ⓜ *Étienne Marcel*

Owner Marthe Desmoulins has taste. Her off-beat, Ali Baba-ish cavern is filled with fashionable clothes and accessories for men and women from such stalwarts as Dries Von Noten and Jamin-Puench. There are also whimsical Palmaccio dresses, made with antique fabrics from the middle of the last century, and the poetic creations of Catalan designer Josep Font. The window displays alone are worth a visit.

Atelier Frederic Delliaux

4 rue du Roi de Sicile (5th). **Tel.** *01.40.29.03.53.* Ⓜ *St. Paul.*

Leather "haute streetware" designer Frédéric Delliaux's shop in the heart of Paris features very stylish and wearable clothes for both men and women, the uniting feature being that all are in possession of gold cards.

Bonnie Cox

38 Rue des Abbesses (18th). **Tel.** *01.42.54.95.68.* **Open** *daily 11am-8pm.* Ⓜ *Abbesses*

Bonnie Cox reinforced her fashion-forward reputation when she became the first in Paris to carry the clothes of Xüly Bet. If this shop is still a bellwether, than we can look for more retro '70s rock'n'roll rags, jazzed up with fun accessories.

Barbara Bui

23 Rue Étienne Marcel (1st). **Tel.** *01.40.26.43.65.* **Open** *Mon 1pm-7pm, Tues-Sat 1030am-730pm.* Ⓜ *Étienne Marcel*

Barbara Bui's terminally hip boutique features both sensual and modern clothes from the most Western of the Eastern designers. Bui's self-named cafe is two doors down, at the corner of Rue Française.

Branch: *50 Ave Montaigne, 8th (tel. 01.42.25.05.25).*

L'Eclaireur

3 ter Rue des Rosiers (4th). **Tel.** *01.48.87.10.22.* **Open** *Mon 2-7pm, Tues-Sat 11am-7pm.* Ⓜ *St-Paul*

A temple to the Fashion Gods, L'Eclaireur is a one-stop-shop for edgy designs by Prada, Dries Van Noten, Ann Demeulemeester, Jil Sander, Martin Margiela and Helmut Lang—all served in warm surroundings that are a pleasant respite from the steely minimalism that pervades other high-fashion outlets.

Branches: *10 Rue Hérold, (1st) and 26 Ave des Champs-Elysées, (8th).*

Kabuki
25 Rue Étienne Marcel (1st). **Tel.** *01.42.33.55.65.* **Open** *Mon 1-730pm, Tues-Sat 1030am-730pm.* M *Étienne-Marcel*
Always up-to-date and to the point, William Halimi's shop is the Cliff Notes of high fashion. Bags and shoes on the ground floor give way to an upper floor full of men's and women's fashions by Prada, Martine Sitbon, Barbara Bui, Helmut Lang and Costume National. Two doors down is a women's wear boutique; and diagonally across the street is a shoe space with everything from DKNY sneakers to mules by Rudolphe Meundier.

Et Vous Stock
15 Rue de Turbigo (2nd). **Tel.** *01.40.13.04.12.* **Open** *Mon-Sat noon-7pm.* M *Étienne-Marcel*
This outlet store sells end-of-season and last-season clothes from the classic brand Et Vous for up to 50% off their original price, all year long. Look for coats priced from €123, jeans starting at €38 and sweaters from €46.

Le Shop
3 Rue d'Argout (2nd). **Tel.** *01.40.28.95.94.* **Open** *Mon 1-7pm, Tues-Sat 11am-7pm. Closed two weeks in Aug.* M *Étienne-Marcel*
Something of a Gen-Y shopping mall, this collection of clothing outlets is aimed at Third Millennium skate rats. You'll see Levi's, Stussy, Homecore, Lady Soul, Crw, Freaks and the like, along with the requisite DJs and on-site Sony PlayStations.

Maria Luisa
2 Rue Cambon (1st). **Tel.** *01.47.03.96.15.* **Open** *Mon-Sat 1030am-7pm.* M *Concorde*
As bewitching as it is expensive, Maria Luisa is all about flamboastful high-end style for avant women. The shops around the corner (19 bis, 38 and 40 Rue Mont Thabor) stock appropriate shoes, accessories, and men's fashions by Alexander McQueen, Andrew Mackenzie, Jean-Paul Gaultier and others.

Zadig & Voltaire
15 Rue du Jour (1st). **Tel.** *01.42.21.88.70.* **Open** *Mon-Sat 1030am-7pm.* M *Châtelet/Les-Halles*
A terrific store for women, Z&V carries lots of Japanese designers (think Junk by Junko Shimada and Indivi by Atsuro Tayama) as well as Occidental staples like Helmut Lang jeans.
Branches: *9 Rue du 29 Juillet, 1st (tel. 01.42.92.00.80); 1 Rue du Vieux Colombier, 6th (tel. 01.43.29.18.29).*

CLOtHiNG—dISCOUNT & ViNtAGE

Didier Ludot

20-24 Galerie Montpensier, Jardin du Palais-Royal (1st). **Tel.** *01.42.96.06.56.* **Open** *Mon-Sat 1030am-7pm.* **M** *Palais-Royal*

Although it looks like junk to some, Didier Ludot's two shops are filled with landmark pieces of fashion history that include an original 1950s Chanel suit and a 1970s beaded Dior dress. One of the shops is dedicated to authentic accessories (crocodile handbags!) by Chanel, Pucci, Hermès, and the like. His boutique La Petite Robe Noir (across the gardens at 125 Galerie de Valois) sells his own label and vintage couture little black dresses.

Alternatives

18 Rue du Roi-de-Sicile (4th). **Tel.** *01.42.78.31.50.* **Open** *Tues-Sat 11am-1pm & 230-7pm. Closed July 15-Aug 15.* **M** *St-Paul*

Second-hand certainly doesn't mean downmarket at Alternatives, where Jean-Paul Gaultier, Hermès, Channel, Dries Van Noten and Comme des Garçons are featured. Everything's in good shape too.

L'Habilleur

44 Rue de Poitou (3rd). **Tel.** *01.48.87.77.12.* **Open** *Mon-Sat 11am-8pm.* **M** *St-Sébastien-Froissart*

Stocked with fashions from last season's collections at up to 50% off, John Crawley's Marais boutique is a prime destination for fashion-hungry men and women. Look for designs by Olivier Strelli, Martine Sitbon, Patrick Cox, Dice Kayek and Barbara Bui.

Kiliwatch

64 Rue Tiquetonne (2nd). **Tel.** *01.42.21.17.37.* **Open** *Mon 2-7pm, Tues-Sat 11am-7pm.* **M** *Étienne Marcel*

The top second-hand clothing destination for club kids and skaters, Kiliwatch is a huge shop full of vintage (and new) Diesel, Levi's, Adidas, DKNY, Polo Jeans, Firetrap and other street-smart labels. You can also pick-up the latest issues of magazines like Purple, Index and Dutch.

La Clef des Marques

20 Place du Marché St-Honoré (1st). **Tel.** *01.47.03.90.40.* **Open** *Mon-Fri 11am-230pm & 330-7pm, Sat 11am-1pm, 2-7pm.* **M** *Tuileries*

New shipments arrive regularly at this chain that stocks staples for men, women and children. It's always a bit of a crapshoot, but with a little luck you can find great deals on designer outfits and shoes.

Branches: 124 Blvd. Raspail, 6th (tel. 01.45.49.31.00); 86 Rue du Fbg-St-Antoine, 11th (tel. 01.40.01.95.15).

Le Mouton à Cinq Pattes

8, 18 Rue St-Placide (6th) **Tel.** *01.45.48.86.26.* **Open** *Mon-Sat 10am-7pm.* M *St-Sulpice*

A fashion zoo if ever there was one, Le Mouton is famous with bargain hounds for last season's designer collections at massively reduced rates. Intrepid shoppers elbow their way through unorganized racks and bins of designerwear, priced 50%, and more, off original retail. Neophytes beware: Labels are cut out so you better know the difference between a Helmut Lang and an H&M or you could end up with less than you bargained for.

Réciproque

88, 89, 92, 95, 97, 101, 123 Rue de la Pompe (16th). **Tel.** *01.47.04.82.24.* **Open** *Tues-Fri 11am-7pm, Sat 1030am-7pm. Closed in August.* M *Rue de la Pompe*

Réciproque's row of seven second-hand stores are the answer for those with champagne taste and beer budgets. All the top designers are represented; though even at half-price, Chanel, Yves St-Laurent, Prada and Christian Lacroix can be mighty expensive. The shops sell men's and women's couture, jewelry and accessories, many of which have barely been worn.

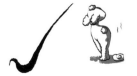

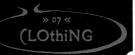

Department Stores

Galeries Lafayette and Printemps, adjacent to each other, are the capital's two largest department stores (*grands magasins*). Le Bon Marché, on the Left Bank, is smaller and more exclusive than its rivals; BHV and Samaritaine are known as mid-priced shops; while Monoprix and Tati are at the bottom end of the market. If you're going to brave the department store world, you can escape the crush by shopping early in the day and avoiding Saturdays altogether.

Tati

4 Blvd. Rochechouart (18th). **Tel.** *01.55.29.50.00.* **Open** *Mon-Sat 10am-7pm.* **M** *Barbès-Rochechouart*

A veritable retail mosh pit, Tati's huge flagship store is a holy Mecca for discount enthusiasts. Where else can you find T-shirts for €1.55, sneakers for €8 and DDD bras for a mere €4.60? Shockingly cheap when it first opened, the store has become something of a curiosity for bargain hunters and contemporary anthropologists.

Branches: *13 Place de la République, 3rd (tel. 01.48.87.72.81);* **Tati Bonbons,** *26 Rue St-Denis, 1st (tel. 01.42.36.51.45);* **Tati Optique,** *11 Rue Belhomme, 18th (tel. 01.55.79.95.00).* **Tati Or** (jewelry) *19 Rue de la Paix, 2nd (tel. 01.40.07.06.76); 132 Blvd. St-Germain, 6th (tel. 01.56.24.93.15).*

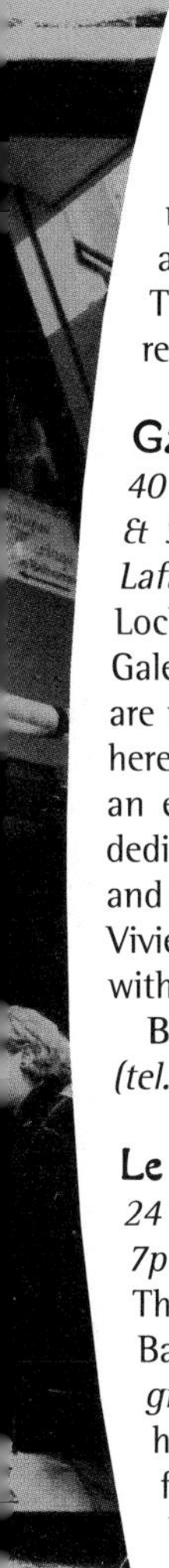

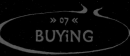

Bazar de l'Hôtel de Ville (BHV)

52 Rue de Rivoli (4th). **Tel.** *01.42.74.90.00.* **Open** *Mon-Tues & Thurs-Sat 930am-7pm; Wed 930am-10pm; Sat 930am-7pm.* **M** *Hôtel de Ville*

Located directly across the street from the monumental Hôtel de Ville, BHV is an equally classic department store known for a comprehensive selection of do-it-yourself supplies ranging from lightbulbs and furniture coasters to power tools and car parts. They've got a large assortment of clothes too. The place is perpetually packed despite the fact that few self-respecting Parisians actually admit to shopping here.

Galeries Lafayette

40 Blvd. Haussmann (9th). **Tel.** *01.42.82.34.56.* **Open** *Mon-Wed & Sat 930am-7pm, Thurs 930am-9pm.* **M** *Chaussée d'Antin-Lafayette*

Locked in a perpetual battle for customers with Printemps, Les Galeries claims to carry more than 75,000 brand names. And who are we to argue? It seems as though you can get almost anything here. There is a huge selection of china, glassware and kitchenware, an enormous home-furnishings department, and a whole floor dedicated to lingerie. Many of the best-known designers are present and accounted for, including Yohji Yamamoto, Claude Montana and Vivienne Westwood. And there are two restaurants on the 6th floor with killer views.

Branch: *22 Rue du Départ, (Maine-Montparnasse) 14th (tel. 01.45.38.52.87).*

Le Bon Marché

24 Rue de Sèvres (7th) **Tel.** *01.44.39.80.00.* **Open** *Fri-Wed 930am-7pm, Thurs 10am-9pm.* **M** *Sèvres Babylone*

The only major department store headquartered on the Left Bank, Le Bon Marché ("good deal" in French) was the first *grand magasin* in Paris. It's a pretty store, with relatively humane proportions (Gustave Eiffel helped design its iron-framed structure), popular with the bourgeoisie for excellent linens, Vuitton and Dior boutiques, and the Théâtre de la Beauté day spa. Lots of young women visit just to check out the designer dresses in the Wedding Shop. Others head straight for the name-brand fashion areas that stock limited-edition collections of some top designers. We love the ground floor Grande Épicerie, a celebrated gourmet supermarket in the store's adjacent annex.

SOLDES

Printemps

64 Blvd. Haussmann (9th). **Tel.** *01.42. 82.50.00.* **Open** *Mon-Wed & Fri-Sat 935am-7pm, Thurs 935am-10pm.* M *Havre Caumartin*

Hugely popular with Japanese tourists, Printemps has the largest perfume department in France, excellent lingerie, a nice selection of upscale ready-to-wear, and solid toy and stationary departments. The Espace Créateurs features the clothes of some of the world's hottest designers, from Alexander McQueen to Jeremy Scott.

Branches: *30 Ave. d'Italie, 13th (tel. 01.40.78.17.17); 21-25 Cour de Vincennes, 20th (tel. 01.43. 71.12.41).*

Monoprix

52 Ave. des Champs-Elysées (8th). **Tel.** *01.53.77.65.65.* **Open** *daily 9am-midnight.* M *Franklin D. Roosevelt*

Almost as ubiquitous as the corner *boulangerie*, Monoprix is perfect for restocking toiletries, loading up on snacks and picking-up low-priced disposable fashions.

Branches: *Numerous.*

La Samaritaine

19 Rue de la Monnaie (1st). **Tel.** *01.40.41.20.20.* **Open** *Mon-Wed & Fri-Sat 930am-7pm, Thurs 930am-10pm.* M *Pont Neuf*

An art nouveau landmark by the Seine, Samaritaine is a multi-building complex that seems to stock everything from pins to pianos. The children's clothing and toy departments have excellent reputations, and the store offers one of the world's greatest selections of kitchenware. Situated opposite the Pont-Neuf, the best thing about La Samaritaine is the 360-degree view from its roof that puts the gargoyles of Notre-Dame at eye-level.

MALLS

Forum des Halles

11 bis Rue de l'Arc en Ciel (4th). **Tel.** *01.44.76.96.56.* **Open** *Mon-Sat 10am-730pm.* M *Les Halles*

Riddled with almost 180 lowbrow stores and restaurants, Forum des Halles is a thoroughly horrible place filled with boring suburban shops that appeal to God knows who. Located completely underground, and riddled with a maze of escalators and passageways, the Forum is a rodent-like non-event that only appeals to mallrats, drug dealers, Ricky Lake Girls and other teen angst rebels.

Carrousel du Louvre

99 Rue de Rivoli (1st). **Tel.** *01.43. 16.47.22.* **Open** *daily 830am-11pm (individual store/restaurant hours vary, usually 10am–8pm).* M *Palais Royal*

The selection at this shopping mall under the Louvre museum is relatively uninspired (read: The Body Shop, Esprit and the like). But it's a good place to pick up some last-minute gifts and clothing. It's also one of the few reliable places you can shop on Sundays.

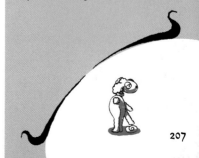

YOUNG TALENT

Tatiana Lebedev

2 rue Piémontési (18th). **Tel.** *01.42.23.66.08.*

Several fresh design shops are sprouting up around Abbesses in Montmartre. At Lebedev's "Futurewearlab" you can find unique waxed cotton bottoms, leather jackets and Lycra tops, most with plenty of appliquée and gold print.

Branch: *64 rue Vielle du Temple (3rd).* **Tel.** *01.42.77.80.89.*

Patricia Louisor

16 rue Houdon (18th). **Tel.** *01.42.62.10.42.* **Open** *daily 1130am-730pm.*

The colorful Caribbean prints here are inspired by the designers origins in Martinique. Look for everything from linin skirts to dimono-type dresses, all at very reasonable prices.

A chic oasis in an otherwise dilapidated section of Barbès' has sprung up on the rue des Gardes to promote young designers. Here are the best:

Dognin

4 Rue des Gardes (18th). **Tel.** *01.44.92.32.16.*

The best-known boutique on the street is a great place for leathergoods, handbags and luggage for globetrotters especially, combining originality and practicality by designer duo Luc Dognin and Rafik Mahiout.

Flux

7 Rue des Gardes (18th). **Tel.** *01.44.92.32.16.*

a.k.a. Fuckin' Fashion System, Flux is a fine jewelry brand by Mathias Chaize, a designer who cut his teeth under Claudie Pierlot, Junko Shimada and Agnès b. His output reflects current Parisian trends and plays on unusual contrasts with gold, ebony and precious stones.

Carvalho & Marinelli

2 Rue des Gardes (18th). **Tel.** *01.44.92.32.16.*

Designers Marcia de Carvalho and Pierina Marinelli are both Brazilian. Together they produce candy-hued collections that are fun and festive: think sexy knits and black lacing.

LifEStYLE BOUtiQUES

Colette

213 Rue St-Honoré (1st). **Tel.** *01.55.35.33.90.* **Open** *Mon-Sat 11am-7pm.* **M** *Tuileries*

The Mother Of All Lifestyle Boutiques, Colette is a multi-level monument to minimalist living, offering a chic and daring take on everything from clothing to home-furnishings on the otherwise restrained Rue St-Honoré. The store's high-priced, design-heavy merchandise runs the gamut from kitchenware to ready-to-wear, and includes top-quality beauty products, dresses by Jeremy Scott, and wacky customizable shoes. The lower-level water bar serves dozens of brands of bottled H2O along with light lunches.

Muji

27 & 30 Rue St-Sulpice (6th). **Tel.** *01.46.34.01.10.* **Open** *Mon-Sat 10am-8pm.* **M** *St-Sulpice*

This fast-growing Tokyo-based style store is an all-purpose, one-stop shop for contemporary Japanese art *de vivre*, from Lucite boxes, cool bags and kitchenware to stationary, mod office supplies, linens and clothes. It's unlikely you'll walk out empty handed. You can even ride off on a fold-up Muji bike. Stop in and see why this is Petra Lustigová's favorite shop.

Branch: *47 Rue Francs-Bourgeois, 4th (tel. 01.49.96.41.41).*

nova
DROLE DE

fEtiSh & LiNGERiE

Sabbia Rosa

73 Rue des Sts-Pères (6th). Tel. *01.45.48.88.37.* Open *Tues-Sat 10am-7pm, Mon 230pm-730pm.* M *St-Germain-des-Prés*
The underwear maker to some of the best-undressed mistresses in Paris, Sabbia Rosa has been well known to high-powered execs and government officials for almost a quarter century. Silk panties, string bikinis, naughty marabou baby dolls... it's what the au pair could be wearing this summer.

Phylea

61 Rue Quincampoix (4th). Hours vary. Tel. *01.42.76.01.80.* M *Châtelet-Les-Halles*
Paris' premiere fetish boutique stocks a terrific selection of one-of-a-kind sexwear that includes leather and latex shoes, PVC bras, and tight-fitting, slippery suits. Whips and accessories too!

ShOES

Michel Perry

4 bis, Rue des Petits Pères (2nd). Tel. *01.42.44.10.07.* Open *Mon-Sat 1030am-7pm.* M *Bourse*
Avant in both form and substance, Perry's shoes regularly play supporting roles to the fashions of star designers.

Accessoire

6 Rue du Cherche-Midi (6th). Tel. *01.45.48.36.08.* Open *Mon-Sat 10am-7pm. Closed two weeks in Aug.*
M *Sèvres Babylone/St-Sulpice*
This popular French chain is known for good quality, up-to-the-moment fashions, and decidedly reasonable prices. Their more casual Détente line is even more affordable.

Branches: *8 Rue du Jour, 1st (tel. 01.40.26.19.84); 11 Rue du Pré-aux-Clercs, 7th (tel. 01.42. 84.26.85).*

Freelance

30 Rue du Four (6th). Tel. *01.45.48.14.78.* Open *Mon-Sat 10am-730pm.*
M *St-Germain-des-Prés*
The place to go for chunky men's shoes, rainbow-colored loafers, embroidered mules, fur-covered scandals, and Gucci-style vamp stilettos. It's not especially cheap, but these dogs are guaranteed to impress.

Branch: *2 Rue Mondétour, 1st (tel. 01.42.33.74.70).*

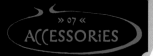

ACCESSORIES

La Droguerie

9 Rue du Jour (1st). Tel. *01.45.08.93.27.* **Open** *Tues-Sat 1030am-645pm.* M *Les Halles*
Like an old-fashioned candy store, La Droguerie tempts with hundreds of varieties of beads, feathers, unusual buttons, colorful yarns and other trimmings for accessorizaion.

Jamin-Puech

61 Rue d'Hauteville (10th). Tel. *01.40.22.08.32.* **Open** *Tues-Fri 10am-7pm, Mon and Sat 11am–7pm.* M *Poissonnière*
The handbags created by Isabelle Puech and Benoît Jamin are almost considered sacred by fashion insiders. Silk-screened satin and unusual juxtapositions of materials are some of the ways these designers bring new life to classic forms. Prices range between €75 and €325.

Ursule Beaugeste

50 rue Charonne (11th). Tel. 01.49.23.02.48. Open Mon-Fri 11am-7pm, Sat noon-7pm. M *Bastille*
The fine craftsmanship and sublime subtlety of Anne Grand-Clément's Raffia shopping bags and engraved leather handbags have made them runway favorites. Definitely a place to check out, even if you end up buying the knock-off at H&M.

Entre des Fournisseurs

8 Rue des Francs-Bourgeois (3rd). Tel. *01.48.87.58.98.*
The amazing buttons and ribbons at this high-end needle shop can make any old off-the-rack jacket look like the lates in haute couture.
Branch: *9 Rue Madame (6th).* Tel. *01.42.84.13.97.*

Yves Gratas

9 Rue Oberkampf (11th). Tel. *01.49.29.00.53.* **Open** *Tues-Sat 10am-1pm & 2-7pm.* M *Filles du Calvaire*
Yves Gratas has created jewelry for both Agnès b. and Marithé & François Girbaud. His boutique highlights precious jewelry with massive, modern lines. Pieces can also be commissioned.

HAUTE COUTURE

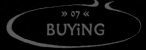

Haute couture refers to one-of-a-kind creations designed by officially recognized couture houses listed with the *Fédération Française de la Couture.* Established in 1943, the rules governing this prestigious classification are so restrictive that many of today's best-known designers are not included. Haute couture is important to the French fashion industry not because the often outrageous creations bring in a lot of money, but because the publicity they generate powers the sales of profitable ready-to-wear lines, as well as accessories, perfume and underwear.

As a rule, couture houses are not open to casual window shoppers. But if you are genuinely interested in dropping a fortune for a unique, hand-made creation (or just want to fake it), then by all means have your concierge call for an appointment.

Pierre Balmain
44 Rue François 1er (8th).
Tel. *01.47.20.35.34*

Chanel
31 Rue Cambon (1st).
Tel. *01.42.86.28.50*

Christian Dior
28–30 Ave. Montaigne (8th).
Tel. *01.40.73.54.00*

Christian Lacroix
73 Rue du Fbg-St-Honoré (8th).
Tel. *01.42.68.79.04*

Givenchy
3 Ave. George V (8th).
Tel. *01.44.31.51.25*

Hanae Mori
5 Place de l'Alma (8th).
Tel. *01.47.23.52.03*

Jean-Louis Scherrer
51 Ave. Montaigne (8th).
Tel. *01.56.59.98.41*

Jean-Paul Gaultier
44 Ave George V (8th).
Tel. *01.44.43.00.44*

Louis Féraud
28 Rue du Faubourg-St-Honoré (8th). Tel. *01.42.65.27.29*

Torrente
1 Rond-Ponit des Champs Elysées (8th).
Tel. *01.42.56.14.14*

Yves St-Laurent
5 Ave. Marceau (8th).
Tel. *01.44.31.64.00*

bEAUtY & PERfUME

By Terry

36 Galerie Véro-Dodat (1st). Tel. *01.44.76.00.76.* Open *Mon-Sat 11am-7pm.* M *Palais Royal*
Terry's beautiful, mahogany-paneled shop is known for custom-made lipsticks, foundations and blushes. There's plenty of ready-made colors too, displayed in gorgeous glass and steel containers.

Comme des Garçons Perfume Shop

23 Place du Marché St-Honoré (1st). Tel. *01.47.03.15.03.* Open *Mon-Sat 11am-7pm.* M *Tuileries/Opéra*
A whole different kind of perfume shop, this space was made to stimulate all your senses. Conceived by architect Rei Kawakudo, the glass-box design of this classic shop has received tons of attention too.

Editions de Parfums Frédéric Malle

37 Rue de Grenelle (7th). Tel. *01.42.22.77.22.*
Like any fashion, perfumes come and go. But not everything that's new is better. This shop sells re-creations of almost a dozen exceptional perfumes, some of which were originally blended by 1950's Dior "nose" Edmond Roudnitska. The jewel box shop itself is also particularly special.

Guerlain

68 Ave. des Champs-Elysées (8th). Tel. *01.45.62.52.57.* Open *Mon-Sat 10am-8pm, Sun 3-7pm.* M *George V*
Built in 1913, in the style of that era's luxury ocean liners and grand hotels, this beautiful, marble-and-mirror Parisian perfumery is known for Jicky (the oldest French perfume still sold), Shalimar, and all the other classic fragrances only available in Guerlain stores.

Sephora

70 Ave. des Champs-Elysées (8th). **Tel.** *01.42.25.37.13.* **Open** *Mon-Sat 10am-midnight, Sun noon-midnight.* Ⓜ *George V*

The flagship of this fast-growing beauty supermarket is an awesome trove of thousands of products from almost 500 different labels. All the major fragrances, cosmetics and skincare products are here, along with a helpful staff and terrific in-store soundtrack.

EYEWEAR

Alain Mikli
74 Rue des Saints Pères (7th). **Tel.** *01.45.49.40.00.* **Open** *Mon-Fri 10am-7pm, Sat 10am-730pm.* **M** *St-Germain-des-Prés*
In this cool store designed by Philippe Starck, you'll find all the Alain Mikli lines, along with some eye-catching models by Monsieur Starck himself.

fLEA MARKEtS

Paris' three main flea markets *(puces)* have been selling everything from junk to gems since time immemorial. Each is situated close to a former gate *(porte)* to the old city. Although they are no longer the haunts of street urchins and back-alley bandits, plenty of pickpockets and conmen remain, so watch your ass. And although they are not always a source of real bargains, *les puces* never fail to entertain. The best deals are said to be gone by 8am.

In addition to the markets listed below, check out the **stamp and postcard market** on avenues Marigny and Gabriel (8th) Thursday, Saturday and Sunday from 10am-7pm; the daily **flower market** on Rue de la Cité on Ile de la Cité (4th); and the **bird and bunny market** on the Quai de la Megisserie (1st), open Monday-Saturday.

Les Puces de Vanves
Porte de Vanves. Open Sat-Sun 9am-7pm. M Porte de Vanves
Stretching from Porte Brancion to Porte de Vanves, hundreds of vendors come here weekly to sell furniture, lamps, silverware and fine art objects. The real bargains are around the market's edges, where, if you're willing to get down on your knees and root around, you can find some very nice decorative pieces for under €11.

Les Puces de Montreuil
Porte de Montreuil.
Open Sat-Mon 8am-6pm.
M Porte de Montreuil
Primarily a second-hand clothes market, Montreuil is the most real of all the fleas. If you've got the nose, this is the place to get the good deals. If you don't, this market will smell like the Salvation Army.

Les Puces de Saint-Ouen

Porte de Clignancourt. **Open** *Sat-Mon 9am-7pm.*
M *Porte de Clignancourt/Porte de St-Ouen*

The largest flea market in Europe, Porte de Clignancourt is actually a massive collection of separate markets that coalesce into a single, chaotic square mile of stalls. Each area has its own specialty; some sections resemble a garage sale, while others seem closer to high-end antique shops, with prices to match. A morning stroll (and you should go in the morning) will take you past collectibles and decorative objects at **Vernaison**; late 18th, 19th and 20th century furniture at Malassis; Scandinavian antiques and **Aubusson** tapestries at **Biron**; and *objects d'art* from the 1950s-1970s at Serpette. Need a pair of worn-out shoes? Some coat hangers? A dented can of green beans? No problem. For true local color, head past the stands selling Celtic jewelry, T-shirts and crêpes to the **Thieves Market**. It's by the Avenue de la Porte de Montmartre underpass, at the market's southernmost edge.

ANtiQUES

The best high-end antiquing on the Right Bank is found along Rue du Faubourg-St-Honoré, where dozens of beautiful shops are filled with a plethora of Empire-period treasures.

The Left Bank is only slightly more egalitarian. The streets surrounding the *Ecole Nationale Supérieure des Beaux-Arts* are flooded with more than 120 antique stores and art galleries specializing in 17th and 18th century art and antiques. Start along the river at Quai Voltaire, then dip into rues de Lille, du Bac, de Verneuil, de l'Université, de Beaune, and des SaintsPères.

Weekend flea markets are a good source for genuine antiques (as well as certified junk). The most famous of these is **Les Puces de Saint-Ouen**, which stretches from Porte de Clignancourt (18th) to Porte de St-Ouen (17th). See Flea Markets, above, for complete information.

The most fun and rewarding place to shop for antiquarian books is at ***les Bouquinistes***, the bookstalls perched against the parapets of the Seine right in the heart of the city. Not only are these outdoor booths some of Paris' most charming details, but with patience and a knack for bargaining, you just might come away with a rare first edition for the price of lunch.

Louvre des Antiquaires

2 Place du Palais Royal (1st). **Tel.** *01.42.97.27.00.* **Open** *Tues-Sun 11am–7pm (closed on Sundays in July, August).* **M** *Palais Royal/Musée du Louvre*

Many of the city's most prestigious antique shops are clustered together in this distinctive building across from the Louvre. The pricey emporium is home to about 250 dealers selling museum-quality antiques, art-deco objects, prints, woodcuts, furniture, dolls, clothing and more. You can find Asian and African antiques here as well.

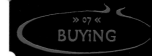

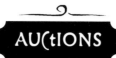

AUCtIONS

Drouot

9 Rue Drouot (9th). **Tel.** *01.48.00.20.20.* **Open** *Mon-Sat 11am-6pm.* M *Richelieu Drouot*

Lively, frenetic and accessible to the masses, Drouot is what an auction house should be. Items up for bid in the house's 16 auction rooms run the gamut from medieval manuscripts and Old Masters paintings to fine wines and estate liquidations. Browsing through the clutter in this startlingly post-modern (some say "ugly") auction house is a day's work; and a fun one at that. Nearly everything can be viewed the day before it goes on the block, from 11am-6pm; and on auction day from 11am-noon. For a comprehensive rundown of the current week's auctions, pick up a copy of ***Gazette de l'Hôtel Drouot***, available at newsstands throughout the city.

Sotheby's

76 Rue du Faubourg-St-Honoré (8th). **Tel.** *01.53.05.53.05.* **Open** *Mon-Fri 10am-6pm.* M *Champs-Elysées-Clémenceau/Miromesnil.*

Until recently, protectionist French laws banned this august London-based auction house from competing with homegrown Drouot. Antiques and fine arts are the specialties of this house. Phone for auctions and previews.

ARt SUPPLiES

Rougier & Plé

13 Blvd. Filles du Calvaire (3rd). **Tel.** *01.44.54.81.00* **Open** *Mon-Sat 930am-7pm.* M *Filles du Calvaire*

Supplying the needs of artists and craftsmakers for three generations, Rougier & Plé is the best place for canvas, oils, watercolors and lots of other creative supplies.

Chez Maman

4 Rue Tiquetonne (2nd). Tel. *01.40.28.46.09.* Open *Mon-Sat noon-8pm.* M *Étienne Marcel*

A visit to Chez Maman is a romanticized journey back to the days of plastic-fantastic furnishings designed with spheres, curves and bubbles. Check out the basement, where the real bargains are.

La Corbeille

5 Passage du Grand Cerf (2nd). Tel. *01.53.40.78.77.* Open *Mon-Sat 1-8pm.* M *Étienne-Marcel*

Literally "the trash can," this bi-level store specializes in stylish furniture and lamps from the '50s and '60s. Some newer pieces include limited-edition plates and paintings by 100drine. Twice a year, the shop organizes *Les Puces du Design*, a flea market specializing in 20th-century furniture and design.

Cuisinophile

28 Rue du Bourg Tibourg (4th). Tel. 01.40.29.07.32. Open Tues-Sat 2-7pm. M Hôtel-de-Ville

Charming, old-fashioned kitchenware includes coffee grinders, spice boxes, thermoses, mixing bowls and kettles that are straight out of Jean Renoir's "A Day in the Country."

Dream On

70 Blvd. Beaumarchais (11th). Tel. *01.43.38.50.25.* Open *Mon-Sat 1-8pm.* M *Chemin Vert*

Retro-kitsch dreams do come true in this warehouse of space-age furniture from the '60s and '70s. There's lots of objects by masters like Mourgue, Eames and Enzo Mari. And the enormous basement is jam-packed with gems, including Vernal Pantan fabrics and Mondrian-inspired rugs.

Lulu Berlu

8, 27 Rue Oberkampf (11th). Tel. *01.43.55.10.19.* Open *Mon-Sat 1130am-830pm.* M *Filles du Calvaire*

This mellow boutique carries furniture, lamps and interior design details from the last century. Look for beautiful silver jewelry from the 1930s, original art from the '40s, lots of examples from the '50s, and blond wood and Scandinavian design from the '70s (#27 has antique toys).

Bo Plastic

31 Rue de Charonne (11th). Tel. *01.53.36.73.16.* Open *Mon-Sat 11am-8pm.* M *Ledru-Rollin*

Hello plastic, my old friend. Familiar molded furniture and decorative items include Knoll pedestal tables, and Colombo and Zanotta lamps. Most everything's in great shape too.

S.O.F.T.
27 Rue de Charonne (11th). **Tel.** *01.43.14.22.50.* **Open** *Mon-Sat 11am-7pm.* Ⓜ *Bastille*
S.O.F.T. is known for good prices on down-market '70s design. The offerings lean toward the ironic, and include everything from deep shag rugs and period stereos, to molded-plastic tables and lamps. The "Me Decade" never looked so good.

Schmock Broc
15 Rue Racine (6th). **Tel.** *01. 46.33.79.98.* **Open** *Mon 3-8pm, Tues-Fri 11am-2pm & 3-730pm, Sat 10am-730pm.* Ⓜ *Odéon*
Check this place out for very cool chairs, lamps and paintings from the second and third millennia.

CAMERAS & ELECTRONICS

Bazar de l'Hôtel de Ville (BHV)

52 Rue de Rivoli (4th). **Tel.** *01.42.74.90.00.* **Open** *Mon-Tues & Thurs-Fri 930am-7pm; Wed 930am-10pm; Sat 930am-7pm.* **M** *Hôtel-de-Ville*

The cluttered basement of this popular department store is the best place to locate hard-to-find electrical transformers and modular telephone jacks.

Fnac

74 Ave. des Champs-Elysées (8th). **Tel.** *01.53.53.64.64.* **Open** *Mon-Sat 10am-midnight.* **M** *George V*

Fnac is where your average Pierre goes for an afternoon of browsing and dreaming. Each giant store is filled with books, music, video, photography equipment, electronics and computers, and not many pesky salespeople hanging around to bother you. Prices are competitive (for France). Fnac is also a convenient place to get film developed and buy concert tickets.

Branches: *Forum des Halles, 1st (tel. 01.40.41.40.00); 136 Rue de Rennes, 6th (tel. 01.49.54.30.00); 24 Blvd. des Italiens, 9th (tel. 01.48.01.02.03); (music only) 4 Place de la Bastille, 12th (tel. 01.43.42.04.04); 26-30 Ave. des Ternes, 17th (tel. 01.44.09.18.00).*

GIFTS

Calao

95 Rue du Faubourg-St-Denis (10th). **Tel.** *01.45.23.59.49.* **Open** *Mon-Tues & Thurs-Sat 1030am-730pm.* **M** *Château d'Eau*

Run by a pair of intrepid travelers, this quirky store is crammed with beautiful handicrafts and jewelry from the four corners of the globe, with emphasis on art from Southeast Asia.

Le Laguiole du Marais

6 Rue du Pas de la Mule (3rd). **Tel.** *01.48.87.46.88.* **Open** *Mon-Sat 1030am-1230pm & 2-7pm.* **M** *Chemin Vert*

Delicately carved Laguiole pocketknives from the Aveyron region can be found at this little shop by the Place des Vosges. There's a wide selection of these hand-tooled collectors items with curved bone, boxwood or mahogany handles, priced from €25-€200.

L'Esprit et le Vin

81 Ave. des Ternes (17th). **Tel.** *01.45.74.80.99.* **Open** *Mon 2-7pm, Tues-Sat 10am-1pm & 2-7pm.* **M** *Chemin Vert*

In the 18th century, when wine bottles were sealed with wax, corkscrews were fitted with tiny brushes. Along with these and other enological gifts and gadgets, this shop has a terrific selection of unique pewter corkscrews priced from €25-€140.

Lagerfeld Gallery

40 Rue de Seine (6th). **Tel.** *01.55.42.75.51.* **Open** *Tues-Sat 11am-7pm.* **M** *Mabillon*

Karl Lagerfeld personally chooses this shop's elegant array of books, photographs, accessories and magazines. The shopping experience is augmented by regular photography and illustration exhibitions.

Pouic-Pouic

4 Rue Hérold (1st). **Tel.** *01.40.26.27.90.* **Open** *Mon-Sat noon-7pm.* **M** *Sentier*

Original Barbie dolls, rubber duckies, plastic soldiers, match box Ferraris... we're talking collectibles here. Grown-ups searching for childhood lost come here *en masse*. And prices can't be beat.

MAGAZiNES

OFR Systeme

30 Rue Beaurepaire (10th). **Tel.** *01.42.45.72.88.* **Open** *Mon-Fri 10am-7pm.* **M** *République*

The most comprehensive selection of magazines and newspapers in the city, OFR is also one of the few places that carries back issues of local avant-style mags like Self-Service, Dutch, Purple and Numero.

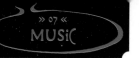

MUSiC

Crocodisc

40-42 Rue des Ecoles (5th).
Tel. *01.43.54.33.22.* Open *Tues-Sat 11am-7pm.* M *Maubert Mutualité*

A terrific indie selection rubs shoulders here with all the usual suspects from the major labels. Crocodisc is the place to find European dub and reggae, along with plenty of French rap.

Le Silence de la Rue

39 Rue Faidherbe (11th).
Tel. *01.40. 24.16.16.* Open *Mon-Sat 10am-7pm.*
M *Charonne*

An interesting selection of analog and digital reggae, noise, techno, jungle and ambient, all at competitive prices. A good source for fanzines and flyers too.

Monster Melodies

9 Rue des Déchargeurs (1st).
Tel. *01.40.28.09.39.* Open *Mon-Sat 11am-7pm.*
M *Châtelet*

Early Eno? Late Sex Pistols? This vintage specialist has lots of otherwise unfindable 1970s vinyl.

O'CD

24 rue Pierre Lescot (1st).
Tel. *01.42.33.58.50.* Open *Mon-Sat 11am-8pm, Sun 3-7pm.*
M *Châtelet*

This spacious store is an amazing place to browse for used CDs, statrting at 3 euros. You can find a hodgepodge of everything here, and can listen before you buy.

Parallèles

47 Rue Saint Honoré (1st). **Tel.** *01.42.33.62.70.* **Open** *Mon-Sat noon-7pm.* M *Palais Royal*

If it's an obscure piece of musical history you're after, Parallèles is a good bet. There's tons of used records (and books), and plenty of rare new stuff as well.

Paris Jazz Corner

5-7 rue de Navarre (5th). **Tel.** *01.43.36.78.92.* **Open** *Mon-Sat 1130am-8pm.* M *Jussieu*

For jazz purists, this Left Bank institution is a must-go for everything from gypsy swing and big band to Latin jazz and fusion.

Virgin Megastore

52-60 Ave. des Champs-Elysées (8th). **Tel.** *01.49.53.50.00.* **Open** *Mon-Sat 10am-midnight, Sun noon-midnight.* M *Franklin D. Roosevelt*

In addition to a mega-selection of CDs, books, videos and computer games, there's a decent cafe on the second level with a terrific view of the Champs-Elysées.

tOYS

Au Nain Bleu

408 Rue de Faubourg-St-Honoré (8th). Tel. *01.42.60.39.01.* Open *Mon-Sat 10am-630pm.* M *Miromesnil*

Once considered to be the world's definitive toy store, by today's FAO standards, this old standby now seems a bit stale. The selection of tin soldiers, stuffed animals and marionettes is fantastic, but there aren't many contemporary toys, and the presentation just isn't, well, fun. Still, it's a great place to pick up presents.

Do You Speak Martian?

8 Rue des Trois Frères (18th). Tel. *01.42.52.89.72.* Open *Tues-Fri 11am-7pm, Sat 11am-730pm, Sun 2-7pm.* M *Abbesses*

For close encounters with flying saucers, men from Mars and other space invaders, look no further than this quirky specialized shop.

Lulu Berlu

27 Rue Oberkampf (11th). Tel. *01.43.55.10.19.* Open *Mon-Sat 1130am-830pm.* M *Filles du Calvaire*

The Promised Land for thirtysomethings looking to baby their inner child, Lulu stocks what seems like a gazillion new and vintage action figurines from Japanese, French and American TV shows, movies and comic books. GI Joes, and dolls with the likenesses of The Incredible Hulk, Kiss, The Simpsons characters, Mohammed Ali... You name it, they've got it.

BOOkS

The banks of the Seine in the heart of the city are lined with stalls selling old books, prints and maps. Most are in French. The majority of stalls are open daily from 10am until dusk. Look especially on the Quai des Grands Augustins and Quai Malaquais on the Left Bank, and the Quai du Louvre and the Quai de la Megisserie on the Right Bank.

Galignani

224 Rue de Rivoli (1st). Tel. *01.42.60.76.07.* Open *Mon-Sat 10am-7pm.* M *Tuileries*

Opened in 1802, Galignani bills itself as the first English-language book shop in continental Europe. Today it stocks fine art tomes, design books and French and English literature. All in a rarefied atmosphere that Henry James would admire.

Gibert Joseph

26 Blvd. St-Michel (6th). Tel. *01.44.41.88.88.* Open *Mon-Sat 930am-730pm.* M *St-Michel*

The place to buy and sell textbooks if you're enrolled at the Sorbonne nearby. This shop includes a small selection of English books along with sidewalk stalls piled high with discount art and photography books.

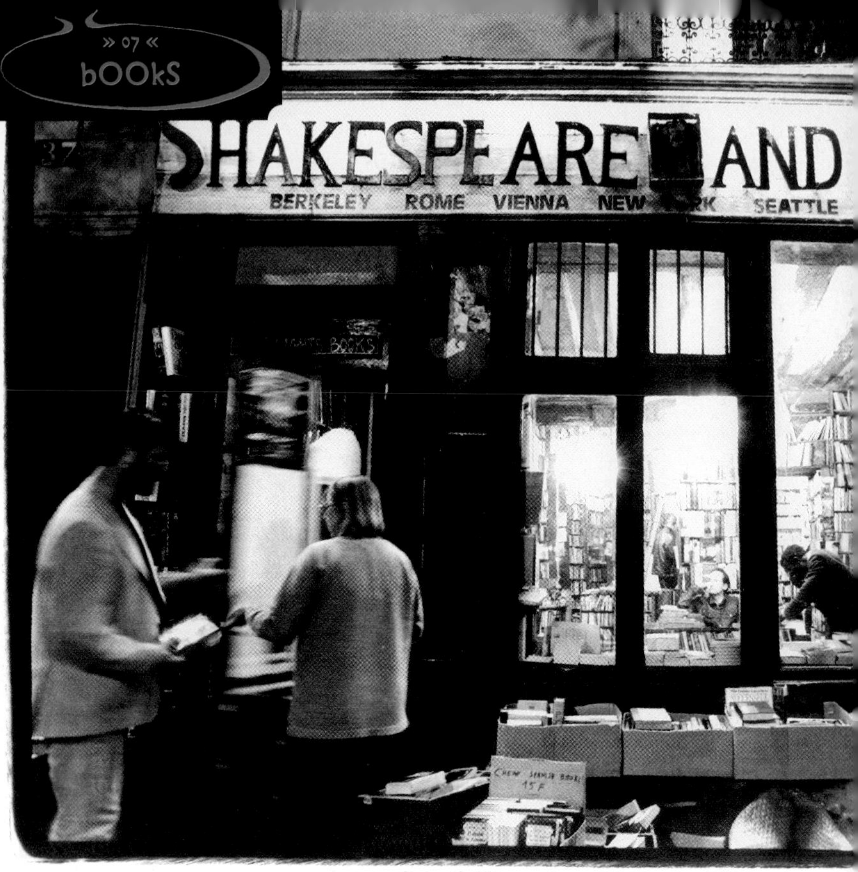

Le Regard Moderne

10 Rue Gît-le-Coeur (6th). **Tel.** *01.43.29.13.93.* **Open** *Mon-Sat 1130am-8pm.* M *St-Michel*

One of the most comprehensive selections of rare, art, sex and underground books you'll ever lay eyes on. A dip into this ocean of images will feed your imagination for months.

Village Voice

6 Rue Princesse (6th). **Tel.** *01.46.33.36.47.* **Open** *Mon 2-8pm, Tues-Sat 10am-8pm, Sun 2-7pm.* M *St-Germain-des-Prés/Mabillon*

A veritable institution, this very Left Bank bookshop carries an excellent selection of contemporary and classic literature as well as a wide range of literary reviews. Regular readings too.

WH Smith

248 Rue de Rivoli (1st). **Tel.** *01.44.77.88.99.* **Open** *Mon-Sat 930am-7pm, Sun 1-7pm.* M *Concorde*

A Mecca for readers of Anglo-American literature, this English-language bookstore is perpetually packed with expats looking for a literary fix in their mother tongue. The selection is decent and the magazine rack rules the Continent!

Brentano's

37 Ave. de l'Opéra (2nd). **Tel.** *01.42.61.52.50.* **Open** *Mon-Sat 10am-730pm.* M *Opéra*

Brentano's is a particularly wonderful place to browse. Bestsellers, guidebooks and plenty of *belles lettres*.

Librairie Japonaise Junku

18 Rue des Pyramides (1st).
Tel. *01.42.60.89.12.* **Open** *Mon-Sat 10am-7pm.* **M** *Pyramides*
Home away from home for Japanese students and *biznizmen,* this hip book shop stocks lots of Nipponese books, mags, manga and CDs. The basement is jammed with comic books and posters featuring those famous round-eyed cartoon heroes.

Shakespeare & Company

37 Rue de la Bûcherie (5th). **Tel.** *01.43.26.96.50.* **Open** *daily noon-midnight.* **M** *Saint-Michel*
Named after Sylvia Beach's original, this Seine-side shop is a Paris landmark in its own right. Squeeze past shelves overflowing with new and used books, and explore the cluttered warren of rooms in the back and upstairs.

Marché aux Livres

Halles de Vaugirard, Parc Georges Brassens, Rue Brançion (15th). **Tel.** *01.45.32.12.75 or 01.47.83.93.91.* **Open** *Sat-Sun 8am-7pm.* **M** *Porte de Vanves*
This weekly gathering speaks volumes about France's love affair with the written word. Held in a former horse market, the Marché brings together hundreds of vendors selling poetry tomes, old detective novels, rare editions and everything else you can think of. Some are pricey, some less so. And even if you don't speak the *lingua franca*, it's doubtful you'll leave empty-handed.

CiGARS

La Civette

157 Rue St-Honoré (1st). **Tel.** *01.42.96.04.99.* **Open** *Mon-Sat 10am-7pm.* **M** *Palais-Royal-Musée du Louvre.*
Jonesing for a Cubano? Head to this upscale corner cigar store with one of the widest selections of singles in the country. A fresh *Montecristo A* will set you back about €38. The shop sells lots of high-end paraphernalia too.

No 08

The Restaurant Scene

Eating

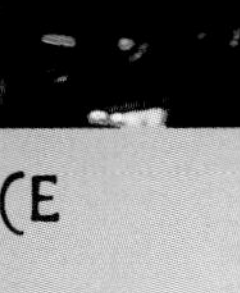

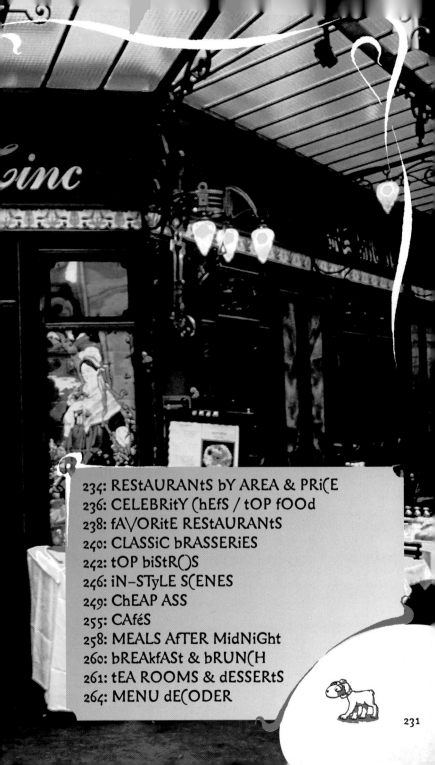

You don't need us to wax lyrical about the intimate relationship Parisians have with their food. But what you might not know is that food and society are so fanatically intertwined that the Ministry of Culture has designated some celebrity cooks "artists" and subsidizes them with huge amounts of money each year to keep them in their kitchens. The city's top chefs are household names and the annual March release of Michelin's star promotions and demotions always makes front-page news.

Yet for all the hype, France's kitchens remain bastions of tradition. Fusion foods that have become commonplace in other major cities of the world are only just beginning to make their way onto local plates. And the hole-in-the-wall Asian places that offer decent, cheap meals in New York City, San Francisco and London are not at all good in the French capital. On the plus side, you can still pop into a random French place and get a reliably decent meal. Complex entrees—richly flavored with time-consuming stock-reductions—are remarkably common. And the ubiquity of foods like *steak au poivre*, on menus both down and *haute*, proves that cholesterol is alive and well in France.

The bottom line is that, despite a decided lack of adventurousness, some of the best dining in the world is still in Paris. It's the result of a confluence of hyperlatives: France's best chefs, finest ingredients and prettiest people converge nightly in Paris' spectacular restaurants.

What's In a Name?

Brasserie, from the word brasseur (brewer), originally indicated establishments that served beer. The famous Bofinger is said to have been the first. Today the designation refers to grand café-restaurants with continuous service. Modern brasseries are large, bright, bustling places that often stay open until 1 or 2 am.

A **café** is someplace where you can stop in for nothing more than a drink and stay as long as you like—that's the all-important distinction. Hot chocolate, coffee and beer are the most typical quaffs, the latter of which is usually on tap (*une pression*). Food-wise, the majority of Paris's 10,000 cafés shine brightest at lunch, when their light meals offer good quality, and at better prices, then many cheap restaurants.

Bistros, from the Russian word for "quick," straddle the fence between café and brasserie; indeed all three these terms are often used interchangeably. Some bistros welcome, at least during specified hours, customers who only a want cup of coffee or a glass of wine. Others open their doors exclusively for lunchers and diners.

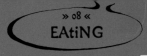

The Reservations Game

If you eat early, say between 7 and 8pm, you should usually have no problem getting a table at most restaurants. Still, reservations are recommended at almost every establishment listed below. It never hurts.

As surely as death and taxes, there's always a restaurant of the moment; one in which every night is like a movie premiere, filled with film stars, models, musicians, the media elite, athletes, restaurateurs, garmentos and generic rich people. Within the first two weeks of opening, everyone will trample through, before quickly heading off to the Next New Thing. If you want to be there too, it's time to use some muscle, work the phones and call-in favors. When white-hot slows to simmering, street-wise mortals can get reservations about a week in advance. Unless you have connections, or don't mind being seated at 6pm or midnight, we advise you to reserve a table as far in advance as possible. The country code for France is 33; then drop the first "0" of the local phone number. From Great Britain dial 00-33-plus the local number (minus the first "0"); from the USA dial 011-33-plus the local number (minus the first "0").

Cheaper Eats

Eating can be expensive in Paris, especially when ordering *a la carte.* The city's best bargains are prix-fixe meals—usually a three-course affair involving an appetizer, entree and dessert—for not much more than a single main course. You should also know that most of the city's restaurants offer lunch menus that are 25%-50% cheaper than the dinner prices quoted below. While eating in Paris is pricier than New York, careful ordering at almost any restaurant can buy some of the world's finest meals without breaking the bank.

Smoking

Fire up. Smoking is common in most restaurants as nicotine-addicts are allowed to get their fixes just about anywhere they please. A few places have separate dining rooms for non-users and these are noted in the listings below.

Tipping

It's hard to believe, but Parisian servers only expect diners to round-up the total bill to the nearest few francs. In fact, many don't even expect that. A relatively recent law requires all restaurants to include the service charge and 20.6% tax in the prices listed on the menu. Because service is officially *compris,* many diners won't leave a franc more. Others just leave some small change, and still others tip another 5%-10%, if service warrants it.

Kibbles & Bits

- Lunch is usually 25-50% cheaper than dinner.
- Although we may say some nasty things in the reviews below, we enthusiastically recommend all the restaurants we list.
- You *can* drink the water.

Our reviewers have no connection with any establishment listed in this guidebook or on the Avant-Guide Web site. All restaurant visits are anonymous, and expenses are paid by *Avant-Guide.*

RESTAURANTS BY AREA, PRICE & CUISINE

The cost (*) reflects the average price of dinner without wine

*	= Under €15	***	= €30-€45
**	= €15-€30	****	= Over €45

1st Arrondissement

Pg	Name	Price	Cuisine
261	Angélina	**	Tea/Dessert
255	Café Marly	***	Café
252	Higuma	*	Japanese
246	Hotel Costes	***	Contemp.
260	Joe Allen	***	American
252	Léon de Bruxelles	**	Belgian
258	Au Pied de Cochon	***	Brasserie

3rd Arrondissement

Pg	Name	Price	Cuisine
238	Au Bascou	**	Basque
241	Chez Jenny	**	Brasserie
238	Chez Omar	**	N. African
253	Restaurant Pho	*	Vietnamese

4th Arrondissement

Pg	Name	Price	Cuisine
249	L'As du Fallafel	*	Falafel
257	Au Petit Fer â Cheval	*	Café
261	Berthillon	*	Dessert
240	Bofinger	***	Brasserie
260	Café Beaubourg	**	Café
248	Georges	***	Contemp.
261	Le Loir dans la Théière	**	Tea/Dessert
263	Mariage Frères	**	Tea/Dessert
243	Nos Ancìtres les Gaulois	**	Bistro
239	L'Ostéria	***	Venetian

5th Arrondissement

Pg	Name	Price	Cuisine
238	Atlas	**	N. African
261	Café Maure de la Mosquee	*	Tea/Dessert

6th Arrondissement

Pg	Name	Price	Cuisine
255	Café de Flore	**	Café
239	Coffee Parisien	**	American
251	Cosi	*	Sandwiches
257	Les Deux Magots	**	Café
252	Léon de Bruxelles	**	Belgian
263	Mariage Frères	**	Tea/Dessert
256	La Palette	*	Café
252	Polidor	**	Bourgeoise
259	Le Select	**	Café
245	Wadja	**	Bistro

7th Arrondissement

Pg	Name	Price	Cuisine
236	L'Arpège	****	Haute
237	Le Jules Verne	****	Haute
243	L'Oeillade	***	Bistro
244	La Petite Chaise	**	Bistro
244	Thoumieux	***	Bistro

8th Arrondissement

Pg	Name	Price	Cuisine
236	Les Ambassadeurs	****	Haute
251	BE-Boulangépicier	**	French
246	Buddha Bar	***	Eurasian
251	Chez Papa	*	Southwest.
263	Ladurée	**	Tea/Dessert
252	Léon de Bruxelles	**	Belgian
246	Lô Sushi	**	Japanese
258	La Maison de l'Alsace	***	Alsatian
248	Man Ray	***	Eurasian
263	Mariage Frères	**	Tea/Dessert
248	Spoon Food & Wine	***	World

9th Arrondissement

Pg	Name	Price	Cuisine
256	Baggi	*	Desert
250	Chartier	*	Bourgeoise
252	Léon de Bruxelles	**	Belgian

10th Arrondissement

Pg	Name	Price	Cuisine
240	Brasserie Julien	***	Brasserie
251	Chez Papa	*	Southwestern

11th Arrondissement

Pg	Name	Price	Cuisine
255	Café de l'Industrie	**	Café
242	Chez Paul	**	Bistro
252	Léon de Bruxelles	**	Belgian

12th Arrondissement

Pg	Name	Price	Cuisine
244	Le Square Trousseau	**	Bistro
241	Le Train Bleu	***	Brasserie

14th Arrondissement

Pg	Name	Price	Cuisine
251	Chez Papa	*	Southwestern
239	Contre-Allée	**	Bistro
240	La Coupole	**	Brasserie
259	Mustang Café	*	Tex-Mex
243	Natacha	**	Bistro
253	Ti Jos	*	Crèpe
245	Le Vin des Rues	**	Bistro

15th Arrondissement

Pg	Name	Price	Cuisine
250	Le Café du Commerce	**	Bourgeoise
251	Chez Papa	*	Southwestern

16th Arrondissement

Pg	Name	Price	Cuisine
241	La Gare	***	Brasserie

17th Arrondissement

Pg	Name	Price	Cuisine
237	Guy Savoy	****	Haute

18th Arrondissement

Pg	Name	Price	Cuisine
253	Rendez-vous des Chauffeurs	**	Bistro

20th Arrondissement

Pg	Name	Price	Cuisine
250	La Boulangerie	*	Bistro

Les Ambassadeurs

Hôtel de Crillon, 10 Place de la Concorde (8th). Tel. 01.44.71.16.16. Kitchen open daily noon-230pm & 7-1030pm. Average meal €150. Prix-fixe €135. Mon-Fri lunch menu €62. AE, MC, V. M Concorde

From the opulent Old World dining room to the truffle-loaded menu, everything about Les Ambassadeurs screams Serious Restaurant! Dressed with spectacular frescoes, marble-and-mirror-and-crystal hallways, and lots of greenery and gilt, this is a formal, gastronomic theme park; a destination place meant to be the main part of an evening, rather than a mere prelude to some other entertainment. Each guest is treated like nobility by a fawning waitstaff that never lets a glass become empty nor an emptied plate lie. Depending on whom you're dining with, Les Ambassadeurs can feel either gentleman's-clubby or amorous—the palatial atmosphere appeals to both corporate-card carriers and romantic couples in search of a quiet meal in beautiful surroundings. And Table 16 puts the Place de la Concorde and all of Paris at your feet. Chef Dominique Bouchet's extraordinary cuisine rises to the surroundings with signature dishes like potato waffles with creamy, garlicked cod casserole; Breton lobster in a golden caviar-flecked cream sauce; and roast chicken basted with mocha-infused clarified butter. There's a great wine cellar too. And when it's time for coffee, the Maître d' himself arrives to describe all the different Arabicas and Robustas on the menu. Les Ambassadeurs is not cheap (only *monsieur* is given a menu with prices), but it's probably the closest you'll ever come to dining at Versailles.

L'Arpège

84 Rue de Varenne (7th). Tel. 01.47.05.09.06. Kitchen open Mon-Fri noon-2pm & 730-1030pm. Average meal €250. Prix-fixe for lunch or dinner €320 (drinks included). AE, MC, V. M Varenne

One of the very best restaurants in Paris, with three Michelin stars and prices to prove it, L'Arpège is a culinary icon, known for extraordinary banquet-length meals. Chef Alain Passard is one of the greatest in the world, creating inventive sauces and surprising flavor combinations that are a perfect synthesis of tradition and mode. Chicken is a signature dish here, either bedded in hay, sealed in casserole, or doused with lemon liqueur. Roast chicken for two, presented whole and carved tableside, is one of the most succulent birds we've ever put to tooth. The *pommes soufflées* are also sublime, and should be ordered when you make your reservations. Sweets are one of the restaurant's strong suits. The final component of a decadent eight-course tasting menu is a multi-part dessert that concludes with a spice-filled crystallized tomato, a plate of homemade chocolates and a multi-tiered tray of mixed petits fours. The French-heavy wine cellar is excellent, but the best on the budget end will set you back around €80. With great food and sublime service, the biggest gripe about L'Arpège has always been the relatively plain dining room.

Guy Savoy

18 Rue Troyon (17th). Tel. 01.43.80.40.61. Kitchen open Tue-Fri 1230-230pm & 7-1030pm; Sat 7-1030pm. Average meal €160. Prix-fixe €188. AE, MC, V. M *Charles de Gaulle-Etoile*

Chef Guy Savoy heads a revolutionary kitchen that has become one of the very best in the world. He has a seemingly natural ability to invent cross-regional dishes that dance in the mouth and are a beauty to behold. Food here is old-skool French with modernist twists. Savoy's seasonal menu might include langoustine soup with lentils, or pan-fried mussels and wild mushrooms in "land and sea" *jus*, a signature dish. And the Savoy magic reaches all the way to dessert where, in addition to the classics, you'll always find a novelty like grapefruit terrine in a tea-based sauce. Over the years, almost everyone has eaten here, from presidents and kings to rock and film stars. Of course, there have been plenty of mortals too. Dinners here are lengthy, multi-course affairs often involving several bottles of wine. The relaxed, modern art-filled dining room is far less *haute*—and that's a good thing. Meals here can wow foodies, but they are also friendly affairs you can enjoy without the food itself being the center of attention. When reserving, request the livelier main dining room.

Le Jules Verne

Second level, Eiffel Tower, Champ de Mars (7th). Tel. 01.45.55.61.44. Kitchen open daily 1215-2pm & 730-930pm. Average meal €120. Prix-fixe €110. Mon-Fri Lunch menu €49. AE, MC, V. M *Bir-Hakeim*

If you can only go to one top restaurant in Paris then really go to the top—of the Eiffel Tower that is—to this stellar dining room with food so yummy you'll almost forget the view. While most first-timers come for the one-of-a-kind panorama, everyone else returns for the exceptional, high-flying cuisine. French fare here is imaginative and delicious. Foie gras—a dish that has made its way onto the menu at practically every expense-account restaurant in town—is served here atop marinated salmon and tuna, and in a terrine of leeks and truffles. Both are memorable appetizers that have become signature dishes here. Notable entrées include crab-and-shrimp-filled puff pastries, pan-roasted langoustines with citrus *jus*, baked veal sweetbreads, and veal with mushrooms. The bottom line is that Chef Alain Reix's meals are always exciting, right down to the last forkful of raspberries with Brouilly sherbet. The older, suburban crowd is less thrilling. But with views and food like this, who cares? Service is impeccable, the wine list is impressive and the ebony dining room is dark and romantic. As you might imagine, scoring a table in this unique restaurant is no easy feat. You'll need to reserve months ahead for dinner (phone right now), though lunch tables can sometimes be booked just days in advance. Say whatever you must to secure a table by the bay window in the "Salle Paris." If they suggest the "Salle Trocadéro," gently explain that you're allergic to sunsets. They'll get the picture.

fAVORitE RESTAURANtS

Atlas

12 Blvd. St-Germain (5th). Tel. 01.46.33.86.98. Kitchen open Tue-Sun noon-3pm & 730-1115pm. Main courses €12-€18. AE, MC, V Ⓜ *Maubert-Mutualité*

A stylish, tiled North African interior and excellent Moroccan food are the hallmarks of this mosque of gastronomy in the corner of St-Germain. Terrific couscous and *tagines* are served with huge chunks of extremely tender meat, and sauces so good you want to ask for a straw. Many of the offerings from the extensive list fall into the category of "avant." The specialty here is classic Moroccan peasant food, updated with inventive sauces and surprising flavor combinations that are never completely incomprehensible to the Moroccan peasants in question. Witness *tagines* with calf's kidneys, sea urchins, or dates and duck *confit.* The *harira* (spicy Moroccan soup) is great too, but portions are so HUGE that ordering appetizers seems like overkill. Service can be hit or miss and, as often as not, the dining room can be crowded or empty. Go hungry, and don't forget to bring a date.

Au Bascou

38 Rue Réaumur (3rd). Tel. 01.42.72.69.25. Kitchen open Mon-Fri noon-2pm & 8-1030pm; Closed Aug. Starters €9, main courses €15. AE, MC, V. Ⓜ *Arts et Métiers*

Forget the tawny country-in-the-city décor and focus on the food; terrific down-home Basque fare paired with very good wines. Au Bascou attracts diners from all over the city and the globe, and has won many awards for serving the best regional cooking in the capital. All the legends of Basquetry are here, including wood pigeon, scallops with peppers, and outstanding *Ttoro du labourd*, a bouillabaisse of cod, salmon, prawns, and mussels. There are also terrific breads and special Ardi Gasna cheese. Morning-fresh ingredients, regular menu updates and a friendly waitstaff round out this exceptional dining experience, all at fair prices that are well within this world.

Chez Omar

47 Rue de Bretagne (3rd). Tel. *01.42.72.36.26.* Kitchen open *Mon-Sat noon-245pm & 7pm-midnight, Sun 7pm-midnight.* Main courses *€11-€24. No cards.* Ⓜ *Arts et Métiers*

In a city brimming with North African restaurants it's hard to choose the best, but Omar is certainly a contender. Here, couscous (steamed semolina, served with grilled meats and a cauldron of vegetables) is perfectly cooked with fine, fluffy grain. And their *tagines* (meat or fish baked with spices in a sealed earthenware pot) are wonderfully aromatic and chunked-out with top cuts of carefully trimmed meat. We love the lively international crowd and simple turn-of-the-century dining room too. Arrive early to avoid the crowds; later if you want to be a part of the moderately trendy scene.

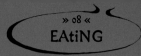

Coffee Parisien

4 Rue Princesse (6th). Tel. 01.43.54.18.18. Kitchen open daily 1130am-midnight. Main courses €8-€12. AE, MC, V. M *Mabillon*

This American-style coffee shop with inauthentically good food draws a trendy lunch crowd that comes for bubbly surroundings and faux JFK-infused Americana. The pan-USA menu reads like a list of suburban hits, from great burgers and spicy chicken wings to creamy tuna salad and well-made omelets. But many of the best dishes are virtually unknown in Iowa, including avocado and grapefruit salad, beef carpaccio and excellent salmon tartare. Ben & Jerry's ice-cream, a dessert that's popping up on some of the swankiest menus in town (including Chef Alain Ducasse's Spoon) is also a staple here. And best of all, mobile phones are prohibited.

Contre-Allée

83 Ave. Denfert-Rochereau (14th). Tel. 01.43.54.99.86. Kitchen open Mon-Fri noon-2pm & 8-11pm; Sat 8-11pm. Closed last week in December. Prix-fixe €25, €29 and €35. AE, MC,V. M *Denfert-Rochereau*

Contre-Allée is a very good, casual restaurant with pleasant decor and wonderful food. The dining room is a relaxed space, built with wooden floors, long mirrors, and minimalist furnishings that appeal to a grooving arts and letters crowd. The contemporary French kitchen is equally comfortable dishing out raw tuna in soy sauce and *confit de canard*, and their extremely flexible, all-inclusive menus always represent a good deal. *Foie gras* with artichokes, prepared with Muscat wine jelly, is a specialty here, as is lamb with garlic cake and sweet peas. And the vanilla crème brûlée is tops. All in all, an excellent dining experience.

L'Ostéria

10 Rue de Sévigné (4th). Tel. 01.42.71.37.08. Kitchen open Mon-Fri noon-2pm & 8-1030pm. Closed Aug. Average meal €40. MC, V. M *St-Paul*

A fabulous restaurant with no name on the door, L'Ostéria is often called the best Italian in France. The draw is awesomely flavorful classic Venetian cooking, chummy service and a fashion-conscious crowd that actually cares about food. The menu changes daily, but superb spaghetti *alle vongole* and gnocchi with white truffles are staples among a strong list of starters and pastas. Meat choices always include excellent veal, and seafood specials that really are. Physically, L'Ostéria is standard new-wave Italian, with a tiny dining room and the occasional limo parked out front. Regulars often come here to graze, and you could easily make a meal exclusively from antipasti, starting with the tomato and buffalo-Mozzarella salad. Make reservations, or fugetaboutit.

CLASSiC bRASSERiES

Brasserie Julien

16 Rue du Fbg-St-Denis (10th). Tel. 01.47.70.12.06. Kitchen open daily noon-3pm & 7pm-1am. Main courses €18-€25. Prix-fixe €23 and €31. AE, MC, V. M Strasbourg-St-Denis

This big, noisy brasserie near the Grands Boulevards serves very good food in an awesome *belle-époque* dining room with abfab decor and a buzzy atmosphere. There's something about Julien that's infused with the spirit of Paris. Maybe it's the entrance, off a grotty street, that transports you into another world. Maybe it's the period decor, which is completely authentic, right down to the high ceilings and street-lamp fixtures hung with antique headgear. And maybe it's the food, classic French fare that hasn't changed in a century. Fans come from across the city to jaw on great southwestern staples like *foie gras* and cassoulet. The menus change frequently, but often include snails, roast lamb and sea bass. And value-oriented fixed-priced meals even include wine. We love this place.

Bofinger

5–7 Rue de la Bastille (4th). Tel. 01.42.72.87.82. Kitchen open Mon-Fri noon-3pm & 630pm-1am; Sat-Sun noon-1am. Main courses €18-€30. Prix-fixe €30.50. Mon-Fri Lunch menu €21. AE, MC, V. M Bastille

Built with a spectacular stained glass cupola, swirling with multi-lingual waiters, and packed to the gills, Bofinger has all the makings of a tourist trap. With all its turn-of-the century clichés in place, it just looks *too* perfect. But perfect it is. Paris' oldest brasserie (opened in 1864) is a genuine *belle-époque* treat with a celebratory atmosphere that's plays equally well to first dates and 50th anniversary parties. And the food is far better than it has to be. Regulars opt for the colossal seafood platters, classic andouillette, or the solid choucroute that's as good as you can get almost anywhere. And the crème brûlée with bourbon vanilla is absolutely one of the best. Set menus are surprisingly affordable, and even include wine. Make reservations or arrive after 1130pm or you won't get a table. And request a seat in the sensational main dining room, where smoking is prohibited.

La Coupole

102 Blvd. du Montparnasse (14th). Tel. 01.43.20.14.20. Kitchen open daily 830am-1030am and noon-1am (until 130am Fri-Sat). Main courses €18-25. Prix-fixe €21.50 and €29. AE, MC, V. M Vavin

One of our favorite Parisian brasseries, La Coupole is an institution with a reputation as big as its massive dining room. Though prices were undoubtedly far lower back when Hemingway, Lenin, Picasso and company hung out here, the quintessential Montparnasse ambiance remains. La Coupole is what a Parisian brasserie is *supposed* to look like, complete with hand-painted columns, art deco decor, and medium-high noise levels. Food here can be excellent, and is rarely disappointing. Hits include choucroute, cassoulet (white beans simmered in goose fat with goose, lamb and sausages), and giant seafood platters brimming with oysters, sea urchins, sweet jumbo shrimp and clams. The Grand Marnier-flamed crèpes suzette are justifiably famous, and the profiteroles are to die for. Service is attentive even when the place is packed, which means almost every night of the week. Arrive late to avoid a wait and you'll also benefit from a discounted prix-fixe menu that's only available after 10pm.

Chez Jenny

39 Blvd. du Temple (3rd). Tel. 01.44.54.39.00. Kitchen open daily noon-1am. Main courses €12-€15. Prix-fixe €17 and €24. AE, MC, V. M République

Jenny is a vast 1930s brasserie known for its festive atmosphere, costumed waitresses and top-of-the-line choucroute with grilled, rather than boiled, meats. Sauerkraut is the specialty of this house; each meal from the extensive menu is full-portioned, full-bodied and intensely flavorful. The mountain of tangy cabbage is redolent with white wine, coriander seed and juniper berries, and perfectly cooked to retain just the right amount of crispness. The seafood platters are equally enormous, and the regional desserts look great, though we've never had room enough to order one. Tucked into a corner of the Place de la République, Jenny is a warm and cheery place, built with inlaid woods and decorations by the celebrated Alsatian artist Charles Spindler. Go with friends, and bring an appetite.

Le Train Bleu

Gare de Lyon, Place Louis-Armand (12th). Tel. 01.43.43.09.06. Kitchen open daily 1130am-3pm & 7-11pm. Main courses €23-€38. Prix-fixe €42. DC, AE, MC, V. M Gare de Lyon

Built for the 1900 Great Exhibition and designated a national historical monument in 1972, many people call Le Train Bleu "the most beautiful restaurant in Paris." Part the heavy curtains at the top of the stairs and you step back into another century, where the gilt-and-mural decor is so amazing they could serve TV dinners and we'd still go back for more. But in fact, the food is very good. Classic starters include caviar and *foie gras*, while mains mean salmon in red wine and steaks. Regulars swear by the veal chops. Order the wafer-thin *pommes gaufrettes* with everything, and save room for Rum Baba only if you love rum; the little sponge cake is served with a full bottle which, after a thorough dosing, is left on the table. There's hardly a bad seat in the house, but the most sought-after table is number 92, which was preferred by François Mitterrand.

La Gare

19 Chaussée de la Muette (16th). Tel. 01.42.15.15.31. Kitchen open daily noon-3pm & 7pm-midnight. Main courses €18-€25. AE, MC, V. M La Muette

Huge and bustling, La Gare is a continuously buzzing grill with excellent sightlines, good food and train station acoustics that are worthy of its name. Created from a former train station, La Gare takes full advantage of its location, with a platform-turned-dining room, waiting room benches, a glass roof, factory lighting, and an exhibition kitchen. Everything about this voguish spot is big, from the colossal windows and warehouse-high ceilings to the lengthy wine list, robust flavors and generous portions of food. The kitchen does best with rôtisserie items: leg of lamb, rosemary chicken, and pork loins that arrive perfectly moist and tender. Start with oysters, and don't miss the chocolate cake with caramel sauce. During warm weather, reserve on the terrace, where dozens of parasol-studded tables overlook the tracks.

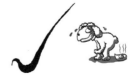

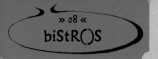

T()P biStROS

Chez Paul

13 Rue de Charonne (11th). Tel. 01.47.00.34.57. Kitchen open daily noon-230pm & 7pm-1230am. Closed for lunch for two weeks in Aug. Main courses €15-€18. AE, MC, V. M *Bastille*

Tight and trendy, Chez Paul is the classic downscale Bastille dining room. It's a happy and hip vintage restaurant that's uncomfortably designed with bare walls, tile floors and tables so tight they'll soon be seating two to a chair. But the food is reliable, the atmosphere is authentic and buzzy, and the crowd can be high on the Cool-O-Meter. Simple starters are followed by classic, meaty Frog fare that runs the gamut from mint-and-*chevre*-stuffed rabbit to Armagnac-infused steak and Jurassic-sized bones filled with slithery dollops of marrow. The waiters are chummy, but service tends to go awry when things get ultra-busy, which means weekends can be disastrous. Make reservations, arrive early and prepare to wait at the cramped zinc bar.

Natacha

17bis Rue Campagne-Première (14th). Tel. 01.43.20.79.27. Kitchen open Mon-Sat noon-230pm and 830pm-1am. Closed three weeks in Aug. Main courses €8-€12. Lunch menu €18. AE, MC, V. M Raspail

Beautiful people, music-industry folks and famous faces pack-in nightly for refined cuisine served in warm, clubby surroundings. It's been that way for years. Wrapped with velvet banquettes and studded with candle-lit tables, Natacha is an intimate and stylish little restaurant in the heart of Montparnasse. But seeing and being sceney is not this place's *raison d'être*. Very good French food, a wonderful hostess (Natacha), and a menu designed to please everyone are the draws. Some of the entrées miss their proverbial marks, but all are intelligently prepared and some are superlative. We love the goat cheese ravioli and the pork filet with honey and ginger. But we could also make a meal from the restaurant's trademark Black Russian cocktails. The scene heats up after 11pm.

L'Oeillade

10 Rue St-Simon (7th). Tel. 01.42.22.01.60. Kitchen open Mon-Fri 1230-2pm & 730-11pm; Sat 730-11pm. Closed last two weeks in Aug. Main courses €15-€20. MC, V. M Rue du Bac

Always busy, this tiny Left Bank charmer serves delicious food that straddles the fence between simple and sophisticated. Generous portions of perfectly-cooked Parisian comfort foods include roast veal, mozzarella fritters, reasonably-priced *foie gras* and top-of-the line terrines. Fixed-price menus change frequently, and usually represent excellent value. And the gently priced wine list recognizes that the clientele is out for a good time too. White linen-topped tables are set on simple terra-cotta floors and surrounded by natural wood paneling. The crowd is a cultured mix of neighborhood types and knowledgeable cross-towners. Round out this almost perfect dining experience with chocolate *fondant*, one of the best of the genre we've had.

Nos Ancìtres les Gaulois

39 Rue St-Louis-en-l'Ile (4th). Tel. 01.46.33.66.07. Kitchen open Mon-Sat 7pm-midnight, Sun noon-3pm. Prix-fixe €35. AE, MC, DC, V. M Pont-Marie

Situated behind Notre-Dame Cathedral, the Ancestors of Gaul is a kitschy theme restaurant that pays tribute to days that probably never were. The dining room is a rustic stone dungeon set with long wooden tables laden with jugs of wine, baskets of uncut vegetables and plates of dried sausages. It's a festive Medieval Times banquet for rowdy groups bent on fun. Everybody shows up here eventually—with Astérix helmet on head and tongue firmly in cheek. Diners are encouraged to gorge on *saucisson* and pâté and to help themselves to as much cheap red plonk as they can drink. Good meats are charred on an open grill and served with excellent home-baked breads and sad veggies that are cooked lifeless. Nobody could mistake this for the most sophisticated food in Paris, but it's certainly the most generous. Nos Ancìtres is a terrifically playful once-in-a-lifetime kind of place—because that's exactly as many times as you should go.

La Petite Chaise

36 Rue de Grenelle (7th). Tel. 01.42.22.13.35. Kitchen open daily noon-2pm & 7-11pm. Main courses €12.50-€16. Prix-fixe €29. AE, MC, V. M Rue du Bac/Sèvres-Babylone

Traditional food, popular prices and an awesome old-world atmosphere (1680s) keep this restaurant humming throughout the week. Tourists and locals, young and old—everybody comes here, drawn by very good food, friendly servers, and a unique ancient atmosphere that's often copied but rarely replicated. Meals run the gamut from poached eggs to an ironclad pot-au-feu, an all-inclusive dish *par excellence* mixing broth, meat, marrow and vegetables. Most of the good-value fixed-price dinners come with a half-bottle of very drinkable wine, and the fine food extends all the way to dessert. A winner.

Le Square Trousseau

1 Rue Antoine-Vollon (12th). Tel. 01.43.43.06.00. Kitchen open daily noon-230pm & 8-1130pm. Main courses €15-€25. Mon-Sat lunch menu €20 and €25. AE, MC, V. M Ledru-Rollin

Good food, beautiful-yet-unpretentious 1900s surroundings and decent prices make Le Square Trousseau a hit with fashion types, the media elite, and countless regulars who pop in for everything from crèpes suzette with caramelized apples to the classic snails in puff-pastry. Other hits from the market-influenced menu include cream of pumpkin soup and rosemary-stuffed rabbit sausage, all accompanied by a strong list of sulfite-free wines. At its core, Le Square is basically a pretty corner bistro with molded ceilings, sturdy wooden school chairs, etched glass windows and a traditional zinc bar. The fact that Jean-Paul Gaultier is regularly spied here doesn't make this a trendy scene spot; just a down-to-earth French diner that has been recognized by the creatives who happen to live and work in the neighborhood. Oh, and there's great brunch food too, including scrambled eggs, bacon, potatoes, OJ, and fresh breads and jams.

Thoumieux

79 Rue St-Dominique (7th). Tel. 01.47.05.49.75. Kitchen open Mon-Sat noon-330pm & 645pm-midnight; Sun noon-midnight. Main courses €14-€19. Prix-fixe €14 and €28. AE, MC, V. M Invalides/La Tour-Maubourg

A neighborhood place in a very nice neighborhood, Thoumieux is a venerable old brasserie/bar with an intensely loyal following. As big and friendly as a Great Dane, the restaurant is known for really good homestyle Southwestern cooking and archetype decor that includes mirrored columns, red banquettes, white table cloths, and sturdy wooden chairs on tile floors. Regulars swear by the huge cassoulet, which is served in earthenware and is rich with meat and beans. Because the prix-fixe is limited, it's worth stretching your finances to the *carte* for wild mushroom omelets, trout with almonds, or toothsome snails, which arrive piping hot in a classic parsley and garlic sauce. Thoumieux seldom disappoints.

Le Vin des Rues

21 Rue Boulard (14th). Tel. 01.43.22.19.78. Kitchen open Tues, Thurs, Sat 1-230pm; Wed, Fri 1-230pm & 9-1030pm (by reservation only). Closed early Aug-Sept & one week in Feb. Main courses €10- €15. No cards.
M *Denfert-Rochereau*

Very good food and the distinctive (if not always lovable) personality of owner Jean Chanrion makes Le Vin de Rues one of the city's most characterful eateries. Chanrion rules his little kingdom with an iron *toque*, and his slightly surly service is an integral part of this bistro's *gestalt.* The owner takes orders from customers, gives them to the servers, pours the wine and tots up the bills with the bullheaded authority of a police officer writing a ticket. Before bistro cooking became so faddish, it was about having a solidly good meal, not a gastronomic vision. Le Vin is from this old school. Here the blackboard menu fills with classic bistro fare that usually includes housemade terrines, terrific snails, and that standard-bearer of simple French cuisine: lentil salad. Many regulars swear by the andouillette Beaujolais. There's a strong list of decently-priced Beaujolais wines too, and even the house plunk is pretty good. Checked paper cloths on red Formica tables and a clutter of cartoon-art decor keeps this place real.

Wadja

10 Rue de la Grande-Chaumière (6th). Tel. 01.46.33.02.02. Kitchen open Mon 730-11pm; Tues-Sat noon-230pm & 730-11pm. Closed Aug. Main courses €14-€18. Prix-fixe €24. MC, V.
M *Vavin*

Tasteful, no-nonsense atmosphere—with food to match—is the secret of Wadja's success. The pocket-sized dining room is all style and elegance, without any of the film-set pretense that characterizes so many lesser restaurants. It's also a youth-infected space, packed with attitude-laden beautiful people speaking a myriad of foreign tongues and sucking filterless Gitanes. Wadja is the kind of place you could enjoy several times a week, and plenty of locals do; drawn by a short, reliable menu of moderately-priced bistro fare. Insiders come for the seven-hour leg of lamb that's so soft it could be eaten with a spoon. Other staples include tuna with lavender, and sautéed chicken with lime. Prices are reasonable too.

iN-StYLE S(ENES

Hotel Costes

239 Rue St-Honoré (1st). Tel. 01.42.44.50.25. Kitchen open daily 7am-1130am, noon-1am. Main courses €26-€35. AE, MC, V. M Concorde

Built with a brilliantly faux Napolén III interior, the Costes restaurant is Paris as the French wish it could be. Trendy and stylish, like everything else the Costes brothers touch, this beautiful restaurant also remains one of the hottest spots in town. Golden light bounces around the room with theatrical illumination, and funky chill-out music keeps conversations to a minimum. And nobody minds the guard-dog hostess or having to wait at the three-deep bar. There's a fireplace in winter (a surprising rarity in Parisian restaurants), and a pleasant patio in summer. And all year round the crowd is hot, hot, hot. The menu is all over the map, and includes everything from veal noisettes and club sandwiches to a Thai-inspired beef dish called "*le tigre qui pleure*" (the tiger that cries). Definitely order dessert: Not only are tarts this kitchen's strongest suit, but it gives you an excuse to linger. And isn't that really what this place is all about?

Lô Sushi

8 Rue de Berri (8th). **Tel.** *01.45.62.01.00.* **Kitchen open** *daily noon-1230am. Average meal €30. AE, MC, V. M George V.*

Conveyor-belt sushi is taken to the next level in this rock 'n' roll Japanese with minimalist pearl white walls, frosted-glass tables, and popular prices aimed squarely at the poverty jetset. The high tech, stainless steel interior, pulsating with projections and techno music, is just oh so Tokyo. And the low-priced, medium-quality sushi is often just what the doctor ordered at 11pm. It's popular with local fashion workers, suburban trendies, and visiting tightwads from around the globe.

Buddha Bar

8 Rue Boissy d'Anglas (8th). Tel. 01.53.05.90.00. Kitchen open Mon-Fri noon-3pm & daily 6pm-2am. Main courses €22-€30. Lunch menu €32. AE, MC, V. M Concorde

Le Buddha invented the hip French/Colonial dining scene in Paris, by way of New York and L.A. A hotspot since 1996 known for sashimi and celebs, Buddha Bar has taken on all comers and remains as hot as a chili-oil stir fry. Few diners doubt that this Asian-themed cellar is more of a feast for the eyes than the palate. But nobody seems to care. The restaurant's black-clad table-hopping loyals are lorded over by a giant golden Buddha, and surrounded with beautiful servers and palm fronds. Models are still ordering nothing but can be seen everywhere. And the delicate Franco-Asian food still feels inventive, if not exotic. There is an interesting variety of crunchy handrolls paired with piquant dipping sauces. Tempura, spicy beef dishes and steamed fish are also on the menu. Wines are not too dear, and a variety of beers are available. The best tables for people-watching are at the bottom of the staircase: If you're not sitting there, there's a good chance you'll recognize who is.

Man Ray

34 Rue Marbeuf (8th). Tel. 01.56.88.36.36. Kitchen open daily noon-230pm & 7pm-1245am. Main courses €28-35. Prix-fixe €46, €61. Lunch €29. AE, MC, V. M Franklin D. Roosevelt

Investors Sean Penn, Johnny Depp, Mick Hucknall and John Malkovich have made Man Ray a scene spot from the get-go. With its pedigree in place, this big restaurant near the Champs has become a magnet for scenesters, mannequins and generic rich people, most of whom come here to ogle each other from plush banquettes and low-rider armchairs. The restaurant reflects Paris' newfound (again) fascination with everything Asian, with a menu that reads like a directory of pseudo-Oriental hits: *nem* rolls, Thai sea scallops, Chinese stir-fries and Japanese sushi. The Eurasian decor includes bubbling fountains, giant statues and colored-glass mosaic ceilings. You can obtain the Man Ray experience without dropping a fortune (or an entire night) by grazing at the mezzanine bar, from which you have a bird's eye view of the action below.

Georges

Centre Pompidou, Place Georges Pompidou (4th). Tel. 01.44.78.47.99. Kitchen open Wed-Mon 1130-3pm & 6pm-midnight. Main courses €9-€25. AE, MC, V. M Rambuteau/Hôtel-de-Ville

The striking art installation architecture of this restaurant on the top floor of the Centre Pompidou is perfectly in keeping with the contemporary art museum in which it's located. So is the fiercely fashionable crowd of well-behaved trendies and twiggy young things who come to make the scene. The interior is truly memorable, designed with mind-bending brushed-aluminum "pods" that hide the kitchen, house a coat room, and make a bold statement about the state of postmodernism. Hyper-modern cutlery, sandblasted glass tables and a terrific terrace with unobstructed views over all of Paris complete the stellar effect. The food is Asian, Italian and French and, although we've been here on numerous occations, we somehow can't remember exactly what we ate.

Spoon Food & Wine

14 Rue de Marignan (8th). Tel. 01.40.76.34.44. Kitchen open Mon-Fri noon-230pm & 7-1130pm. Closed mid July-mid Aug. Average meal €80. AE, MC, V. M Franklin D. Roosevelt

One of the newest ventures from super chef Alain Ducasse, Spoon is a decidedly offbeat round-the-world adventure offering everything from Asian ravioli and Italian pasta to grilled fish and BLTs from the USA. Created by anyone else, this multi-culti approach would probably end up insulting several cuisines at once. From Ducasse it's fusion at its simplest and most elegant: international ingredients combined with *haute* French technique. While much of the menu is somewhat familiar to New Yorkers, Los Angelinos, and even some Londoners, French are only beginning to experiment with the whole world on a single plate. Even the decidedly un-French wine list is designed to provoke. Consequently, diners here are among the most adventurous local eaters; international travelers who are wooed by the open plan dining room, recessed lighting, plum-colored walls, and minimalist chairs covered in muted pastels. Come here to experience local dining on the edge.

ChEAP ASS

L'As du Fallafel

34 Rue des Rosiers (4th). **Tel.** *01.48.87.63.60.* **Kitchen open** *Sun-Thurs noon-midnight, Fri noon-5pm, Sat 8pm-midnight. Closed Saturday. Falafel €3.50-€4. Cash only.* Ⓜ *St-Paul*

The best fast-food joint on the Marais' "Falafel Row" serves top-quality pita sandwiches stuffed with perfectly-made fried chickpeas and salad. The owners like to boast that Lenny Kravitz eats here, and why wouldn't he? Everyone else does. Cheap and delicious, it's no wonder that this place is legendary with students and backpackers worldwide. Prices rise slightly if you add humus or fried eggplant, or if you want to sit down inside.

La Boulangerie

15 Rue des Panoyaux (20th). Tel. 01.43.58.45.45. Kitchen open Sat 730-11pm, Mon-Fri noon-2pm & 730-11pm; Sun 1130-4pm. Main courses €6.50-€11. Prix-fixe €15 and €18; lunch €11 and €12. MC, V. M Ménilmontant

We could hardly be more enthusiastic about this excellent and affordable bakery-turned-restaurant. There's just so much to like. Each night young chef Jerémie Ogé whips up a new set of value-packed, fixed-priced bistro meals that are so good you can hardly keep your eyes on the crowd. And that's saying a lot. You never know what's going to be on the market menu, but there is always a generous selection of meat and fish dishes. Signature meals include stuffed cabbage, veal kidneys, and tuna tartare. The dining room is pleasant too, decorated with bas-reliefs, mosaic floors, and hand-painted walls that riff on the baking theme. La Boulangerie is one of the very best meals in Ménilmontant—at any price.

Chartier

7 Rue du Fbg-Montmartre (9th). Tel. 01.47.70.86.29. Kitchen open daily noon-3pm & 7-10pm. Main courses €5-€8. Prix-fixe €15, €25. V. M Grands Boulevards

Decent food, excellent prices, and a frenetic, buzzy atmosphere are the hallmarks of this landmarked, turn-of-the-century soup kitchen. Chartier is an art nouveau institution with a glass roof, wood paneling, and overhead bag-racks built to hold workers' belongings. White-apron-clad waiters dash from table to table with steaming plates of soul food from the bedrock of French bourgeois cooking. Bouillon is a specialty here, especially on Mondays when pot-au-feu with vermicelli and toast hits the menu—just as it has since 1896. And the fact that the restaurant was awarded a "diploma" from the Egg Mayonnaise Protection Society might just be enough to convince you to order the egg salad. Or maybe not. Other dishes can be hit or miss, but few people seem to care. Keep it simple, stick to beef or lamb, and avoid dessert at all costs.

Le Café du Commerce

51 Rue du Commerce (15th). Tel. 01.45.75.03.27. Kitchen open daily noon-midnight. Main courses €8-12. Prix-fixe €13.50 (lunch), €20. AE, MC, V. M Émile-Zola

Unusually decent food at unusually low prices could be the motto of this relentlessly marketed restaurant in the far reaches of the 15th. What is also unusual is the tri-level dining room, built around a plant-filled atrium with a roof that retracts in summer. There are lots of tables, occupied by everyone from neighborhood secretaries and older locals to a nonstop parade of travelers who've heard about this bargain from afar. The atmosphere is always lively and the food is fine, straightforward bistro fare. Stick to simple preparations (steak *frites* is our fave) and it's a completely satisfying affair. And in case you're wondering, the fresco is of French industrialist Marcel Dassault.

Chez Papa—Espace Sud-Ouest

206 Rue La Fayette (10th). Tel. 01.40.05.06.41 Kitchen open daily 1130am-1am. Main courses €5-€7.50. Prix-fixe Mon-Fri until 10pm €10. AE, MC, V. M *Louis-Blanc*

When your wallet is crying "uncle" and your stomach is not far behind, Chez Papa comes to the rescue with artery-clogging comfort foods like cassoulet and *confit de canard.* The early-bird prix-fixe is the stuff of student dreams, and the meals are far better than the value pricing and ample portions would suggest. There's not much to the non-decor, but boring walls are countered by boisterous diners excited about good food and inexpensive wines. Chez Papa's brothers are recommended too. We only wish there were more places in Paris like this.

Branches: *29 Rue de l'Arcade, 8th (tel. 01.42. 65.43.68); 6 Rue Gassendi, 14th (tel. 01.43.22.41.19); 101 Rue de la Croix Nivert, 15th (tel. 01.48. 28.31.88).*

BE-Boulangépicier

73 Boulevard de Courcelles (8th). Tel. *01.46.22.20.20. Lunch €20.*

Alain Ducasse, one of Paris's most famous Michelin three-star chefs, is now courting the budget-minded with this sleek little bakery and food shop. Everything here is made on the premises, including fantastic sandwiches on homemade bread that you can pair with a doughnut and take to the nearby Parc Monceau for lunch.

Cosi

54 Rue de Seine (6th). Tel. *01.46. 33.35.36.* Kitchen open *daily 11am-11pm. Sandwiches €5-€8. V, MC.* M *Odéon/St-Germain-des-Prés*

The working-class hero turns *haute* at this upscale sandwich shop, where crusty flat breads are baked in wood-fired ovens, then filled with an astounding choice of delicacies that range from smoked meats and fishes to gourmet vegetables and cheeses. Like their sister shop in New York, this designer lunch spot is especially known for its seasoned breads and flavorful, baked fillings. It's a zoo at the height of lunch hour. After the midday rush, you'll enjoy a fantastic meal surrounded by local office workers pretending they don't have real jobs. Decent wines are served by the glass.

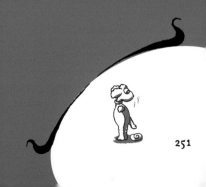

Higuma

32bis Rue St-Anne (1st). Tel. 01.47.03.38.59. Kitchen open daily noon-10pm. Main courses €5-€8. Prix-fixe €20 . V, MC. M Pyramides

A deep bow to the fine art of noodles, Higuma is a downscale Japanese pasta parlor specializing in Hokkaido-style *ramen* swimming in huge bowls of seductively subtle broth. Unless you've spent a lot of time poking around the Shinjuku, these are probably the finest noodles you've ever had. Tucked away on a small side street close to the Opéra Garnier, Higuma is a real find in an otherwise tab-happy neighborhood. The sounds of noodle slurps and chopstick clacks are oh so Japanese, but the low prices and Formica-and-neon decor are decidedly not. There's good *yakisoba* (fried noodles), dumplings and *donburi* (meat- or fish-topped rice bowls), along with many vegetarian options. Singles are catered to at the bar, and their no-smoking policy will appeal to Americans.

Léon de Bruxelles

120 Rue Rambuteau (1st). Tel. 01.42.36.18.50. Kitchen open Sun-Thurs 1145am-midnight; Fri-Sat 1145am-1am. Main courses €9-€15. Prix-fixe €9.90 (lunch) and €11.60. AE, MC, V. M Les Halles

The McDonalds of mussels is a great place to conquer a *moules* jones. The menu is basic—15 versions of steamed mussels, all-you-can-eat fries, and an excellent selection of Belgian beer. There is little subtlety when it comes to the sauces, and the *frites* are shockingly bad for a place that features them so prominently. But service is the epitome of haste cuisine, and it's hard to screw-up steamed shellfish too badly—even at mimimum wage.

Branches: *131 Blvd. St-Germain, 6th (tel. 01.43.26.45.95); 63 Ave. des Champs-Elysées, 8th (tel. 01.42.25.96.16); 1 Place Pigalle, 9th (tel. 01.42.80.28.33); 8 Place République, 11th (tel. 01.43.38.65.11).*

Polidor

41 Rue Monsieur-le-Prince (6th). Tel. 01.43.26.95.34. Kitchen open Mon-Sat noon-230pm & 7pm-1230am, Sun noon-230pm & 7pm-11pm. Main courses €8 - €12. Prix-fixe €18; Mon-Fri lunch €9. No cards. M Odéon

Hard by the Luxembourg Gardens, Polidor is a century-old Left Bank canteen that oozes authenticity. The shabby-chic interior is complimented by a no-airs crowd and career waiters who are auditioning for nothing. Everything about Polidor is straightforward and old-fashioned, including the prices. Good, heavy peasant fare includes dynamite shepherd's pie, meaty *boeuf bourguignon*, and creamy veal *blanquette* with rice pilaf, a peasant-food staple that's served here daily. Although Polidor offers one of the city's best-priced lunch menus, their time-consuming stock reductions and strong wine list prove the kitchen's integrity. Even the desserts are good. Tightly packed tables are one of our few gripes—especially in the back room

Rendez-vous des Chauffeurs

11 Rue des Portes-Blanches (18th). Tel. 01.42.64.04.17. Kitchen open Thurs-Tues noon-230pm & 730-11pm. Closed first two weeks in Aug. Main courses €7.50-€11.50. Prix-fixe until 830pm €13. MC, V. M Marcadet-Poissoniers

You have to travel to the outer reaches of the 18th for one of the city's best-value finds. It's worth the trip for excellent bistro fare at prices that time forgot. There's not much to the décor, but that's countered in spades by excellent Parisian comfort food that runs the gamut from zucchini terrine to juicy steaks and phat fries. The crowd is an egalitarian mix of everybody, with a few dogs thrown in for good measure. Parisians know good food, and they definitely know a good deal when they see one. Rendez-vous des Chauffeurs bats two out of two, then throws in very drinkable house wine to make this place a standout. And although the restaurant is a wee bit from the center, it's conveniently situated in a tiny side street close to the Métro.

Restaurant Pho

3 Rue Volta (3rd). Tel. 01.42.78.31.70. Kitchen open Mon-Sat 10m-4pm. Closed Aug. Main courses €5-€7.50. No cards. M Arts et Métiers

Faux-nothing, this authentic Vietnamese is named for its best main dish, pho, a beautifully-spiced traditional noodle soup. This is truly a specialty restaurant, as there are only two other regular menu items, both of which are out-of-this-world delicious. Bo bun (rice vermicelli with sautéed beef, peanuts, fresh mint and beansprouts) is an excellent meal we could eat every day. Alternatively, choose the broth full of wheat noodles and roast duck; a delicious winter warmer. The small dining room, tight tables and bullet service are not meant for lingering. But for a great feed on the cusp of the Marais, you can't say "phooey" to Pho.

Ti Jos

30 Rue Delambre (14th). Tel. 01.43.22.57.69. Open Mon & Wed-Fri noon-230pm & 7pm-1230am, Tues noon-230pm. Crepes €5.50-€8.50. V. M Vavin

There are, of course, hundreds of crèperies all over Paris, the majority of which make very respectable crèpes. Good ingredients are integral, but when bellying up to a bar for a one-handed meal, even a layperson should insist on a freshly made pancake, as opposed to getting a pre-cooked one off the stack. There's no worry about quality or authenticity at Ti Jos, perhaps the best exponent of the genre in the city. It's a thoroughly Bretonesque place, with traditional ham-and-cheese fillings that are a long way from avant. There are a few non-crèpe options, but why? Apple cider is the traditional drink of choice and, like the best crèperies in Paris, this one is located near Montparnasse rail station, where the Bretons who eat here can catch the train north.

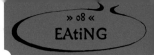

Café de Flore

172 Blvd. St-Germain (6th). Tel. 01.45.48.55.26. Open daily 7am-130am. Snacks served all day. Average meal €25; drinks €4-€6. AE, MC, V. M St-Germain-des-Prés

Café de Flore is in a perpetual duel with Deux Magots (across the street) for the mantle of "most famous Left Bank café." Luckily for them both, there are plenty of locals and visitors who are happy to shell-out €4 for coffee and a coveted sidewalk seat. And shell out they should, because Flore is an institution that remains worthy of Hemingway and Fitzgerald. And the girl watching is great too. Little has changed since its 1920s and '30s heydays. Many of the servers even appear to be the same. But today's artists and intellectuals tend to congregate upstairs, farther away from the tourists. If you must eat, order the scrambled eggs, one of the few menu items that's really outstanding.

Café Marly

93 Rue de Rivoli, Cour Napoléon du Louvre (1st). Tel. 01.49.26.06.60. Open daily 8am-2am. Food served 11am-1am. Average meal €45; drinks €4.20-€8. AE, MC, V. M Palais-Royal

On a warm day or night there is no better *al fresco* dining than in the Louvre courtyard facing IM Pei's famous *pyramide*. Nestled under the arcade, between the Cour Napoléon and the Richelieu wing of the Louvre museum, it's hard to find a better setting. It's both beautiful and chic, with no stinky cars zipping by. Like other hotspots from the brothers' Costes, the crowd here is fashion-heavy, but also includes a healthy mix of mortals. When the weather cools, the action moves indoors to an understated Napoleon III-era dining room set with comfortable armchairs. Service can be sloppy, but the *nouvelle* brasserie fare remains solid, and includes everything from designer salads and grilled salmon to cheeseburgers. Reservations are essential, though you might get lucky if you just drop in. Café Marly is recommended for classic Continental breakfasts too. And whatever you do, don't let them banish you to a table on the pavement out front.

Café de l'Industrie

16 Rue St-Sabin (11th). Tel. 01.47.00.13.53. Open Mon-Fri & Sun 10am-2am. Food served noon-midnight. Average meal €25; drinks €2-€4. MC, V. M Bastille

Inexpensive and worth it, l'Industrie is a well-trodden Bastille hang for good-looking students and trendies of all ages. Pseudo-colonial bric-a-brac anti-decor includes live flora and stuffed fauna that brings back memories of Africa. Tortoise shells (on the walls) mix with turtlenecks (on the patrons) and, day and night, the café buzzes with intensity. The model waitstaff serves Continental meals and copious bottles of wine. But nobody minds if you linger for hours over a single beer or espresso.

Baggi

33 Rue Chaptal (9th). **Tel.** *01.48.74.01.39. About €4.* **M** *Pigalle*

Mad mobs flock to the Île St-Louis for Berthillon's (see page 261), but those who want a quietier scene choose Baggi for its wonderful early-19th-century atmosphere and to-die-for mokalina ice cream (coffee and caramel with chocolate bits).

Branch: *29 Rue de Mogador (9th).* **Tel.** *01.48.78.38.30*

Les Deux Magots

6 Place St-Germain-des-Prés (6th). Tel. 01.45.48.55.25. Open daily 730am-2am. Food served all day. Average meal €30; drinks €4-€11. AE, MC, V. M St-Germain-des-Prés

Once a chill-out space for the likes of Simone de Beauvoir, Jean-Paul Sartre and other intellectual elitists from the 1920s onwards, this landmark St-Germain café never misses an opportunity to point out how it inspired generations of writers and thinkers. The result is that most of the customers are tourists who jostle for the perfectly positioned sidewalk tables. It's not a bad place to hang, especially on a warm afternoon when the fashion parade is in full gear. The hot chocolate is good, as are the omelets, salads and plates of warm goat cheese.

Au Petit Fer â Cheval

30 Rue Vieille-du-Temple (4th). Tel. 01.42.72.47.47. Open daily 9am-2am. Food served noon-1am. Average meal €15; drinks €2-€6. MC, V. M Hôtel-de-Ville/St-Paul

The ever-popular "Little Horseshoe," near the pinkest part of the Marais, is the perfect place to linger with a drink facing one of the best-looking little streets anywhere. In good weather the small handful of sidewalk seats become some of the most desired real estate in the city. The inside bar is beautiful, and the little dining area behind it is a hidden gem of a place for salads and first-rate steak tartare. This place is a fave.

La Palette

43 Rue de Seine (6th). Tel. *01.43.26.68.15. Open Mon-Sat 8am-2am. Food served noon-3pm; snacks until close. Average meal €12; drinks €2.50-€4. Closed three weeks in Aug. V. M Mabillon*

We absolutely love this vintage café and would be happy to come here every day. Hidden in plain sight a few blocks from the touristy madness, our favorite Left Bank café is frequented by local art dealers, students from the nearby Academie des Beaux-Arts, and just about everyone we know. There's ample outdoor seating (facing a car-free zone), a zinc bar and a back room where snacks and simple meals are served.

MEALS AftER MidNiGht

One of the very best things about the Parisian foodscape are the many places—in all price ranges—to relieve late-night munchies. Most of the restaurants listed above keep their kitchens open until 11pm or midnight. Those that serve later include **Brasserie Julien** (130am), **La Coupole** (2am), **Buddha Bar** (2am), **Café de Flore** (130am), **Les Deux Magots** (2am), and **La Palette** (2am). Recommended restaurants, open very late or nonstop, are listed below.

La Maison de l'Alsace

39 Ave. des Champs-Elysées (8th). Tel. 01.53.83.10.00. Kitchen open nonstop. Main courses €12-€18.50. Prix-fixe €30. AE, MC, V. M Franklin D. Roosevelt

It's easy to fear the worst on a street that's becoming something of a McDonaldland. But La Maison surprises with very good cooking that includes trout in white wine, shellfish platters, bæckœff (baked lamb, beef, pork & potatoes) and stereotype choucroute lavished with sausages, ham hock and other *charcuterie*. The ground-zero location, blazing red awning and flashy interior attracts everyone from jet-lagged Japanese and late-working businessmen to hardcore partiers just out of Le Queen.

Au Pied de Cochon

6 Rue Coquillière (1st). Tel. 01.40.13.77.00. Kitchen open nonstop. Average meal €43. AE, MC, V. M Les Halles

It's great to see such a good restaurant plugging away in the wee hours, and this lively brasserie is often hopping even at 4am. It's a pretty place, with gilt-and-mirror decor, painted ceilings and old-fashioned red banquettes. The down-home French fare evokes the Les Halles wholesale food market that used to be nearby; the place that Émile Zola called the "belly of Paris." Like the name says, grilled pig's feet are the house specialty. Served with béarnaise sauce, they practically melt off the bone. "The Temptation of St. Anthony" reunites the pig's trotters with his tail, ears and snout, and is only for the brave. But don't worry, there's plenty of normal food here too. Lots of late-niters come here for a bowl of onion soup gratinée, or the mighty platters of seafood.

Mustang Café

34 Blvd. du Montparnasse (14th). Tel. 01.43.35.36.12. Kitchen open daily 1130am-5pm & 7pm-5am (kitchen until 1am on Sun). Average meal €20. MC, V. M Montparnasse-Bienvenüe

Bright, boisterous and seriously boozy, this Tex-Mex late-niter is the perfect place to satisfy a bout of 4am munchies. The garish interior is offset by decent food that seems only to get better as the hours become later. Tacos, enchiladas, burritos... all the hits are here. And vegetarians are amply catered for. When the sun is about to rise, Mustang Café is the next best thing to Taco Bell.

Le Select

99 Blvd. du Montparnasse (6th). Tel. 01.42.22.65.27. Open Mon-Thurs & Sun 7am-230am, Fri-Sat 7am-4am. Kitchen open 11am-close. Main courses €8.50-€12.50. MC, V. M Vavin

Situated on the most popular stretch of Montparnasse's most famous boulevard, Select is a deco café from a former age with a terrific traditional terrace that offers some of the best car-watching in the capital. It's also one of the few cafés with a barman who knows how to make cocktails, an important consideration if you're not willing to dilute your buzz with food. When it's time to eat, there's a good selection of salads, sandwiches and steaks. While standards here never fell below what the French describe as "correct," meaning acceptable, Select is no Cordon Bleu. Rather its a place to fuel up, meet a friend, and linger over a bowl of soup or a cup of coffee.

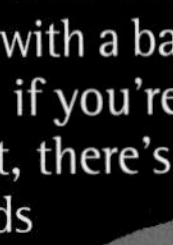

bREAkfASt & BRUNCh

Parisians seldom eat breakfast in restaurants, if at all. For most locals the "most important meal of the day" consists of little more than a croissant and coffee. Artists, writers and visitors are luckier. For us, every day is brunchable, and we can always find a seat. Most cafés are perfect for morning meals (see above), though you may prefer to pop into the corner patisserie or boulangerie.

Many of the restaurants listed above serve breakfast and/or brunch, including **Angélina, Café Marly,** Le Loir dans la Théière, **Le Square Trousseau,** and **Coffee Parisien.** Some restaurants listed under "Meals After Midnight" are also serving 24/seven. The places below are especially known for morning meals and are highly recommendable.

Café Beaubourg

43 Rue St-Merri (4th). **Tel.** *01.48.87.63.96. Open Mon-Thurs & Sun 8am-1am, Fri-Sat 8am-2am.* **Kitchen open** *Mon-Thurs & Sun 8am-midnight, Fri-Sat 8am-1am;* **Main Courses** *€13.70-€16.75. AE , MC. V.* M *Hôtel-de-Ville*

The brothers' Costes stylish postmodern Café Beaubourg overlooks the crowded Pompidou Centre plaza with one of the finest terraces around. This ultimate 1980s designer café remains a haven for hipsters who hold court with their cell phones while watching the world go by. The simple fare is perfect for breakfast or brunch, and they do a great flash-fried steak tartare.

Joe Allen

30 Rue Pierre-Lescot (1st). Tel. 01.42.36.70.13. Kitchen open daily noon-1am. Average meal €25. AE, MC, V. M *Etienne-Marcel*

With outposts in New York, London and Paris, Joe Allen has become something of an upscale Planet Hollywood to the theater world. The restaurant earns mention here for its excellent American-style weekend brunches, which include such soul-stirrers as pancakes, eggs, bacon, toast, sausage, fresh juices and American coffee. Brunch is served Saturday and Sunday from noon to 2pm.

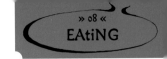

tEA ROOMS & dESSERtS

Angélina

226 Rue de Rivoli (1st). **Tel.** *01.42.60.82.00.* **Kitchen open** *Mon-Fri 9am-7pm, Sat-Sun 9am-730pm. Complete tea service about €18. AE, MC, V.* **M** *Tuileries*

Everyone from tourists to local grandmothers goes to this celebrated salon de thé with marble-topped tables and belle époque decor for two treats: mud-thick hot cocoa (called "l'Africain" and served in a pitcher with a side of unsweetened whipped cream) and the equally rich Mont Blanc pastries (meringue and Chantilly cream covered with strands of chestnut cream). Never mind that the service is *blasé* and there's always a line. The shabby-chic interior and waitresses who look like they've been here since the beginning make this Tuileries-area hotspot a fashionable teatime favorite. It's great for breakfast and light lunches too.

Berthillon

31 Rue Saint Louis en l'Ile (4th). **Tel.** *01.43.54.31.61. Open Wed-Sun 10am-8pm. Closed school hols. From €3.20. No cards.* **M** *Pont-Marie*

There's a place behind Notre-Dame on the Ile St-Louis where ice cream dreams are made. Berthillon is Paris' most legendary spot to enjoy some of the world's best frozen desserts (the wild-strawberry sorbet!). No artificial ingredients defile its 60-plus ice cream flavors, which run from traditional chocolate to wild whiskey. But beware grouchy servers and sunny weekend days, when the wait can be interminable.

Café Maure de la Mosquee

39 Rue Geoffroy St-Hillaire (5th). **Tel.** *01.43.31.18.14. Open daily 9am-midnight. Tea and pastries about €6 V.* **M** *Monge/Jussieu*

Because luxury, calm and voluptuousness aren't everyone's cup of thé, we offer the café at the Mosquee de Paris, an exotic, tile-wrapped hangoutery that buzzes with Left Bank students, visiting foreigners, and the occasional African president. Terra-cotta tile and wrought-iron wall sconces prevail, giving the impression of the Moorish temple it is. The lights are dim and the tea is minty and sweet. Order a plate of flaky, honey-laced pastries and pray that heaven is this good.

Le Loir dans la Théière

3 Rue des Rosiers (4th). **Tel.** *01.42.72.90.61.* **Kitchen open** *daily 10am-7pm. Complete tea service about €15. MC, V.* **M** *St-Paul*

As comfortable as an old beret, this tearoom in the heart of the Marais is the ideal place to snuggle into an overstuffed armchair and install yourself for an afternoon. Good tea, homemade pastries and jumbo portions of homespun food (quiches are a specialty) mean you can curl up with a book or a friend and relax, chat or just daydream.

Mariage Frères

30-32 Rue du Bourg-Tibourg (4th). Tel. 01.42.72.28.11. Kitchen open daily noon-7pm. Brunch and afternoon tea menus €23. AE, MC, V. M *Hôtel-de-Ville*

Studded with handsome teapots, potted palms and ceiling fans, this Right Bank landmark still feels like the elegant colonial tea merchant it was. An island of serenity in the maddening Marais, Mariage Frères has been Paris' pre-eminent tea shop since its founding in 1854. Serving a mosaic of sandwiches and croques between 3 and 6pm, the dining room is perfect for lunch, or just a cuppa, along with cakes tarts, muffins and scones. The shop offers hundreds of varieties of leaves, buds and blends, served on clothed tables by knowledgeable (and good looking!) waiters in colonial attire. It aint cheap, but it's unforgettable.

Branches: *13 Rue des Grands-Augustins, 6th (tel. 01.40.51.82.50); 260 Rue du Faubourg St-Honoré, 8th (tel. 01.46. 22.18.54).*

Ladurée

16 Rue Royale (8th). Tel. *01.42. 60.21.79.* Kitchen open *Mon-Sat 830am-7pm, Sun 10am-7pm. Complete tea service about €25. AE, MC, V.* M *Madeleine*

Opened in 1862, a half-block from the Place de la Madeleine, Ladurée is the Nutcracker Suite come to life with romantic murals, enormous mirrors and an abundance of gilt trim. We love Ladurée's entire tea menu, from their infinitesimal cucumber sandwiches and state-of-the-art croissants, to their legendary macaroons (coffee, chocolate, pistachio, vanilla) and exquisite pastry selection. Ten different teas are served in heavy silver-plated pots. Regulars are happy to wait for a seat at one of the tiny marble-topped tables downstairs rather than be banished to the more spacious—but less animated—nonsmoking room up top.

Branch: *75 Ave. des Champs-Elysées, 8th (tel. 01.40.75.08.75).*

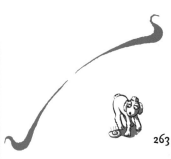

MENU dECOdER

Abats · · · · · · · · offal
Abricots · · · · · · · apricots
Agneau · · · · · · · lamb
Agnelet · · · · · · · young lamb
Aiglefin · · · · · · · haddock
Aiguillettes · · · · · thin slices
Ail · · · · · · · · · · · garlic
Aile · · · · · · · · · · wing
Aïoli · · · · · · · · · · mayonnaise, garlic, olive oil
Airelles · · · · · · · · cranberries
Algues · · · · · · · · seaweed
Allemande (à l') · · German style: with sauerkraut, sausages
Alose · · · · · · · · · shad
Alouette de mer · sandpiper
Aloyau · · · · · · · · beef sirloin
Alsacienne (à l') · Alsace style: with sauerkraut, sausage, foie gras (occasionally)
Amandes · · · · · · almonds
Amourettes · · · · ox or calf marrow
Ananas · · · · · · · · pineapple
Anchois · · · · · · · anchovy
Andalouse (à l') · Andalusian style: with rice, tomatoes, sweet red peppers
Andouille · · · · · · cold smoked sausage
Andouillette · · · · tripe sausage
Angevine (à l') · · Anjou style: with dry white wine, cream, mushrooms, onions
Anglaise (à l') · · · English style: plain boiled
Anguilles · · · · · · eels
Arachides · · · · · · peanuts
Ardennaise (à l') · Ardenne style: with juniper berries
Artichaut · · · · · · artichoke
Asperges · · · · · · · asparagus
Assiette (de) · · · · plate (of)
Aubergine · · · · · eggplant
Aulx · · · · · · · · · · garlic (plural)
Aumonière · · · · · pancake
Auvergnate (à l') · Auvergne style: with cabbage, sausage, bacon
Avelines · · · · · · · hazelnuts

Baies · · · · · · · · · berries
Baigné · · · · · · · · bathed in
Bar · · · · · · · · · · · sea bass
Barbarie · · · · · · · Barbary duck
Basilic · · · · · · · · basil
Basquaise (à l') · · Basque style: with ham, rice, peppers
Bavette · · · · · · · skirt of beef
Béatilles (Malin de) livers, kidneys, sweetbreads, cocks-combs
Belons · · · · · · · · flat-shelled oysters
Beurre · · · · · · · · butter
Bifteck · · · · · · · · steak
Bisque · · · · · · · · shellfish soup
Bombe · · · · · · · · ice cream
Bordelaise (à la) · Bordeaux style: with shallots, red wine, beef marrow
Bouquet · · · · · · · prawn
Bourguignonne (à la) Burgundy style: with red wine, onions, bacon, mushrooms
Braisé · · · · · · · · · braised
Brési · · · · · · · · · · thin slices of dried beef
Bretonne (à la) · · Brittany style: with celery, leeks, beans, mushrooms
Brochettes (de) · · meat or fish on a skewer
Broutard · · · · · · young goat
Brugnon · · · · · · · nectarine

Cagouilles · · · · · snails
Caille (Caillette) · quail
Calmars · · · · · · · squid
Canard · · · · · · · · duck
Caneton (canette) duckling
Cannelle · · · · · · · cinnamon
Carpe · · · · · · · · · carp
Carré (de) · · · · · · loin (of)
Carrelet · · · · · · · flounder/plaice
Carvi · · · · · · · · · caraway seeds
Cassis · · · · · · · · · blackcurrants
Céleri · · · · · · · · · celery
Cerises (noires) · · cherries (black)
Cerneaux · · · · · · walnuts
Cervelas · · · · · · · garlicky pork sausage
Cervelle · · · · · · · brains
Champignons · · · mushrooms
Chanterelles · · · · apricot-coloured mushrooms
Chantilly · · · · · · sweetened whipped-cream
Chapon · · · · · · · capon
Charcuterie · · · · · coldcut meats
Châtaignes · · · · · chestnuts
Chaude · · · · · · · · hot
Chevreuil · · · · · · roe-deer
Chicon · · · · · · · · chicory
Chicorée · · · · · · · curly endive
Chinois (à la) · · · Chinese style: with bean sprouts, soy sauce
Chou (vert) · · · · · cabbage
Chou rouge · · · · red cabbage
Chou-fleur · · · · · cauliflower
Choucroute · · · · kraut, pepper-corns, boiled ham, potatoes, sausages
Choux de Bruxelles Brussels sprouts
Ciboules · · · · · · · onions
Ciboulettes · · · · · chives
Cidre · · · · · · · · · cider
Citron · · · · · · · · · lemon
Citron vert · · · · · lime
Civet · · · · · · · · · · stew
Cochon · · · · · · · pig
Colin · · · · · · · · · hake
Colvert · · · · · · · · wild duck
Concombres · · · · cucumbers
Confit(e) · · · · · · · preserved in fat
Congre · · · · · · · · conger eel
Coques · · · · · · · · cockles
Coquillages · · · · shellfish
Coquilles St-Jacques scallops
Côte d'agneau · · lamb chop
Côte de boeuf · · side of beef
Côte de veau · · · veal chop
Coulis (de) · · · · · thick sauce (of)
Courge · · · · · · · · pumpkin
Crabe · · · · · · · · · crab
Cresson · · · · · · · watercress
Crêtes · · · · · · · · · cocks-combs
Crevettes grises · · shrimp
Crevettes roses · · prawns
Cru · · · · · · · · · · · raw
Cuisses (de) · · · · legs (of)
Cuissot (de) · · · · haunch (of)
Cul · · · · · · · · · · · haunch or rear
Culotte · · · · · · · · rump (usually steak)

Dattes · · · · · · · dates
Dieppoise (à la) · · Dieppe style: with white wine, cream, mussels, shrimp
Dinde · · · · · · · · · young turkey hen
Dindon · · · · · · · · turkey
Douceurs · · · · · · desserts

Echalotes · · · · · shallots
Echine · · · · · · · · spare ribs
Ecrevisses · · · · · · freshwater crayfish
Encornets · · · · · · cuttlefish
Endive · · · · · · · · chicory
Entrecôte · · · · · · rib steak
Epaule · · · · · · · · shoulder
Eperlan · · · · · · · smelt
Epinards · · · · · · · spinach
Epis de maïs · · · · sweetcorn
Escalope · · · · · · · thinly cut (meat or fish)
Escargots · · · · · · snails
Espadon · · · · · · · swordfish
Estrilles · · · · · · · crabs
Exocet · · · · · · · · flying fish

Faisan(e) · · · · · · pheasant
Farci(e) · · · · · · · · stuffed
Faux-fillet · · · · · sirloin steak
Favouilles · · · · · · spider crabs
Fenouil · · · · · · · · fennel
Fèves · · · · · · · · · broad beans
Figues · · · · · · · · figs
Flageolets · · · · · · kidney beans
Flétan · · · · · · · · halibut
Foie · · · · · · · · · · liver
Foie gras · · · · · · goose liver
Fraises · · · · · · · · strawberries
Framboises · · · · · rasberries
Fricedelles · · · · · meat balls
Frit · · · · · · · · · · · fried
Froid · · · · · · · · · cold
Fromage · · · · · · · cheese
Fruits de mer · · · seafood
Fumé · · · · · · · · · smoked
Fumet · · · · · · · · fish stock

Gambas	big prawns
Gardons	small roach
Gaufre	waffle
Géline	chicken
Genièvre	juniper
Gésier	gizzard
Gibier	game
Gigot	leg
Gingembre	ginger
Girofle	clove
Glace	ice cream
Graisse	fat
Granité	water ice
Gratin	browned
Grenade	pomegranate
Grenadin	thick veal escalope
Grenouilles	frogs
Grillé(e)	grilled
Grisets	mushrooms
Groseilles	currants
Groseilles	gooseberries
Gyromitres	fungi
Hachis	minced or chopped-up
Hareng	herring
Haricot (de)	stew (of)
Haricots	beans
Hochepot	thick stew
Homard	lobster
Huile	oil
Huîtres	oysters
Jambon	ham
Joue (de)	cheek (of)
Judru	pork sausage
Jus	juice
Lait	milk
Laitue	lettuce
Langouste	spiny lobster or crawfish
Langue	tongue
Lapereau	young rabbit
Lapin	rabbit
Lard	bacon
Lardons	strips of bacon
Lèche	thin slice
Légumes	vegetables
Lièvre	hare
Limande	lemon sole
Limon	lime
Longe	loin
Lotte de mer	monkfish
Loup de mer	sea bass
Lyonnaise (à la)	Lyonnaise style: with wine, onions, vinegar
Magret (de canard)	breast (of duck)
Mandarine	tangerine
Mangues	pea pods
Maquereaux	mackerel
Marcassin	young wild boar
Marjolaine	marjoram
Marrons	chestnuts
Merlan	whiting/hake
Mérou	grouper
Miel	honey
Milanaise (à la)	Milan style: dipped in breadcrumbs, egg, cheese
Oeufs durs	hard-boiled eggs
Oie	goose
Oignon	onion
Oison	gosling
Onglet	flank of beef
Oreilles	ears
Orléannaise (à la)	Orléans style: with chicory, potatoes
Oursins	sea urchins
Pain	bread
Paleron	shoulder
Pamplemousse	grapefruit
Panais	parsnip
Panier	basket
Paon	peacock
Parisienne (à la)	Paris style: with leeks, potatoes
Parmentier	potatoes
Passe-pierres	seaweed
Pastèque	watermelon
Pâté	baked chopped meats, served cold
Pâte	pastry/dough
Pâtes (fraîches)	fresh pasta
Patte	claw/foot/leg
Peau (de)	skin (of)
Pêche	peach
Perche	perch
Perdreau	partridge
Persil	parsley
Pigeonneau	young pigeon
Pilou	drumstick
Piments doux	sweet peppers
Pintadeau	young guinea fowl
Pleurotes	mushrooms
Plie franche	plaice
Poêlé	fried
Poire	pear
Poireaux	leeks
Pois	peas
Poisson	fish
Poitrine	breast
Polonaise (à la)	Polish style: with buttered breadcrumbs, parsley, hard-boiled eggs
Pommes	apples
Pommes de terre	potatoes
Porc	pork
Porcelet	suckling pig
Portugaise (à la)	Portuguese style: with fried onions, tomatoes
Potage	thick soup
Poulet	chicken
Poulette	young chicken
Poulpe	octopus
Poussin	small baby chicken
Praslin	caramelised
Primeurs	young vegetables
Provençale (à la)	Provençal style: with tomatoes, garlic, olive oil
Pruneaux	prunes
Prunes	plums
Purée	mashed
Queues	tails
Radis	radish
Ragoût	stew
Raifort	horseradish
Raisins	grapes
Ravioles	ravioli
Rissettes	small sweetbreads
Riz	rice
Rognons	kidneys
Romarin	rosemary
Rôti	roast
Rouget	red mullet
Royans	fresh sardines
Salé	salted
Sang	blood
Sanglier	wild boar
Saucisson	dry sausage
Saumon	salmon
Sauvage	wild
Scarole	endive/chicory
Scipion	cuttlefish
Seiches	squid
Sel	salt
Selle	saddle
Sourdons	cockles
Spaghettis (de)	thin strips (of)
St-Jacques	scallops
Strasbourgeoise (à la)	Strasbourg style: choucroute, foie gras, bacon
Sucre	sugar
Suppions	small cuttlefish
Tapé(e)	dried
Tartare	raw minced beef
Thé	tea
Thon	tuna
Thym	thyme
Tomates	tomatoes
Tortue	turtle
Tourteaux	large crabs
Tranche	slice
Tripettes	small tripe
Truffes	truffles
Truite	trout
Valenciennes (à la)	Valencia style: with rice, red peppers, onions, tomatoes, white wine
Vapeur (à la)	steamed
Veau	veal
Venaison	venison
Ventre	belly/breast
Vernis	clams
Viande	meat
Vinaigre	vinegar
Vol au vent	puff-pastry case
Volaille	poultry
Xérès	sherry
Yaourt	yogurt
Zeste (d'orange)	rubbing from (orange)

Nº 09

ENtERtAiNiNG

NiGhtLifE

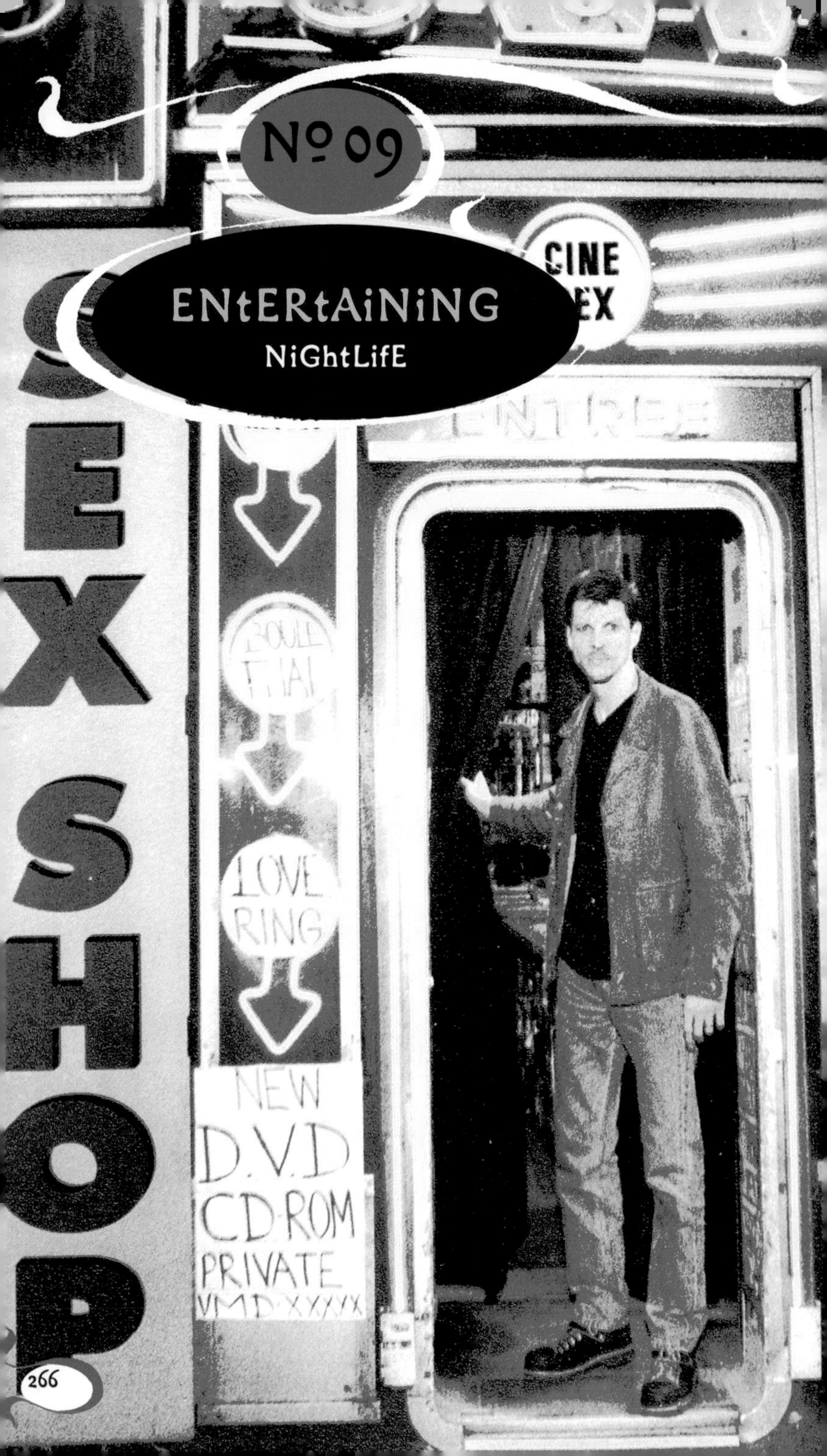

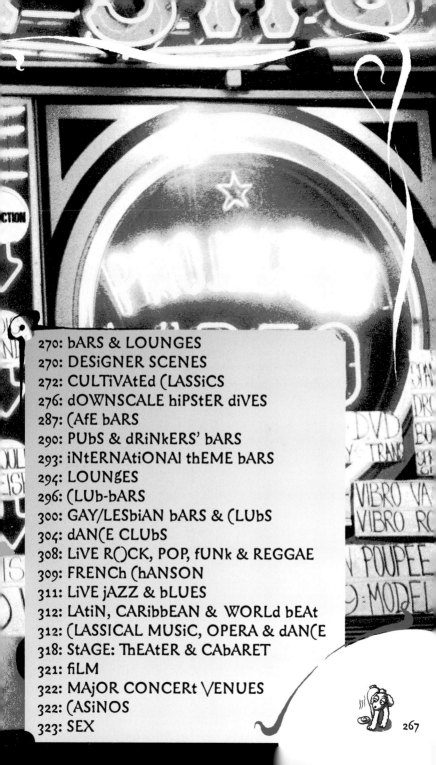

"Paris folks are quite content with gazing at the gazers" wrote Victor Hugo, "and can even regard a wall with intense interest when they think there is something going on behind it." The world capital of fashion still has plenty of places in which to flaunt ones feathers.

In addition to traditional cafes, British-style pubs and upscale, old skool bars, Paris sports a growing number of designer scenes catering to the usual smattering of media elite and modelizers. The city has also taken a page from New York's nightlife scene with the establishment of the lounge—relaxed, cozy spaces designed with comfy couches and low tables, perfectly positioned to accommodate Y-shaped glasses and small plates of food. Often attached to a kitchen, lounges blur the line between restaurant and bar. They are places where you are meant to *install* yourself and imbibe on an expensive roster of retro cocktails—Martinis, Manhattans, Negronis and Cosmopolitans.

Paris' nightlife is thriving and intense, with dozens of passionate subcultures: experimental turntablism, hardcore jungle, decadent cabaret, artistic "happenings," post-ironic raves... all this despite the fact that drugs are far less common in Paris than they are in London and New York.

Vast public subsidies have created a "serious" music scene in Paris that positively hums with activity. Of course, public money comes with the burden of political interference, so that the local music culture seems perpetually broiled in Gallic scandal. A change of government usually comes with a corresponding artistic shake up, whereby a conductor can suddenly find herself without an orchestra. Fashion plays a big role too. As quickly as a chamber ensemble became the flavor of the month, they spoil into box office poison. *C'est la vie.*

To find out what's happening before you get to town, check out *avantguide.com*, where you'll find links to everything cultural that's happening in the city from theater and music to film, fashion and food. Once you arrive, head to the nearest newsstand, check-out the metropolis' mediascape and stock-up on the city's listings magazines.

Pariscope, published Wednesdays, is indispensable for its comprehensive inventory of current cultural events. Unfortunately it's all in French, except for the last few pages which are prepared in English by Time Out magazine. It's available at newsstands throughout the city.

Novamagazine, a French-language monthly, has the Capital's most avant bar and club listings.

Time Out Paris Free Guide, published quarterly, is an excellent cultural update. It's distributed in hotels, bars and shops frequented by Anglophones.

Paris Voice is a decent arts and entertainment monthly that usually has a juicy nugget or two tossed into an otherwise lackluster mix of upcoming cultural events. It's available free at book shops and bars around town.

NIGHTLIFE AREAS

Most of the city's nightspots are huddled together in the 3rd, 6th, 8th, and 11th arrondissements.

The Bastille is the hottest area for mainstream clubs and bars, followed by Oberkampf (artsy hipsters), Marais (rhymes with "gay") and Ménilmontant (the next wave). St-Germain is known for studenty bars, live jazz, and some fun and friendly Latin dance clubs. The Arc de Triomphe area is home to Eurotrash clubs like Le Queen, and Pigalle is known for sex, sex, sex, along with some excellent jazzeries hidden down side streets.

bARS & LOUNgES

dESiGNER S(ENES

B*fly

49 Ave. George V (8th). **Tel.** *01.53.67.84.60.* **Open** *Mon-Fri noon-3pm and 6pm-2am, Sat 7pm-2am, Sun noon-4pm and 7pm-2am.* **M** *George V*

Fooling plenty with its self-conscious hipness, B*fly remains a mega-popular extravaganza for rich and single Euro men, and the Versace-wearing women who love them. If you enjoyed "Barfly," the cult book by writer-cum-functioning-alcoholic Charles Bukowski, be advised: This place would give him the dry heaves. Firstly, young Bukowski couldn't have afforded a drink here–much less the sushi. Second, because his idea of a nightspot was what he would probably call "a real bar" (and we might call "an old-man bar"), he wouldn't even attempt to peacock past the Neanderthal bouncers, take attitude from the sharply dressed host and servers, and sardine in with best-quaffed crowd in Europe. Then again, Bukowski is dead, and the aforementioned sardines are attractive indeed....

China Club

50 Rue de Charenton (12th). **Tel.** *01.43.43.82.02.* **Open** *Mon-Thurs and Sun 7pm-2 am, Fri-Sat 7pm-3am. Closed mid-July to mid-August.* **M** *Ledru-Rollin*

One of the most romantic spaces in town, this elegant favorite just off the Bastille track is worth seeking out–and returning to. It's all good. The cellar speakeasy (open from 10pm) features live jazz on weekends and the ground-level lounge is exceedingly comfortable. But what we really treasure is the sexy upstairs bar, in which you and, ideally, a date, can plunge into an opium dream of old Hong Kong. Lavish furnishings, wooden flooring, lacquered walls, Chinese lamps—sadly, only the opium is absent. Substitute it with The Chinaman (gin fizz with mint) or another pricey-but-worth-it cocktail.

Chao-Ba Café

22 Blvd. de Clichy (18th) Tel. 01.46.06.72.90. Open Sun-Wed 11am-2am, Thurs 11am-4am, Fri-Sat 11am-5am. **M** *Pigalle*

To anyone who says Pigalle is merely a sordid waste dump of Parisian nightlife, we offer Chao-Ba, a splendid lounge which occupies the former premises of the grand old Café Pigalle. Damn-near everything about this subdued-yet-glamorous evocation of French-Indochina is stylishly *au courant*: The exotic drinks, the decent pan-Asian food, the cushioned bamboo armchairs, the unobtrusively funky music, and the upscale and unpretentious crowd. The bar itself is one of the sleekest in town, featuring a curious, continuously-moving booze delivery apparatus. Perhaps that gadget is too showy by half, but everyone's enjoying themselves too much to mind. And that huge bust by the door? By golly, it's Ho Chi Minh—the very man who helped to put Colonial style out of business.

Le Comptoir

37 rue Berger (1st). **Tel.** *01.40.26.26.66.* **Open** *Mon-Thurs and Sun noon-2am, Fri-Sat noon-3am.* M *Châtelet*

Mate a *tres*-glossy Parisian café with a mysterious Moorish salon, add a beautiful poseur crowd, and you start to picture this superb Les Halles hangoutery. For every North African touch–every exotic couch, carpet, lamp and mosaic–there's a Continental analogue. Witness the glamorous curved bar, the iridescent lighting and the better-than-adequate canned music. There's plenty of room to lounge and a fairly extensive bar menu to boot.

Costes Bar

Hôtel Costes, 239 Rue St-Honoré (1st). **Tel.** *01.42.44.50.25.* **Open** *nonstop.* M *Tuileries*

As minuscule as it is magical, the bar of Paris' hippest hotel is an appropriately upscale nightspot known as the place where fashion and film folk flock for great champagne cocktails. On weekends the bar spins sophisticated house and dub compilations by DJ Stéphane Pompougnac. And any day of the week you can expect modelicious miniskirts and macroscopic prices.

Le Fumoir

6 Rue de l'Amiral-de-Coligny (1st). **Tel.** *01.42.92.00.24.* **Open** *daily 11am-2am.* M *Louvre-Rivoli*

The owners of China Club have built on their loungy success with this stylish spot. The secret here is lots of space, contemporary European décor, better-than-average art, good music, and a prize location near the Louvre. We also love the back library, which has a more extensive and eccentric collection than some local book shops (Where else can you find *The Art Of Kissing* and *Trouble With Lichens* on the same shelf?). The crowd is reliably *branche* (plugged-in) and the international waitstaff (Claire from San Francisco, Astrid from former Yugoslavia, and Maha from Mars) is always extremely welcoming. There's also a full menu of sturdy, if overpriced, food.

Le Zorba

137 Rue du Faubourg-du-Temple (10th). **Tel.** *01.42.39.68.68.* **Open** *daily 5am-2am.* M *Belleville.*

If you happen to be in Belleville, trot over to this small joint that's almost always brimming with sexy people with names like Matthieu and Tatiana. Forget the nondécor, order a strong cocktail and enjoy the rattle and hum that you've come for. And when you're done, you can stumble over to the Métro station in about thirty seconds.

CULTiVATEd CLASSiCS

La Closerie Des Lilas

171 Blvd. de Montparnasse (6th). **Tel.** *01.40.51.34.50.* **Open** *daily noon–1am.* M *Vavin*

Chic, low-key thirtysomethings, Montparnasse intellectuals, and a smattering of celebs (Woody Allen was spied here) favor the "Lily Hothouse" for its relaxing atmosphere, live piano music and top-notch cocktails. The warm brown decor includes stylish mosaic flooring, marble lamps and some of the loveliest rest rooms in the city. A large, 19th-century tintype photograph depicts the bar in a former heyday, when Picasso, Man Ray, Apollinaire, Vladimir Lenin and other stars got drunk here. Gold plaques set into each table indicate where the famous regulars sat. Like the bar, the adjacent restaurant/brasserie is costly but superb.

Harry's New York Bar

5 Rue Daunou (2nd). **Tel.** *01.42.61.71.14.* **Open** *daily 1030am-4am.* M *Opéra*

Harry's is a bona fide Paris institution; so you probably thought we'd hate it. But in truth, the birthplace of the Bloody Mary and the Sidecar is a stone delight. The bar at "Sank Roo Doe Noo" has had a devoted following for almost a century. And not just with readers of the *International Herald Tribune*. Frenchies love this place too. So make light of the high prices, ignore the tourists and focus on the task at hand. Dig the speakeasy exterior and the slick cherrywood walls. Dig the graceful curlicues on the ceiling, the ancient, polished tables and the spotless aprons the barmen still wear. If you can, snag the round banquette near the staircase, from which you have unobstructed views. And be sure to check out the circular piano bar downstairs.

Hemingway Bar

Hôtel Ritz, 15 Place Vendôme (1st). **Tel.** *01.43.16.33.65.* **Open** *Tues-Sat 630pm-2am. Closed July 25-Aug 25.* M *Madeleine/Tuileries/Concorde*

To reach "Le Petit Bar," as it was called in the 1920s when Ernest Hemingway frequently drank here, you have to negotiate your way through what seems like a kilometer-long corridor of glass cases containing even more gemstones than Diana ever owned. It's intolerably ostentatious, of course, but nevertheless instructive, as it none-too-subtly signals the prices you're about to pay for drinks. And pay you should, because it's a terrific bar with an understated elegance that's nowhere as stuffy as the ultra-exclusive Ritz Hôtel in which it's located. And when they wind up the mint-condition Victrola, the vibe's not just romantic, it's downright magical. Blond-wood walls, *faux* bookshelves behind the bar, tons of photos of Guess Who everywhere, and a surprisingly friendly staff would all make Papa proud.

La Closerie des Lilas
AMERICAN BAR
LENINE

Bar Lutèce

Hôtel Lutétia, 45 Blvd. Raspail (6th). **Tel.** *01.49.54.46.76.* **Open** *daily 11am-1am.* M *Sèvres-Babylone*

Frequented by a rare mix of staid tourists, buttoned-up businessmen, Left Bank literary types and the occasional actor ("La Deneuve" included), the Hôtel Lutétia bar is one of the best all-purpose watering holes around. Attractions include whiffs of romance and intrigue created by exquisite shabby-chic décor. The pink-marble flooring and colored glass ceiling sandwiches über-comfy red velvet chairs, oversized drapery, iron grillwork, and bronze sculptures by Arman and Cesar, some of which incorporate working lamps. Drinks are excellent, and live jazz combos entertain Wednesday through Saturday evenings from 10pm.

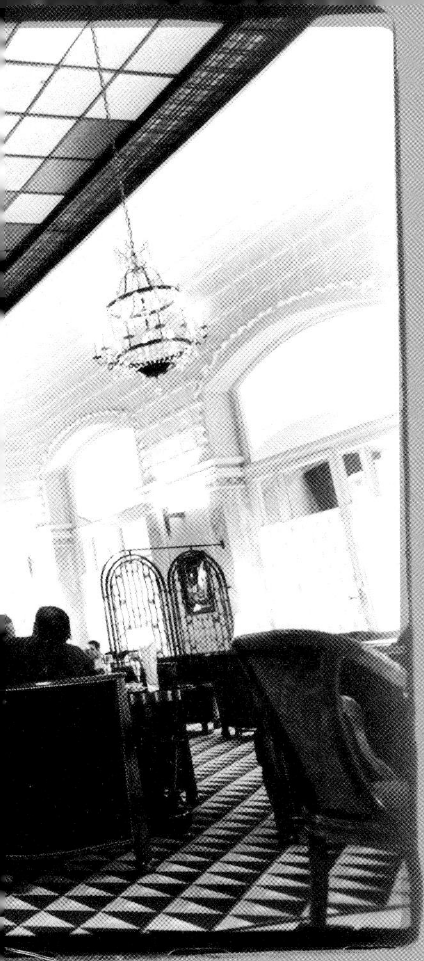

La Muse Vin

101 rue de Charonne (11th). **Tel.** *01.40.09.93.05.* **Open** *Mon-Sat noon-2pm and 8-11pm.* M *Charonne*

Popular, stylish, groovy and all that, this fabulousnes wine bar draws a terrific crowd and feels like a happening party almost every night of the week. There's an excellent selection of offbeat wines from throughout France, served with simple, small dishes that will want to make you stay all night. Reservations are essential.

Le Rosebud

11 bis Rue Delambre (14th). **Tel.** *01.43.20. 44.13.* **Open** *daily 7pm-2am.* M *Vavin*

If Harry's Bar were stripped of all its quasi-American trappings, thoroughly doused with old Montparnasse ambiance and filled with the echoes of vintage jazz, you'd have something very like the Rosebud. The art nouveau front door opens into a room that's all low lights, polished surfaces, red lacquered tables, black banquettes and white-jacketed waiters who will actually keep your cell phone safe, should you accidentally leave it here in a drunken stupor (as we ourselves discovered!). The cocktails are potent and several nooks and crannies seem purpose-built for snogging. Le Rosebud attracts a graying clientele on the prowl for–well, each other. Which is to say, the joint ain't exactly hopping with tight young things, but is a far more egalitarian cross-section of everyone.

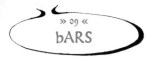

Downscale Hipster Dives

Le Bar Dix

10 Rue de l'Odéon (6th). **Tel.** *01.43.26.66.83.* **Open** *Mon–Sat 5pm–2am, Sun 5pm–1230am.* M *Odéon*

One of our favorite bars in the Odéon area, Le Dix attracts a hippy-ish French-and-expat crowd with a "10" on the front door (the address and name in one package), a vast collection of art nouveau posters, a jukebox that runs the gamut from Guns'n'Roses and Yves Montant to Pink Floyd and Pachabel's Canon, and lip-smackingly good Sangria (no one here seems to drink anything else). To be against this place is to be against life.

Bob Cool

15 Rue des Grands Augustins (6th). **Tel.** *01.46.33.33.77.* **Open** *daily 5pm–2am.* M *Odéon*

A fun little hipster bar near L'Assignat, appropriately-named le Bob has cool cocktails, a cool collection of vintage shakers, a cool old oak bar, cool board games (including our sentimental favorite, "Shut The Box"), and a clientele that's, quite frankly, often cooler than the rest of the Odéon crowd.

Chez Georges

11 Rue des Cannettes (6th). **Tel.** *01.43.26.79.15.* **Open** *Tues–Sat noon–2am. Closed Aug.* M *Mabillon*

There's a whole slew of bars on the lively Rue des Cannettes and this is our favorite of the slew. The reason? Freedom of choice. First, there's an impressively atmospheric basement cave (think candles, long wooden tables, and music that ranges from "New York, New York" and Spanish flamenco to French *chansons* and Jorge Ben's "Pais Tropical"). But when you weary of guzzling beer and making a beast of yourself in a basement full of students and expats, you can retreat to the equally atmospheric street-level bar, a mellower environment infused with the rich history of its cabaret beginnings (Those photos!). As George's children (the current owners) are fond of saying, "When you prefer the upstairs to the downstairs, you know your youth is behind you." Hence, Chez Georges is capable of doing what only the greatest people, places, and things can do: It teaches you something important about yourself.

The Bottle Shop

5 Rue Trousseau (11th). **Tel.** *01.43.14.28.04.* **Open** *daily 1130am-2am.* M *Ledru-Rollin*

With a copper ceiling and luminous orange walls, this small local dive on the edge of the Bastille is pretty, um, "pretty," for lack of a better adjective. Though British in name, it's most popular with American backpackers who are not only the primary customers (a popular, cheap hotel is around the corner), they're also the employees. The BS is situated close the Père Lachaise cemetery, making it a fine stop after visiting the grave of Jim Morrison.

VINS

Café Charbon

109 Rue Oberkampf (11th).
Tel. *01.43.57.55.13.* **Open** *daily 9am-2am.* M *Parmentier*

A pioneer of Oberkampf nightlife some half-dozen years ago, le Charbon remains the *sin qua non* of hotspots there, for the simple reason that few settings in Paris are as enchanting. Built as a typical *fin-de-siècle* dancehall in 1895, the Charbon is set with luscious banquets, gas lamps, cut-glass chandeliers, gilded mirrors, enchanting murals and a quartz-topped bar. The key to Café Charbon's charm is not that it has been *restored,* but *preserved.* The color of chocolate–which is the color of practically everything inside–has never seemed so soulful. Meanwhile, the drinks are cheap, the service is not quite as lackadaisical as at many other "Oberkampferies" (though, come closing time, they'll eject you with less delicacy than you'd like), the toilets—well, never mind the toilets, and the crowd is from all over the hipster map. An absolute must.

Les Etages

35 Rue Vielle-du-Temple (3rd). **Tel.** *01.42.78.72.00.* **Open** *Mon-Fri 5pm-2am, Sat-Sun noon-2am.* M *Saint-Paul*

It's a safe bet that the door will get stuck as you enter this ramshackle and quite affordable little tapas bar–it's been that way for years. Go further into the core of Les Etages, where the staircase at the bartender's right leads you into what unexpectedly turns out to be a bohemian dream: five story's worth of sparsely furnished rooms just waiting to be filled by you and your friends. So come, see and colonize. It's whatever you make of it–and who doesn't dig a blank slate every now and then?

La Folie En Tête

33 Rue de la Butte-aux-Cailles (13th). **Tel.** *01.45.80.65.99.*
Open *Mon-Sat 5pm-2am.* M *Place d'Italie*

"Lunacy in the head" is a terrific little bar in the bohemian enclave of Butte-aux-Cailles. In the 1970s the Butte was punk-rock ground zero, a history the bar celebrates by sponsoring its own anarchistic cable-access TV show. The old punky frisson is here too, in the *faux* absinthe advertisement *("Toujours fort"),* the inexpensive drinks, the traffic light outside the squatter-toilet that signals "free" or "occupied," the exotic musical instruments on the walls, the comic book library, the pair of old skis stashed behind the seats. Matter of fact, the only thing *not* punky about La Folie are the patrons, who are just affably grungy students and locals.

Le Lèche-Vin

13 Rue Daval (11th). **Tel.** *01.43.55.98.91.* **Open** *daily 630pm-130am.* **M** *Bastille*

Le Lèche-Vin is French for "lick wine" but it's called "the Jesus bar" by regulars because the walls are completely covered with hardcore Christian imagery–plus a few photos of Hasidic rabbis thrown in for good measure. Lest you think they mean business, step into the toilet which is adorned with "hardcore" of a rather different sort. Rather than being a run-of-the-mill theme bar with a compelling bathroom, Le Lèche-Vin is a Bastille institution; one in which a beautiful Norwegian woman is rumored to have turned water into wine. It's an authentic bohemian hole-in-the-wall, where drinks are cheap and wonderful, the music is exquisitely funky and the atmosphere is always welcoming. *Bibamus Papaliter* (Let us drink like the popes).

Le Mecano

99 Rue Oberkampf (11th). **Tel.** *01.40.21.35.28.* **Open** *daily 9am-2am.* **M** *Parmentier*

Le Mecano is another Oberkampf mainstay featuring the classic Oberkampf decay-décor, which local fashion designer Wingnut refers to as "cozily destroyed nostalgia." The shabby-chic she's referring to are the peeling murals, askew picture frames on bare ruby-red walls, battered old lamps, bent-up chandeliers, and grotty furniture... you know, cool stuff. It's all counterbalanced by an attractive, young boho mob scene most every night of the week.

Megalo

6 Rue de Lappe (11th). **Tel.** *01.48.05.05.12.* **Open** *daily 6pm-2am.* **M** *Bastille*

You have to love a joint where the burly bouncer actually greets strangers with a smile and a handshake, and appears sincere about it. Then there's the superb music–loud, happy and often deliciously obscure rock, the hilariously grotesque wall murals, and the earthy crowd. Megalo has what it takes for a great night out.

La Mercerie

98 Rue Oberkampf (11th). **Tel.** *01.43.38.81.30.* **Open** *Mon-Fri 5pm-2am, Sat-Sun 3pm-2am.* **M** *Parmentier*

Empty, you might think you've walked into the world's first Museum Of Shockingly Bad Wallpaper. Practically every surface in this newly expanded Oberkampf favorite has a different pattern to offend the eye. Most likely, though, this rocking bar will be full with the usual Oberkampf arts crowd and all you'll notice is truly wonderful music, the funky pseudo-stone cave in back, and Max, one of Paris' sexiest and most congenial barkeeps.

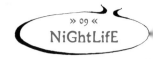

La Patache

60 Rue de Lancry (10th). **Tel.** *01.42.08.14.35.* **Open** *daily 7pm-2am.* **M** *Jacques Bonsergent*

La Patache is so old it's almost prehistoric. The entire bar is scorched and yellowed, the pictures have been there so long they've grafted to the walls, and the bartenders could know Jesus, literally. Needless to say, drinks are cheap, the clientele is the usual art-damaged suspects, and the jukebox is gonzo, containing everything from gospel and Gainsbourg to Morricone, Melanie and someone—or something—called "Fanny." Other notable artsy bars in this Canal Saint-Martin neighborhood are **L'Atmosphere**, 49 Rue Lucien-Sampaix, 10th (tel. 01.40.38.09.21) a chatty, cramped and "atmospheric" space featuring live and canned eclectica, and **La 25th Image**, 9 Rue des Recollets, 10th (tel. 01.40.35.80.88), across the street, which has a brighter and much more relaxed "image." **M** Château d'Eau.

Le Piano Vache

8 Rue Laplace (5th). **Tel.** *01.46.33.75.03.* **Open** *during school term Mon-Fri noon-2am, Sat-Sun 9pm-2am.* **M** *Maubert-Mutualite*

Goths of the world unite every Wednesday at this immensely lovable Latin Quarter tavern. That's when the *soirees gothique* attracts every dark-clad doom-and-gloomer in Gaul. What you get the rest of the week is a tiny, hundred-plus-year-old bar with rustic stone-and-wood décor, deliciously diverse DJ-spun sounds, poster wallpaper, and so many Sorbonne students that the joint should be declared an official branch of the school.

Pick-Clops

16 Rue Vielle-du-Temple (4th). Tel. 01.40.29.02.18. Open Mon-Sat 8am-2am, Sun 230pm-midnight (from 10am in summer). Ⓜ *Saint-Paul*

Although the bar's name evokes a French childhood game, the bar itself more closely resembles the bedroom of a slovenly teenager in the 1970s (the funny lighting, the rock music, the Stones poster–everything but the bed). The rough-and-tumble staff do their jobs adequately enough, though the beery customers hardly seem to care. In short, Pick-Clops is where straight people go slumming in the Marais, and its a great place for a delightfully crazy night.

Impala Lounge

2 Rue de Berri (8th). **Tel.** *01.43.59.12.66.*
Open *Mon-Tues 930am-2am, Wed-Thurs 930am-3am, Fri-Sat 930am-5am, Sun 930am-2am.* **M** *George V*

African in theme, Euro in style, the Impala Lounge is a tres chic style spot serving swanky cocktails along with chilly Afro beats and electro tunes, very much in the Buddha Bar mold (read: sceney crowd that draws from media, fashion and other trendy corners). The design is tribal masks and zebra skins, augmented by a kitchen that cooks Ostrich steaks.

Le Scherkhan

144 Rue Oberkampf (11th). **Tel.** *01.43.57.29.34.*
Open *daily 5pm-2am.*
M *Ménilmontant*

"Men Of The Sea Welcome" reads a crusty old sign in this equally crusty and wonderfully old-looking dive on Oberkampf's main drag. In addition to seamen (of which there is plenty), you'll find a more subdued genus of Oberkampf party warrior here, plus a quasi-café atmosphere, low lighting, plenty of seats, a stuffed tiger, and service that's not typical of the district—which is to say, pretty good. Oh yeah, cheap cocktails too. Extremely cheap ones.

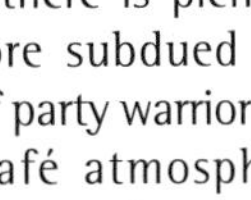

Le Sous Bock

49 Rue Saint-Honoré (1st). **Tel.** *01.40.26.46.61.* **Open** *daily 11am-5am.* **M** *Châtelet*

You want beer? There's beer here–four hundred brands. You want a dark-wood interior that's so hazy you can enjoy the sensation of smoking without buying cigarettes? You want the perfect place to hide from creditors, assassins, outraged parents, jealous spouses, other tourists, or the director of your latest pornographic film who's demanding that you shoot a few more scenes you simply don't have the energy for? Here's your ticket. Best of all, The Beer Mat is open very, very late.

Tabac Des Templiers

35 Rue de Rivoli (1st). Tel.01.42.72.00.07. **Open** *daily noon-2am.* **M** *Hôtel-de-Ville*

In a city rife with oddball bars, this low-rent nutter stands out to the point that we considered listing it in the Museums section of this book. Like the name says, this is not just a place to buy cigarettes, but a shrine to the Templar Knights, a mysterious order of Medieval crusaders whose leader was executed on the Pont-Neuf. Crammed with relics in glass cases, along with respectful photos of the latest uncrowned "dauphin," visitors quickly discover that this Tabac also pays tribute to the currently throneless French royals. Each year they hold a special ceremony mourning the beheading of Louis XVI. Are these people serious? We don't know; ask the cashier with the ZZ Top beard and the piercing eyes.

Le Tambour

41 Rue Montmartre (2nd). **Tel.** *01.42.33.06.90.* **Open** *nonstop.* **M** *Sentier*

It's been a week and we're still recovering from our latest visit to this one-in-a-million, round-the-clock bohemian mainstay. It's not just boozy mirth and merriment, but sheer aesthetic overload. How does one mentally process a joint where even the Swiss chalet-meets-Chinatown facade hardly prepares you for the visual cacophony inside? We're talking tables made of glazed psychedelic mosaics, and seats made from ancient Métro saddles. Miniature basketball nets hanging from the ceiling, Santa Claus grinning from the front window, an astronaut gaping from the rear wall, a makeshift library with Paris' second copy of *Trouble With Lichen* (see Le Fumoir, above), and an "Entrance For Artists" sign outside the toilets. The food and drink are cheap and plentiful, the music is old French *chanson,* the crowd is anything goes (and we do mean anything), and the barman–well, you'll have to see him for yourself. As you've gleaned by now, you have to see the whole thing for yourself. *Comprendez-vous?*

Café Iguana

15 Rue de la Roquette (11th). **Tel.** *01.40.21.39.99.* **Open** *Sun-Thurs 9am-4am, Fri-Sat 9am-5am.* M *Bastille*

Café Iguana is a clean well-located place that stays open very late indeed. But is it a bar or a café? Evidence for café status: It says "café" in the name, they serve solid café fare and, during the day, people come here to sip coffee, read, write, play backgammon, and argue about their troubled love affairs. Evidence for bar status: The décor is postmodernly frigid and, at night, the lighting is dimmed, dance music blares, and a bouncer warily eyes newcomers. Unusually in a neighborhood that gets increasingly less civilized as dawn approaches, the Iguana remains a reasonably civilized spot until closing time.

Café Thoumieux

4 Rue de la Comète (7th). **Tel.** *01.45.51.50.40.* **Open** *Mon-Fri noon-2am, Sat 5pm-2am.* M *La Tour-Maubourg*

When you find yourself with a yen to fraternize with the locals in the bourgeois, residential wasteland of the 7th, head directly to this impeccably decorated little lounge full of chic young Frenchies. Just a bit too dark to see beyond anyone's makeup, Thoumieux is known for world music in the air, wonderful tapas on the tables, and great servers by the bar. There's a terrific selection of flavored vodkas and one of the most beautiful red-velvet banquettes in Paris.

Au Général Lafayette

52 Rue Lafayette (9th). **Tel.** *01.47.70.59.08.* **Open** *daily 10am-4am.* M *Le Peletier*

Smack dab in the middle of an unexceptional neighborhood is an exceptional bar/restaurant/café that elegantly straddles the fence between loopy bohemian dive and cultivated snob emporium. An exemplar of tasteful mid-range drinking culture, le General is a light and airy 1920s-era dream, with chocolate banquettes, mint and lime mosaics, and a diverse, poseur-free crowd. There's an equally diverse cocktail selection and lots of rare beers. The onion soup kicks ass too–and they serve it until 4am.

iNtERNEt CAfES

Access Academy

60-62 rue St-André-des-Arts (6th). No phone. *www.accessacademy.com.* **Open** *daily 8am-2am.* M *Odéon.*

The largest Internet cafe in Paris, AA is a light and bright cyberspot with 400 software-packed PCs. The entire environment is automated, including paying, so that you don't have to deal with any pesky human beings.

Ars Longa

94 rue Jean-Pierre-Timbaud (11th). **Tel.** *01.43.55.47.71.* **Open** *Mon-Sat noon-8pm.* M *Couronnes.*

Ars Longa is one of the reasons that Oberkampf is hip: part contemporary-art exhibition space, part-Internet café, and part venue for twice-monthly "pluricultural" parties, this is a great space almost any day of the week. Music leans towards electronica, and prices are lights.

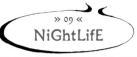

OthER CAfES

Breakfast in America

17 rue des Ecoles, Cardinal Lemoine, (5th). **Tel.** *01.43.54.50.28.*
Open *Mon-Thurs 830am-10pm, Fri-Sat 830am-1030pm, Sun 9am-9pm.*
M *Cardinal LeMoine or Jussieu*
Homesick Americans, and others who are simply hankering for a decent breakfast that consists of more than a croissant and coffee, flock to American Craig Carlson's Sorbonne-area spot. There aren't too many other places in Paris that pour filter coffee just like a real McCoy American-style coffee-shop. And the meat-and-egg morning meals are tops. BiA even has red-vinyl upholstered benches and gray Formica tabletops. Thankfully, Supertramp is not on the cafe's playlist.

Le Café Constant

139 rue St-Dominique (7th). **Tel.** *01.47.53.73.34.*
Open *Mon-Sat 730am-1030pm.* **M** *Ecole Militaire*
A terrific cafe by any measure, this is a friendly corner meeting place smack-dab in the heart of one of the lively little neighborhoods in Paris. Named for it's chef/owner, Christian Constant (whose pricier Le Violon d'Ingres is just down the block), this is a neighborhood place through and through, serving terrific traditional French bistro cooking just a short walk from the Eiffel Tower. Simple surrounding belie a thoughtful menu that changes daily, but is always full of inexpensive local comfort foods.

Café Léa

5 rue Claude-Bernard (5th). **Tel.** *01.43.31.46.30.*
Open *Mon-Sat 830am-2am, Sun 10am-2am.* **M** *Censier-Daubenton.*
Situated hard by the universities, and close to the Mouffetard market, this is an intensely popular student hangout with good sightlines, conversational sound levels, and an appealing surroundings built with urban déco brick-and-concrete. There are several other cafes on the same street, but this one is our favorite for low-key friendly welcome.

Le Tournesol

9 rue de la (14th). Montparnasse. **Tel.** *01.43.27.65.72.*
Open *daily 830am-1am.* **M** *Edgar-Quinet.*
The rue de la Gaîté is packed with gaudy sex shops, but it's also swimming with budget bistros and good cafes, and Le Tournesol is the best of the lot. The look here is nice industrial chic, complimented with eponymous sun-flowers. The good-looking multi-culti waitstaff keeps an ear on the music, which ranges from French chanson to classic jazz. You can just pop in for coffee, but if you need other fuel, you can count on good salads and other light meals.

PUbS & dRiNkERS' bARS

Le Bar Du Marche

16 Rue de Buci (6th). Tel. 01.43. 26.55.15. Open *daily 8am-2am.*
M *Mabillon*

Stroll into the triangle between the Métro stations Mabillon, Odéon and Seine and you'll find nondescript, studenty bars, cafes and restaurants galore. There's little distinctive about the immediate neighborhood, and little to distinguish this bar either, except that this is one of the hardest-partying places we know. Despite the fact that the waiters wear silly plaid berets, this place is never less than mobbed, even by day. When you're ready to rock hard, put Bar du Marche at the start of your Odéon crawl.

Boca Chica

58 Rue de Charonne (11th). Tel. 01.43.57.93.13. Open Sun-Thurs 10am-1 or 2am, Fri-Sat 10am-5am.
M *Ledru Rollin*

Boca Chica does for tapas in Paris what Spaniard Luis Buñuel did for film here. That's another way of saying that this chic Bastille hotspot is definitely a fave. We like the intimate front patio and the roomy, crimson interior. We like the iron tables, the Latin music and the fruity, powerful sangria. And we definitely like those tapas, which, at €4.50-€7.50 a pop, are priced just right. A fun crowd, too. You might even find Buñuel's "obscure object of desire" here, though ours had already left to a suite at Hôtel Costes....

Bugsy's

15 Rue Montalivet (8th). Tel. *01.42. 68.18.44.* Open *daily 9am-1am.*
M *Champs-Elysées Clémenceau*

If you get lost, ask a policeman for directions to this homey, good-time bar in the moneyed hinterland behind the Tuileries, because the motif here is gangsters, gangsters, gangsters. You can survey wall photos of the bad boys (and actors who played them) from an attractive metal bar, all the while getting rat-a-tat-tatted on honestly-priced drinks. Bugsy's is situated directly across the road from the monolithic Ministry of the Interior and, fittingly, has bathrooms labeled "Hoods" and "Molls." Despite the tourist-heavy crowd, Bugsy's is an eminently likable theme bar.

Café Oz

18 Rue Saint-Denis (1st). **Tel.** *01.40.39.00.18.* **Open** *daily 3pm-3am.* M *Châtelet*

"Good on ya," "fair dinkum" and all that, to this cavernous dose of Down Under in the heart of "Light City." Far more comfortable, and a tad less "Australian" than its cramped sister in the Latin Quarter (184 Rue St-Jacques, 5th; tel. 01.43.54.30.48), this rustic, wood-lined dance pub is busy nightly, attracting a predominately Anglo crowd, along with the odd Frog. By midnight, the music is locked into overdrive, courtesy of live combos and decent trip-hop/house deejays. But waltzing Matildas have to arrive before 11pm if they hope to get in the door. Prices are reasonable, there's Fosters on tap.

Freedom And Firkin

8 Rue de Berri (8th). **Tel.** *01.53. 75.25.50.* **Open** *daily 11am-2am.* M *Franklin D. Roosevelt*

After becoming one of the largest pub chains in London, the Firkin group is looking to colonize Paris with its trademark country-in-the-city decor and on-site micro-breweries. Like those back home, this Firkin is known to transform itself into a riotous sing-along party. Only it's better because they don't shoo everyone away at 11pm. The Firkin jokes, however, are wearing thin (The Firkin food! The Firkin toilets! The Firkin beers!). The pub is just a dart's throw from the Champs-Elysées.

Branch: Financier & Firkin, 15, Rue du Départ, 14th (tel. 01.40.47.60.33). M Montparnasse-Bienvenüe.

Le Violon Dingue

46 rue de la Montagne (5th). **Tel.** *01.43.25.79.93.* **Open** *Tues-Sat 8pm-5am.* M *Maubert Mutualité*

Where are all the American students in Paris, you ask? Look no further than this late-opening bar near the Panthéon. Blessed with a good selection of bottled beers, and bartenders who actually know how to mix cocktails, this is a loud and lively spot heaving with expats on the make, which makes this a good last stop on an otherwise unsuccessful night on the town.

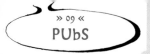

Kitty O'Shea's

10 Rue des Capucines (2nd). **Tel.** *01.40.15.00.30.* **Open** *daily noon-2am.* **M** *Opéra*

Convert the francs to lucre, escort the Frenchies to the door, and Kitty O'Shea's is channeling Dublin. A dead-ringer for any number of pubs in Eire, Kitty's is extremely friendly, intensely popular, and frequently rollicking with daily-breaders, here to loosen their chokers for a little bit of all right. The stained glass and Gaelic street signs are authentic, the booze is fairly priced for the neighborhood, and the food in the upstairs restaurant is so good that visiting Irish complain it isn't authentic. As an experiment, try chatting-up the bartender using the vernacular of a James Joyce novel. Either you'll get a discount—or kicked out.

The Frog & Princess

9 Rue Princesse (6th). **Tel.** *01.40.51.77.38.* **Open** *Mon-Fri 530pm-2am, Sat-Sun noon-2am.* **M** *Mabillon*

Rue Princesse, one of the liveliest streets in the lively 6th, is home to a spirited American restaurant (Coffee Parisien), a superb English-language book shop (The Village Voice), and several British-style pubs of variable quality. So why shouldn't there also be a big English brew-pub? From Mash Tun to Copper Hop Back, some very respectable beers are brewed on the premises, in exposed silver vats. There's serviceable pub grub too. The volume is high and the young crowd is Benneton-cultural. How popular is the Frog? Even on a cold and sleepy night in January it can be difficult to find a seat. And there are lots of seats. How good is the service? Extremely attentive, and mainly English. How good is the music? The last time we popped in they played Toni Basil's "Hey Mickey." Twice. You can't have everything.

Their sister pubs, **The Frog And Rosbif** (116 Rue Saint-Denis, 2nd; tel. 01.42.36.34.73), can get even wild and woollier, but without that great Rue Princesse location. **M** Etienne Marcel. **The Frog at Bercy Village** (25, cour St-Emilion, 12th; tel.01.43.40.70.71) is the largest of the Frog pubs located in a renovated historical wine warehouse. **M** St-Emilion. **The Frog & British Library** (113 Ave de France, 13th; tel. 01.45.84.34.26) is a bit out of the way unless you happen to be visiting Chinatown or the monolithical new Bibliothèque François Mitterand. **M** Bibliothèque.

PARiS: iNTERNAtIONAL CITY Of ThEME BARS»

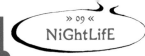

AUSTRALIA

Café Oz, *18 Rue Saint-Denis (1st).* **Tel.** *01.40.39.00.18. Open daily noon-3am.* M *Châtelet. Branch: 184 Rue Saint-Jacques (5th)* Tel. *01.43.54.30.48. Open daily noon-2am.* M *Luxembourg.*

The Outback, 42 Rue Cardinal Lemoine (5th). Tel. 01.43.26.96.59. Open Mon-Sat 2pm-2am. M Cardinal Lemoine.

BELGIUM

La Gueuze, *19 Rue Soufflot (5th).* **Tel.** *01.43.54.63.00. Open Sun-Thurs 11am-2am, Fri-Sat noon-4am.* M *Luxembourg.*

BRAZIL/LEBANON

L'Area, *10 Rue des Tournelles (4th).* **Tel.** *01.42.72.96.50. Open Tues-Sun 5pm-2am.* M *Bastille.*

CANADA

The Moosehead, *16 Rue des Quatre-Vents (6th). Open Sun-Wed noon-2am, Thurs-Sat noon-5am.* M *Odéon.*

ENGLAND

The Cricketer, *41 Rue des Mathurins (8th).* **Tel.** *01.40.07.01.45. Open Mon-Fri 10am-2am, Sat-Sun 4pm-2am.* M *St-Augustin.*

The Bowler, *13 Rue d'Artois (8th).* **Tel.** *01.75.61.16.60. Open Mon-Fri 10am-2am, Sat-Sun 4pm-2am.* M *St-Philippe-du-Roule.*

HOLLAND

Port d'Amsterdam, *20 Rue due Croissart (2nd).* **Tel.** *01.40.39.02.63. Open daily 5pm-2am.* M *Bourse.*

Café Klein-Holland, *36 Rue du Roi de Sicile (3rd).* **Tel.** *01.42.71.43.13. Open daily 5pm-2am.* M *Saint-Paul.*

IRELAND

Flann O'Brien, *6 Rue Bailleul (1st).* **Tel.** *01.42.60.13.58. Open daily 4pm-2am.* M *Louvre-Rivoli.*

Finnegan's Wake, *9 Rue des Boulangers (5th).* **Tel.** *01.46.34.23.65). Open during school term Mon-Fri 11am-2am, Sat-Sun 6pm-2am; during school breaks daily 6pm-2am.* M *Jussieu.*

SCOTLAND

The Auld Alliance, *80 Rue François Miron (3rd).* **Tel.** *01.48.04.30.40. Open daily 11am-2am.* M *Saint-Paul.*

UNITED STATES

Le Violon Dingue, *46 Rue de la Montagne-St-Genevieve (5th).* **Tel.** *01.43.25.79.93. Open Sun-Thurs 6pm-2am, Fri-Sat 8pm-4am.* M *Maubert Mutualité.*

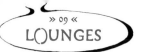

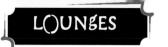

LOUNGES

Le Bar Sans Nom

49 Rue de Lappe (11th). **Tel.** *01.48.05.59.36.*
Open *Mon-Sat 6pm-2am.* Ⓜ *Bastille*

Apart from the tired conundrum of having no name, this is one of the most charming mid-scale bars in Paris. Situated in the heart of Rue de Lappe-land, Sans Nom flickers with candles galore, and is hung with a bird's-nest chandelier, and wall tapestries that are intentionally slashed open for the peek-a-boo positioning of lamps (*warning*: don't try this at home). The music is eclectic, ranging from Joe Cocker and Cuban mambo to the "Pink Panther Theme." There's a long, comfortable couch, sexy lighting and conversational sound levels that are perfect for PoDs (People on Dates).

La Belle Hortense

31 Rue Vielle-du-Temple (3rd). Tel. 01.48.04.71.60. Open Mon-Fri 5pm-2am, Sat-Sun 1pm-2am. M Saint-Paul

If you're like us, you've occasionally found yourself in a bar and wished you had a book. And if you're really like us, you've also stepped into a bookstore and suddenly craved a stiff drink. At LBH, books and booze go together like, well, Georges Perec and Alabama Slammers. This ain't no disco, and it ain't no café, either; it's a winsome gem of a place in which you can sip the hard stuff while browsing French literature and nonfiction.

La Paillotte

45 Rue Monsieur le Prince (6th). Tel. 01.43.26.45.69. Open Sun-Thurs 8pm-2am, Fri-Sat 9pm-5am. M Odéon

La Paillotte is the best quirky lounge in Paris; an eccentric, kitschy flashback to the early '60s fascination with all things Polynesian. It's also supremely romantic and the best place to hear jazz on vinyl (they claim to have the city's largest collection, and we believe them). Built with red lanterns and tiki-hut tables, the bar hasn't changed since it opened in 1959–and looks like it. It's a tight, dark and sexy space that appeals to playful hipsters, partying city workers, the odd tourist and amorous couples, some of whom have surely "gotten lucky" in a discrete corner. The friendly barmen are happy to chat you up as they ladle-out powerful homemade punch. But we could drink Evian here all alone and still be in lounge heaven.

Le Sanz Sans

49 Rue du Faubourg Saint-Antoine (11th). Tel. 01.44.75.78.78. Open Tues-Sat 9am-6am, Sun-Mon 9am-2am. M Bastille

If you could buy gloom in a bottle it would probably have a "Sanz Sans" label. But while gloom is the primary decorative motif, it doesn't describe the *tres chic* atmosphere and well-dressed hipster crowd. Le Sanz Sans is a popular place with good cocktails, reasonable prices, brisk dance tunes, and a labyrinth of salons decadently decorated with deep couches and red velvetry. Upstairs is quieter, slightly brighter and more our speed. We especially like the television screen that lets you gaze at the bar-side beauties without all the bother of having to get up from the comfort of your seat.

CLUb-BARS

Barrio Latino

46-48 Rue du Faubourg-Saint-Antoine (11th) Tel. *01.55.78.84.75. Main room open daily noon-2am; upper rooms open daily 730pm-2am.* M *Bastille*

You want rum? You want cacti? You want a Che Guevera mural? Brought to you by the owners of "Barfly," this hot-as-a-jalapeño-enema Bastille nightspot has all its Hispanic-American clichés in place. Yet the result is less "Latino Disneyland" than it is unmitigated F-U-N. Unlike the real thing, this Barrio is a boisterous, guilty pleasure, decked with three gorgeous bars, oodles of beautiful people (though not necessarily *the* beautiful people), good dining, and a terrific chill-out room in back. And of course there's great music. Lots of nooks include a voyeur's perch on the balcony, a pool table lounge, and jubilant dancing everywhere; which is no mean feat, considering there's no proper dance floor.

Le Cithéa

114 Rue Oberkampf (11th). Tel. 01.40.21.70.95. Open Tues-Sat 5pm-530am. Admission Tues-Thurs free, Fri-Sat €4-€6. M *Parmentier*

Lively and multiethnic, Le Cithéa is what the Latin Quarter should be all about. There's something live happening almost every night of the week from 10pm, with DJs usually taking over after 2am. Wednesday "workshops" are most experimental, and weekends are jam-packed.

Les Trois Maillets

56 Rue Galande (5th). Tel. *01.43.54.42.94.* Open *6pm-5am. Cover (for the cabaret only) €15-€20.* M *St-Michel*

On weekend nights there is no place in Paris that's more fun than this great Latin Quarter cabaret. Cross you're fingers there's room, then happily pay the cover charge, because a drunken night here is not easily forgotten. The action is in the cellar, where nonstop entertainment runs the gamut from Russian singer-songwriters to North African belly dancers and top European instrumentalists. The night usually degenerates into massive table-dancing and over-the-top merry-making. We'll say it again: This is one of the funnest places in Paris.

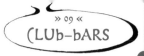

Flèche d'Or

102 bis Rue de Bagnolet (20th).
Tel. *01.43.72.04.23.* **Open** *Tue-Sun 10am-2am.* M *Alexandre Dumas*

Situated in a smartly converted defunct train station, the "Golden Arrow" is a major cultural hotspot with a bar, restaurant, café, theater and concert venue all rolled into one. Despite its relatively distant location, there's something going on here almost every night of the week. Each day brings with it a carnival of alt-punk youths and artists who roll up to enjoy diverse live music, techno DJs, video programs, tango shows and even the occasional late-night "psychology session." There's a restaurant too, but its international menu strives for too much and ends up insulting too many cultures at once. Admission is usually free, and fairly-priced drinks are served from an ingeniously constructed bar.

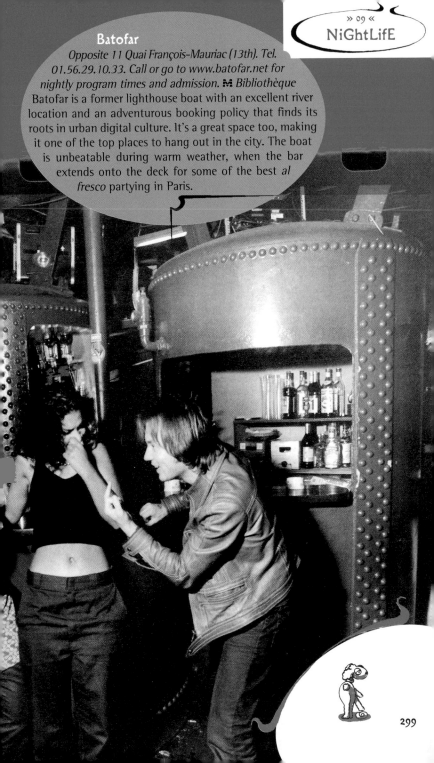

Batofar

Opposite 11 Quai François-Mauriac (13th). Tel. 01.56.29.10.33. Call or go to www.batofar.net for nightly program times and admission. **M** *Bibliothèque*

Batofar is a former lighthouse boat with an excellent river location and an adventurous booking policy that finds its roots in urban digital culture. It's a great space too, making it one of the top places to hang out in the city. The boat is unbeatable during warm weather, when the bar extends onto the deck for some of the best *al fresco* partying in Paris.

GAY-LESBIAN BARS

While the Marais is the center of gay nightlife, the queer city is slowly expanding beyond the borders of its most famous ghetto. As is common most everywhere in the world, the scene is decidedly less exciting for Paris' lesbians, though there are a surprising number of good girl-clubs in the city. Some of the best events are one-off parties at various venues around town. Check the listings magazines for the latest.

Amnésia

42 Rue Vielle-du-Temple (4th). **Tel.** *01.42.72.16.94.* **Open** *daily 930-2am.* **M** *Saint-Paul*
Five things to remember about this bar: 1. It's often as busy by day as it is by night—which is French slang for very busy. 2. With its spacious banquettes, eerily lit bar, and wonderful semi-private mini-mezzanine in the rear (grab it if you can), it's slightly more sumptuously appointed than other bars in its category. 3. The music is dancy and sensational. 4. The weekend brunch draws a large mixed crowd. And 5...we forget what 5 is....

Banana Café

13 Rue de la Ferronnerie (1st). **Tel.** *01.42.33.35.31.* **Open** *daily 6pm-3am.* **M** *Châtelet*
A slam-bang, wham-bam, confetti-strewn, always stuffed-to-the-rafters extravaganza of a bar with a queer, thirtysomething crowd augmented by straights and women, Le Banana is one of the most celebrated bars in town thanks to its extensive theme nights, crazy costumes, and show tunes belted out in the cellar.

La Champmeslé

4 Rue Chabanais (2nd). **Tel.** *01.42.96.85.20.* **Open** *Mon-Sat 5pm-2am.* M *Bourse*

La Champmeslé is Paris' premier lesbian bar, and justifiably so. It's the oldest and coziest, there's a winning cabaret show every Thursday night at ten, you get a free drink on your birthday, and they give you some "freedom of choice," that is, if you tire of the women-only crowd in the rear of the bar, you can wander to the mixed area up front, where the décor is prosaic but the fun never stops—at least not until five in the morning, which makes "la Champ" not only the premier bar for girl-on-girl action, but one of the last to close.

Le Cox

15 Rue des Archives (4th). **Tel.** *01.42.72.08.00.* **Open** *daily 1pm-2am.* M *Hôtel de Ville*

As the provocative name implies, Le Cox is a cruisy Marais hotspot, known for its sexy staff, buff gym queens, and party atmosphere. You can't miss this place: just look for the crowd spilling onto the sidewalk. Sometime during the night you should duck into the equally popular **Open Bar**, 17 Rue des Archives, next door. Most people seem to go back and forth all night.

Le Pulp

25 Blvd. Poissonière (2nd). Tel. 01.40.26.01.93. Open Wed-Sat from midnight until dawn. Free admission Wed-Thur, €9 Fri-Sat. M *Bonne-Nouvelle*

A bastion of dykedom of the lipstick variety—along with plenty of LUGs (lesbians until graduation), this trendy club is one of the world's precious few major dance spaces catering (almost) exclusively to women. Tunes run the gamut from techno and house to Madonna.

Mixer Bar

23 Rue Sainte-Croix de la-Bretonnerie (4th). **Tel.** *01.48. 87.55.44.* **Open** *daily 4pm-2am.* M *Saint-Paul*

Mixer is a fun little bar with an eccentric-colored industrial interior, throbbing music and a modest dance mezzanine that's ideal for getting close and personal. Just a few doors down the same narrow street–which is an increasingly busy charmer–is **The Coffee Shop**, 3 Rue Sainte-Croix de la-Bretonnerie (tel. 01.42.74.24.21), a tiny dance space featuring a clothesline full of club invites strung across its entire length. It's open daily noon-2am.

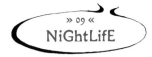

Les Scandaleuses

8 Rue des Ecouffes (4th). **Tel.** *01.48.87.39.26.*
Open *daily 6pm-2am.* M *Hôtel-de-Ville*

The name of this lesbian bar–a bastion of hip and techno music on a long, lean, picturesque Marais street–means "The Scandalous Females," and need we tell you how apt it is? The prices aren't exactly low, and the décor is a bit chilly—we prefer the multi-room cellar. But the paintings on the walls (exclusively by scandalous females) are often quite good, and the crowd can be great. As with most girl zones in Paris, men are welcome only when accompanied by women.

Le Tropic Café

66 Rue des Lombards (1st). **Tel.** *01.40.13.92.62.* **Open** *daily noon-dawn.* M *Châtelet*

Demarcating the western edge of Paris' gay neighborhood, Le Tropic is an eminently likable and welcoming bar with a big terrace. Or should we say "terrace with small bar?" Tropic is indeed a fitting name, although "Leafy" would nail it better: branches in full flower provide an overhead canopy as laid-back loungers relax and converse, both of which are easy to do thanks to not-overly-loud dance tracks and a pleasantly unrushed closing time.

Utopia

15 Rue Michel-le-Comte (3rd). **Tel.** *01.42.71.63.43.*
Open *Mon-Sat 5pm-2am.* M *Rambuteau*

Sapphic sisters rock this house. Too popular for words, "Le Tope" gives good value for a visit: affordable firewater, costumed theme nights, excellent techno music, a pool table and pinball machine, and occasional theater presentations. We love this place.

DANCE CLUBS

Paris' mega-clubs are the epicenter of the world's Eurotrash scene. And there seems to be no lack of idiotic poseurs willing to wait in line at Neanderthal-manned velvet ropes, pay lots of money for badly made drinks, and sardine into an earsplitting space where conversation is impossible.

You can often find discount passes at record stores in Les Halles, the Marais, and the Bastille, but they won't help you avoid the invariably long queues. Places start to hop around 1am, and most clubs stay open until dawn.

The clubs below are Paris' current crop of hot spots. Often, however, the best parties in town are one-offs, and not weekly events.

Novamagazine, a French-language monthly, has the Capital's most avant bar and club listings. **Pariscope**, published Wednesdays, offer the most comprehensive inventory of current events.

Les Bains

7 Rue du Bourg-l'Abbé (3rd). **Tel.** *01.48.87.01.80.*
Open *daily 1130pm-6am; restaurant daily 830-1130pm.*
Admission *€15-€20.* M *Réaumur-Sébastopol*

The space–Turkish baths from the turn of the century revamped by Philippe Starck–is undeniably cool. The crowd–Eurotrash *nouveau riche*, beautiful young girls, plus the occasional celeb-singer or starlet–isn't. The music is mainstream (think Ibiza), and the door policy is downright ridiculous. Proof positive of the power of marketing, Les Bains is the ultimate velvet ropes club, offering plenty of sizzle with very little steak. Last decade's Club of the Moment is now a pretentious scene, catering to the best-looking, and most vapid out-of-towners. Posing and flamboasting (atop Miu Miu stilettos) are such high priorities here that having a good time seems secondary. Go with Nutrasweet friends and wear Prada to get past the velvet ropes.

Le Queen

102 Ave. de Champs-Elysées (8th). Tel. 08.92.70.73.30. Open daily midnight-6am. Admission Mon €12, Tue-Thurs and Sun €10, Fri-Sat €20 (with free drink).
M George V

It's amazing how many people can mistake an aggressive door policy for "exclusive" or "chic." Le Queen is neither. Popular for well over a decade, the club remains a bastion of bottle-blondness; full of celebutants and sauced mannequins. Getting in is another matter, as the doormen separate the wheat from the chaff as zealously as a rabbi separates milk from meat. The club is best on Thursdays and Saturdays when it's strictly gay and women are grudgingly admitted.

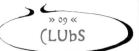

Rex Club

5 Blvd. Poissonière (2nd). Tel. 01.42.36.83.98 (recorded program). Open Thurs-Sat 1130pm-dawn. Admission €11-€13. M Bonne-Nouvelle

Rex sports the best sound system in town and an adventurous booking policy that means there's something happening here almost every night of the week. The door policy isn't as primitive as the competition, and the crowd is far less superficial.

Le Gibus

18 Rue du Faubourg-du-Temple (11th). Tel. 01.47.00.78.88. Open Tues-Sat 1130pm-530am, Sun 5pm-5am. M *République*

One of the largest clubs in Paris, Le Gibus is a multilevel disco theme park, with a chest-thumping sound system and a laser show that would make a Vegas hotel proud. From rock to house, there's usually something for everyone. On any given night, the club attracts the entire spectrum of clubbers, from frat boys to homeboys, the majority of whom are gay. If you're not "on the list" forget weekends before 2am, unless you enjoy standing behind velvet ropes with the *pont-et-tunel* crowd. Hardcore club kids flock here after-hours, when the place fills with blissed-out scenesters, buff muscle boys, winsome fashion plates, and a hundred other varieties of beautiful people.

LiVE ROCk, POP, fUNk & REGGAE

The French pop scene has undergone big changes in the last twenty years. Gone are the days when most pop stars resembled Brell or Brassens, and rock meant desperate Elvis clones like Johnny Hallyday or Eddy Mitchell. Actually, Hallyday is still wildly popular, but so too are the new sounds of French Algerian rockers, Afro-Caribbean soul groups, and home-grown suburban rap. Major balladeers like Mylène Farmer and Lara Fabian have large gay followings, and Charles Aznavour and Mireille Mathieu can still sell out the legendary Olympia.

The music scene in the capital is eclectic and fun. Be it North African Raï in the persons of Khaled and Feudal, or a popular boy-band like 2 B 3, the only thing you can be sure of is that the concert will never start on time. In addition to the venues listed below, many bars offer evenings of rock, jazz and blues and, along the banks of the Seine, a number of barges stage concerts with a particulary good atmosphere. Check the listings magazines for the latest.

Chesterfield Café

124 Rue la Boëtie (8th). **Tel.** *01.42.25.18.06.* **Open** *daily 10am-5am; concerts Tues-Sat from 1130pm.* **Admission** *free.* **M** *Franklin D Roosevelt*

Quality blues and rock, cheap beer and high volume are the secrets of success for this bastion of American-oriented bar rock. Youthquakers are drawn by talent they've vaguely heard of—a one-hit wonder guitar band, perhaps—that usually takes the stage after a local garage band does a set. Chesterfield is often packed to the rafters, so get there early to ensure you get in the door.

La Cigale

120 Blvd. Rochechouart (18th). **Tel.** *01.49.25.89.99.* **Open** *7pm-1030pm.* **Admission** *€15-€40.* **M** *Pigalle*

A vast and characterful venue located in a former theater, La Cigale offers vastly mixed programs that can be Latin/Asian/jazzy/French/you-name-it. Some bigger international names too.

Le Gambetta

104 Rue de Bagnolet (20th) Tel. *01.43.70.52.01. Bar daily 10am-2am; concerts from 9pm.* Admission *free-€7.* M *Alexandre-Dumas*

One of the edgiest live-rock venues in town, Le Gambetta is a small post-punk dive with no-name thrasher bands served-up nightly. It's a good place to hear up-and-comers, along with an occasional came-and-wenter debuting a new project. Few audience members stay an entire night, unless they're "with the band." But, because there's no cover, and it's located next to Flèche d'Or, you can easily add this place to your crawl.

Le Réservoir

16 Rue de la Forge-Royale (11th). Tel. *01.43.56.39.60. Bar daily 8pm-2am; concerts Mon-Sat 1130pm.* Admission *free.* M *Faidherbe-Chaligny*

In addition to presenting a wide range of bands on the cusp of stardom, Le Réservoir books the more-than-occasional national name and draws a knowledgeable, and good-looking crowd.

MCM Café

90 Blvd. de Clichy (18th). Tel. *08.36.68.22.19. Bar daily 5pm-5am; concerts Mon-Tues & Thurs-Fri 11pm.* Admission *free.* M *Blanche*

Good local alternateen bands and a plusher-then-usual environment are the hallmarks of this outpost of French music cable TV station MCM. It's an intimate venue with decent sound and unobstructed sightlines, and some bigger names play on weekends.

fRENCh (HANSON

Even before Edith Piaf's sentimental ballads caught the world's fancy, French music has had that certain *je ne sais quoi.* The best places to hear local balladeers and songsters are:

Cabaret Sauvage,
Bord du Canal, 59 Blvd MacDonald Parc de la Villette, 19th (tel. 01.40.03.75.15).
M *Porte de la Villette*

Chez Adel,
10 Rue de la Grange-aux-Belles, 10th (tel. 01.42.08.24.61).
M *Gare de l'Est*

La Folie en Tête,
33 Rue de la Butte-aux-Cailles, 13th (tel. 01.45.80.65.99).
M *Place d'Italie*

Au Limonaire,
18 Cité Bergère, 9th (tel. 01.45.23.33.33).
M *Grands Boulevards*

Le Sentier des Halles,
50 Rue d'Aboukir, 2nd (tel. 01.42.36.37.27).
M *Sentier*

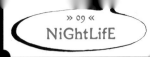

Baiser Salé Jazz

58 Rue des Lombards (1st). Tel. 01.42.33.37.71. Open Mon-Sat 6pm-6am. 10pm-2am. Admission €10-€15. M Châtelet-les-Halles

Dirty Kiss is best known for Afro-fusion, R&B, and Latino music of all kinds.

Le Bilboquet

13 Rue Saint Benoît (6th). Tel. 01.45.48.81.84. Open daily 815pm-4am. Admission €21, incl. 1 drink. M Saint-Germain-des-Prés

One of the oldest and most famous Left Bank jazz clubs, the atmospheric Bilboquet still presents some of the biggest names in the jazz, blues, R&B and even soul.

Lionel Hampton

Meridien Hotel, 81 Blvd. Gouvion St-Cyr (17th). Tel. 01.40.68.30.42. Nightly concerts 1030pm-2am. Admission €20 incl. 1 drink. M Porte Maillot

Like the man himself, the Lionel Hampton club represents the top of the food chain for successful boppers. What we're trying to say is that, although this place is not that old, it's legendary. So are the surprisingly decent prices.

New Morning

7-9 Rue des Petites Ecuries (10th). Tel. 01.45.23.51.41. Live music usually from 830pm. Admission from €18. M Château-d'Eau

Hot, crowded and smoky, New Morning is everything a jazz club is supposed to be. It's also one of the most popular venues in town, attracting lots of big-name international stars, along with the most exciting newcomers.

Petit Journal Montparnasse

13 Rue du Commandant Mouchotte (14th). Tel. 01.43.21.56.70. Open Mon-Sat 8pm-2am. Admission €15-€20, incl. 1 drink. Closed mid-July to mid-August. M Montparnasse-Bienvenüe

Cheap and friendly, this no-frills blues landmark is full of locals enjoying good jams in a lighthearted environment. Arrive early, reserve for dinner, or just be plain lucky if you want a table.

LATIN, CARIBBEAN & WORLD BEAT

Le Divan du Monde

75 Rue des Martyrs (18th). Tel. *01.44.92.77.66.* Open *daily 1130pm-dawn.* M *Pigalle*

There's always something going on in this former cabaret, where musical styles run the gamut from African and salsa to world-music and electronica. The tunes are often live and the slightly alternative crowd comes here to dance. A fun night out.

Elysée Montmartre

72 Blvd. Rochechouart (18th). Tel. *01. 55.07.06.00. Performance times and admission prices vary. Closed in August.* M *Anvers*

An old-fashioned music hall in the heart of disreputable Pigalle, the Elysée offers a wide variety of evenings ranging from Salsa to Reggae.

Institut du Monde Arabe

1 Rue des Fossés Saint Bernard (5th). Tel. 01.40.51.38.11. Concerts Friday and Saturday. Admission €11.50-€16 for performances. No shows in summer. M *Jussieu/Maubert-Mutualité*

This great building is one of the best places in Europe to hear classical Arabic music.

CLASSICAL MUSIC, OPÉRA & DANCE

Paris is home to three major symphony orchestras–**Orchestre National de France, Orchestre de Paris** and **Orchestre Philharmonique de Radio France**–all of which concentrate on a similar, fairly conservative repertoire. Each of these venerable institutions are excellent and, at one time or another, each has found itself under the baton of the great maestri of the world.

Augmenting the big-name symphony orchestras are a host of worthy, smaller ensembles with broadly divergent repertoires. Early music is currently *en vogue*, and "stringent authenticity" are the by-words that draw full houses. The biggest name in this genre is William Christie, an American who was bestowed with honorary French citizenship for his work with the **Arts Florissants** ensemble.

At the other end of the chronological spectrum, the avant-garde thrives under the influence of Pierre Boulez, France's greatest living musical guru. Keep an eye out for performances by the **Ensemble Intercontemporain,** which Boulez founded and still occasionally conducts. **IRCAM,** a veritable hotbed of atonality (and an internationally-renown center for musical research) is currently the venue to watch for edgy new music.

The operatic world is not neglected in Paris. One of President Mitterand's grand projects was the new opera house at the Bastille, which now runs in parallel with the Opéra Garnier (where international divas and controversial productions go hand in hand). The **TMP at the Châtelet Théâtre** is the only major rival to the national houses, offering full and varied seasons. The privately-run **Théâtre des Champs-Elysées** is also equipped for full-scale operatic productions.

Ticket prices at the big venues vary depending on who is performing, but they generally range from €7 to €200.

GETTING TICKETS

Tickets can be purchased in advance or on the day of performance at most theater box offices. You can also buy tickets to most shows from **FNAC Forum**, Forum des Halles, Level -3, 1 Rue Pierre Lescot, 1st (tel. 01.40.41.40.00). They're open Mon-Sat 10am-730pm. **Virgin Megastore**, 52 Ave. des Champs Elysées, 8th (tel. 01.49.53.50.00) also sells tickets. They're open daily 10am-midnight.

The **Kiosque Théâtre**, Place de la Madeleine (8th), sells same-day tickets to all the major theaters–except for the Palais Garnier and the Opéra Bastille–for up to 50% off box office prices, plus a small commission. They're located behind the church, are open Tues-Sat 1230-745pm, Sun 1230-345pm, and only accept cash. There's a second location on the **Esplanade de la Tour Montparnasse**, between Montparnasse Tower and the Montparnasse railway station (15th).

Just because the performance you want to see is sold out doesn't mean you're SOL. When no VIPs appear to claim them, theaters offer their best "house" seats to the general public on the day of the show. Ask about these when you belly up to the box office.

Some theaters offer low-priced standing-room only tickets on the day of each show and, once your in, it's rare not to find an empty seat. When all else fails, take a deep breath and talk to a hotel concierge or a legalized scalper like **Agence Marivaux**, 7 Rue Marivaux, 2nd (tel. 01.42.97.46.70) or **Agence Théâtre des Champs-Elysées**, 33 Rue Le Peletier, 9th (tel. 01.43.59.24.60.).

Opéra National de Paris—Bastille

Place de la Bastille (12th). Tel. 08.92.69.78.68. Box office Mon-Sat 11am-630pm. Tickets €7-€109. M Bastille

The building Parisians love to hate is settling down, under the leadership of Hugues Gall and conductor James Conlon, to produce seasons of a respectable international standard. Recent fare from the untraditional Paris Opéra included a new production of Prokofiev's "War and Peace," based on the Tolstoy bestseller, and "Kát'a Kabanová," based on a 19th century Russian play called "The Storm." Booing still greets most of the new productions... a favorite and frequently unjustified sport of Parisian music lovers. If the technical prowess of the house is no longer in question, then the public areas remain resolutely utilitarian with all the charm of an international airport.

Opéra National de Paris—Palais Garnier

Place de l'Opéra (9th). Tel. 08.92.89.90.90. Box office Mon-Sat 11am-630pm. Tickets €7-€200. M Opéra

Palais Garnier recently emerged from a daring renovation that restored the building's Second Empire facade to its 19th-century polychrome glory. In sharp contrast to the Bastille (above), the Opéra Garnier is probably the most glamorous theater in the world, with the show in the foyers almost as extravagant as any on stage. The Garnier is home to both the Opéra National de Paris and the Paris Ballet Company. And it's not just for traditionalists. A recent over-the-top production of Rossini's "L'Italiana in Algeri" called for an appearance by an enormous pair of breasts, while the ballet "Casanova," by Angelin Preljocaj, included an original score that was part classical and part techno, with the odd electrocardiogram thrown in for good measure.

Châtelet Théâtre Musical de Paris (TMP)

1 Place du Châtelet (1st). Tel. 01.40.28.28.40. Box office daily 11am-7pm. Tickets €7-€130. M Châtelet

Newly opened after extensive renovations, the venerable old Châtelet has transformed from a simple stage for operettas to the prestigious Théâtre Musical de Paris. The new director Jean-Pierre Brossmann is continuing the fine work of his predecessor and operatic productions and concerts here often compete favorably with the work of the big national houses.

Cité de la Musique

221 Ave. Jean-Jaurès (19th). Tel. 01.44.84.44.84. Box office Tues-Sat noon-6pm (8pm on concert nights), Sun 10am-6pm. Tickets €16-€40. M Porte de Pantin

The Cité de la Musique is home to a new *conservatoire*, a concert hall and the Musée de la Musique. The concert hall is a well-designed space, with adventurously varied programming and occasional excursions into unfamiliar repertoire. The *conservatoire* provides the chance to hear gifted youngsters at bargain prices before the media hype.

IRCAM

1 Place Igor Stravinsky (4th). Tel. 01.44.78.48.43. Box office daily 10am-6pm. Tickets €9.50-€20. M Hôtel de Ville

The underground musical center at the Centre Pompidou was in danger of becoming something of a white elephant. But now, with new efforts to interest a wider public in the goings-on of the young generation of modernist composers, it's becoming one of the hottest tickets in town.

Maison de Radio France

116 Ave. du Président Kennedy (16th). Tel. 01.56.40.15.16. Box office daily 11am-6pm. Tickets free-€55. M Passy/Ranelagh

Home to the Orchestre Philharmonique de France and the Orchestre National de France, the cylindrical Maison de la Radio has a rather bleak and cheerless main concert hall. But the music making is pretty reliable and the programming more varied than it is downtown.

Opéra Comique

Place Boiëldieu (2nd). Tel. 08.25.00.00.58. Box office Mon-Sat 9am-9pm, Sun 11am-7pm. Tickets €7-€90. M Richelieu-Drouot

Currently undergoing a change of direction, the sleepy Opéra Comique is hoping that theater producer Jérôme Savary will be able to reverse its fortunes. The beautiful interior, which saw the première of *Carmen,* is in bad need of restoration, as is the second-rate programming the theater has offered in recent seasons.

Salle Gaveau

45 Rue La Boétie (8th). Tel. 01.49.53.05.07. Box office Mon-Fri 1130am-630pm. Tickets €16-€50. M Miromesnil.

Recently refurbished, but still charming, the Salle Gaveau is a great place to hear chamber music and vocal recitals. The hall has just been transformed into a more comfortable venue, and extended stage facilities allow larger Baroque ensembles to perform here.

Salle Pleyel

252 Rue du Faubourg Saint Honoré (8th). Tel. 01.45.61.53.00. Box office Mon-Sat 11am-6pm. Tickets €15.40-€69.25. M Ternes

This leading concert hall has recently been purchased by the State (for a figurative song) and re-opened in 2004 after massive renovation. Still not the most attractive of venues, the hall is nonetheless the most prestigious in Paris (Chopin gave his last recital here) and home to an impressive series of big name concerts.

Théâtre de la Bastille

76 Rue de la Roquette (11th). Tel. *01.43.57.42.14. Box office Mon-Fri 10am-6pm, Sat 2-6pm. Closed July-Aug.* Tickets *€12.50-€9.* M *Bastille*

This theater is known for giving a stage to top quality modern dance companies, and other international fare.

Théâtre des Champs-Elysées

15 Ave. Montaigne (8th). Tel. *01.49.52.50.50. Box office Mon-Sat 1-7pm. Closed July-Aug.* Tickets *€5-€110.* M *Alma-Marceau*

With its pale pink carpeting and turn-of-the-century frescoes, the Théâtre des Champs-Elysées is the most elegant and attractive of Parisian theaters. Free from the constraints of state funding, the season here features visits from leading orchestras from around the world and an enviable list of soloists, as well as full opera and ballet seasons. Accordingly, tickets are slightly more expensive than elsewhere.

Théâtre de la Ville

2 Place du Châtelet (4th). Tel. *01.42.74.22.77. Box office Mon 11am-7pm; Tues-Sat 11am-8pm.* Tickets *€11-€22.* M *Châtelet.*

The modern, raked auditorium is mostly used for dance, but features the occasional world music concert as well.

STAGE: THEATER & CABARET

There are almost 150 theaters in Paris, offering drama, musicals and everything in-between. But since the vast majority of the productions are in French, they are not particularly accessible to most visitors. Check the listings magazines for the latest. For better or worse, Paris clings to its tradition of cancan (some say "can't can't") girls, many of whom wear costumes that aren't much more than the banana skirt made famous by Josephine Baker.

Comédie Française

2 Rue de Richelieu (1st). Tel. 01.44. 58.15.15. Box office 11am-6pm. Admission €6-€30. M *Palais-Royal*

Founded by Louis XIV, this is a venerable French institution for plays by Ibsen, Shakespeare, Camus and others.

Théâtre de Nesle

8 Rue de Nesle (6th). Tel. 01.46. 34.61.04. Box office Tues-Sat 230-630pm. Admission €6-€16. M *Odéon*

In addition to regular French fare, this theater usually stages performances in English on Mondays.

Moulin Rouge

82 Blvd. de Clichy (18th). Tel. 01.53.09. 82.82. Shows daily at 9pm & 11pm. Dinner and show (starts 7pm) €130-€160. Show only from €92 at 9pm; €82 at 11pm. Reservations recommended. M *Blanche*

The cabaret made famous by Toulouse-Lautrec is our top choice (if you have to choose), mainly because it's more than 100 years old (ah, history!). Five dozen leggy dancers high-step for applause.

Crazy Horse

12 Ave. George V (8th). Tel. 01.47.23. 32.32. Shows Sept-Mar, Sun-Fri 830pm & 11pm, Sat 730pm, 945pm & 1150pm; Apr-June, Sun-Fri 830pm & 11pm, Sat 8pm, 1015pm & 1250am; July-Aug daily 830pm & 11pm. Admission €29-€165 Reservations recommended. M *George V*

Topless women with names like Roxy Tornado, Choo Choo Nightrain and Pussy Duty-Free perform a classic tits-and-feathers cabaret show.

Lido de Paris

116bis Champs-Élysées. Tel. 01.40.76.56.10. Shows daily 1pm, 3pm, 10pm and midnight. Admission €70-€90 at bar (incl. 1/2 bottle Champagne per person); Dinner and show €115-€160. M *George V*

Yet another cheezy Vegas-style show. Watch the promo video in the entrance hall, and save yourself time and money.

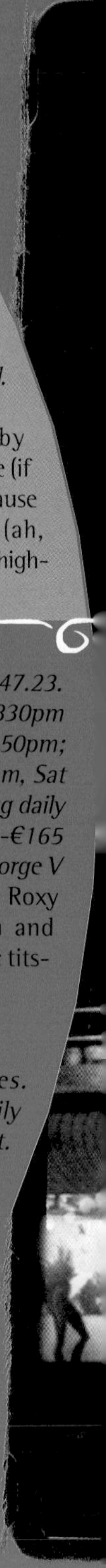

OULIN ROUGE

fiLM

The world's first public film premiere wasn't in Hollywood, but in Paris, held by the Lumière brothers on Rue Scribe on December 28th, 1895. Paris has reigned as one of the movie capitals of the world ever since. In addition to the usual mainstream fare, the city boasts about a dozen arthouse cinemas, ensuring that there's always something interesting playing. Many foreign films are dubbed into French, but plenty are screened in *version originale* (marked "v.o." on posters and in listings magazines).

Gaumont Grand Ecran Italie

30 Place d'Italie (13th). Tel. *08.92.69.66.96.* M *Place d'Italie*

Earns its listing here for having the largest screen in the city. A great place to see almost any film.

Racine Odéon

6 Rue de l'Ecole-de-Médecine (6th). Tel. *01.43.26.19.68.*
M *Odéon/Cluny-La Sorbonne*

Usually serves two or three kitschy classics back-to-back. The place to go for an all-night fix, breakfast included.

Studio Galande

42 Rue Galande (5th). Tel. *01.43.54.72.71.* M *St-Michel*

They still screen The Rocky Horror Picture Show here, each Friday at 10pm.

La Géode

26 Ave. Corentin-Cariou (19th). Tel. 01.40.05.79.99.
Tickets €6.75-€8.75; two films €11 (from 630pm).
M *Porte de la Villette*

The Geode brings big-screen technology to the masses, showing the most popular titles in heavy rotation.

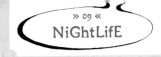

MAjOR CONCERT VENUES

Olympia
28 Blvd. des Capucines (9th). Tel. *08.92.68.33.68.* M *Madeleine*
A legendary Parisian concert hall booking mostly French acts. Playing Olympia remains the pinnacle of any artist's career.

Palais des Sports
Porte de Versailles (15th). Tel. *01. 48.28.40.10.* M *Porte de Versailles*
Huge sports arena hosting the odd rock and jazz concert.

Palais Omnisports de Paris Bercy
8 Blvd. de Bercy (12th). Tel. *08. 92.69.23.00.* M *Bercy/Gare de Lyon*
Cool grass-covered sports stadium for the largest rock events.

Le Bataclan
50 Blvd. Voltaire (11th). Tel. 01.43.14.35.35. M *Oberkampf*
Relatively intimate theater for bands and French singer/songwriters. Good place to see a show.

CASiNOS

Cercle Clichy Montmartre
84 Rue de Clichy (9th). Tel. *01.48.78.32.85.* Open *daily 10am-6am.* M *Place Clichy*
A good-looking casino offering roulette, blackjack and stud poker. There are also a dozen billiards tables to retire to when your money runs out. You must show ID to get in the door.

Le Club-Casino
2 Rue de la Chaussée d'Antin (9th). Tel. *01.48.24.91.40. Open daily noon-dawn.* M *Opéra*
Located near the Opéra, this semi-stylish spot offers baccarat, blackjack and stud poker. There's a decent restaurant on the premises too.

SeX

Pigalle and the Rue St-Denis are the traditional bastions of heterosexual prostitution in Paris. Hooking isn't illegal in the city, but soliciting business is. Thus, the most danger a customer faces is the memory of what he did last night. Women stand alongside their doors asking men for a light. If you want to give them more, it'll cost €50-€75.

Take the Métro to Blanche or Clichy and you can't miss the action. There's plenty of porn here too, including lots of video places for doing the "five-finger shuffle."

There's also plenty of prostitution in the **Bois de Boulogne**. So much, in fact, that the local government has taken to closing parts of the park at night, supposedly to protect citizens from AIDS. The Bois remains the best place to pick up a dazzling Brazilian transvestite, but you need a car, unless you want to roll around in the bushes.

If you want to see a live sex show, head to Rue des Halles, where you'll find several theaters, including **Show Girls "Jade"**, 5 Rue des Halles, 1st (tel. 01.42.33.85.88), in which nonstop action costs €50.

Deux Plus Deux, 9 Blvd. Edgar Quinet, 14th (tel. 01.43.35.14.00) is one of many swing clubs in Paris, most of which are open to couples (and single women) only. And remember: Be safe out there.

№ 10

DAY TRIPS & SLEEP-AWAYS

TRIPPING

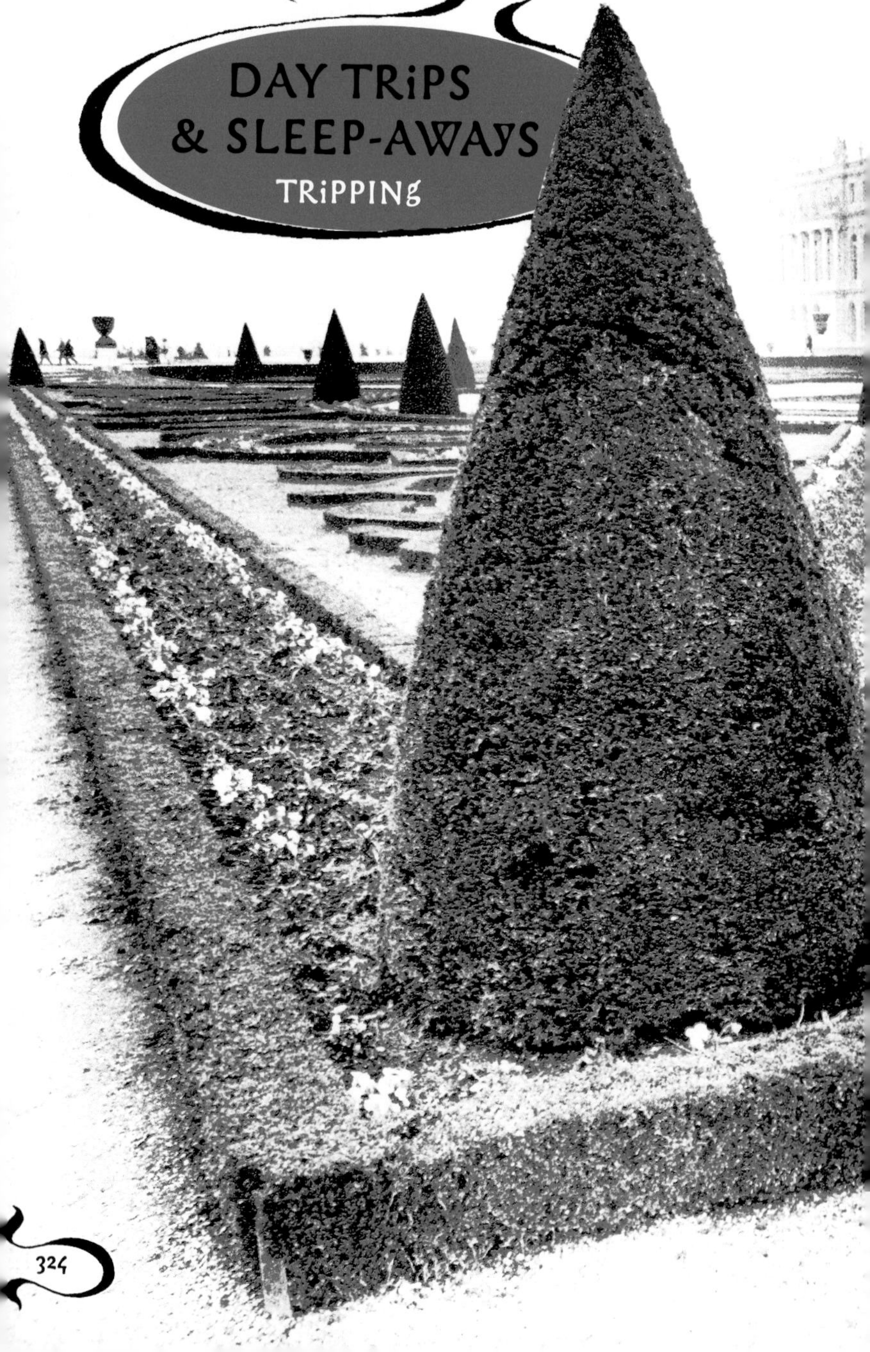

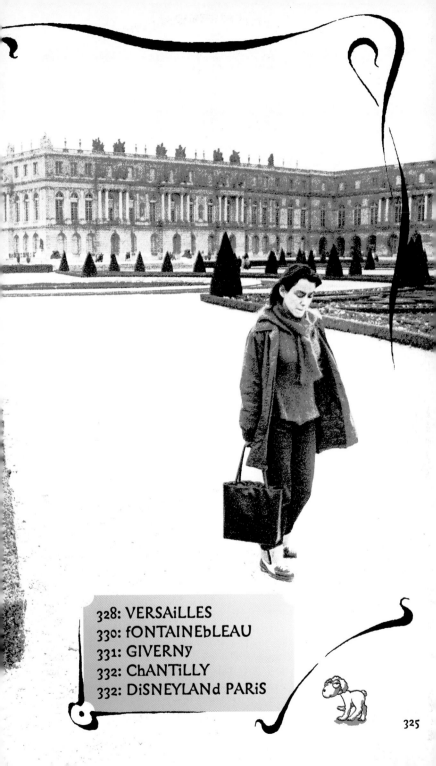

Just a short distance from the Champs-Elysées you'll be confronted with a France that's strikingly different from the inner city. The air is cleaner, the people are friendlier and everything is cheaper.

Getting Around by Train

French Rail—SNCF (www.sncf.fr) is both extensive and efficient. Seats can be purchased up until the moment of departure, but pre-booking is recommended, especially on weekends and in summer. You can make reservations in most travel agencies and train stations, which also have automatic ticket and reservations machines (*biletterie automatique*). VISA and MasterCard are accepted. You can purchase tickets onboard, but you will pay a stiff supplement.

The high speed TGV (*train à grande vitesse*) can cut many long-distance journeys in half. It currently serves the Paris-Lyon-Marseilles line to the south, Geneva and Lausanne to the east, and Bordeaux to the southwest. The TGV also runs north to Lille, where it connects with the EuroTunnel to Great Britain.

Each of Paris' six main rail stations are conveniently located on Métro lines. Information offices are usually open daily from 8am-6pm. For information and reservations call **SNCF** (tel. 08.92. 35.35.35. or 08.36.35.35.35).

There are a confusing variety of train fares offering reductions on various destinations, dates, and times. Travel is usually cheapest from noon Saturday until 3pm on Sunday. And dogs pay half fare.

Train travel within France is nominally based on the honor system; before boarding validate your ticket in the automatic cancellation machines located at the head of each platform. Most tickets are valid for two months from the date stamped on the face.

Which Station?

Gare du Nord serves the north, including the Channel ports, where trains connect with ferries and hovercrafts to Britain; also Belgium, Holland and Scandinavian countries.

Gare de l'Est serves the east, Nancy and Strasbourg, as well as Germany and Eastern Europe.

Gare d'Austerlitz serves the southwest; Bordeaux, Toulouse, and Spain and Portugal via Orléans, Tours, Poitiers and Angoulême.

Gare St-Lazare serves Normandy and Dieppe.

Gare Montparnasse serves western France up to Bretagne.

Gare de Lyon serves southwestern France, Switzerland, Italy and Greece.

Getting Around by Coach

Buses typically cost half the price of trains, and reservations should be made as far in advance as possible.

The major long-distance coach operators are **Eurolines** (tel. 08. 92.89.90.91), **Nouvelles Frontiers** (tel. 08.25.00.08.25), **Fédération Nationale des Transports Routiers** (tel. 01.44.29.04.29), and **Usit Voyages** (tel. 01.44.55.32.60).

Information

Espace du Tourisme d'Ile de France, Carrousel du Louvre 99, Rue de Rivoli, 1st (tel. 01.44.50.19.98), can help you plan trips throughout the Île-de-France region, including transportation, hotels, gourmet weekends, walks, château visits and more.

When to Go

Really, the question is when not to go. Because of vacations, it can be murder getting in and out of the city on the first and last days of July and August. The 15th of each summer month can be difficult for traveling too.

DISTANCES FROM PARIS

	Km	Mi.
Amsterdam	504	315
Athens	2918	1824
Berlin	1054	659
Brussels	308	193
Budapest	1257	786
Dublin	854	534
Edinburgh	867	542
Florence	878	549
Frankfurt	465	291
Geneva	402	251
Helsinki	1894	1184
Lisbon	1817	1136
London	414	259
Lyon	460	288
Madrid	1316	823
Marseilles	776	465
Milan	826	516
Moscow	2851	1782
Munich	832	520
Oslo	1337	836
Prague	1035	647
Rome	1388	868
Stockholm	1549	968
Venice	838	524
Vienna	1227	767
Warsaw	1044	653

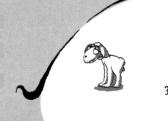

VERSAiLLES CHÂTEAU

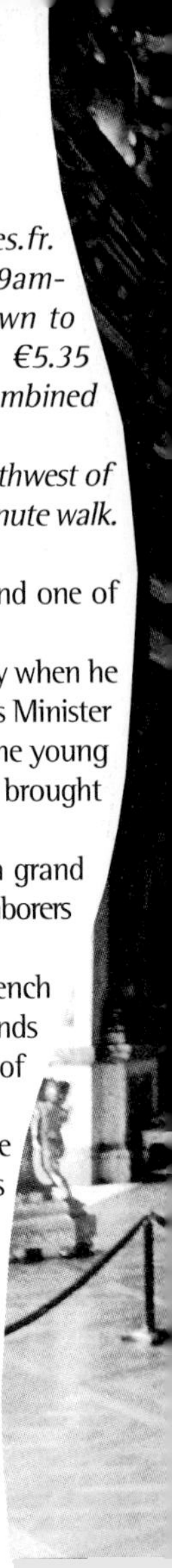

Tel. *01.30.83.78.00 or 01.39.50.36.22. www.chateauversailles.fr.* **Open** *Oct-Apr, Tues-Sun 9am-530pm; May-Sept, Tues-Sun 9am-630pm. Closed Mon and public hols. Gardens open daily dawn to dusk, weather permitting.* **Château admission** *€6.90 adults, €5.35 18-25s, free under 18; €5.35 for all after 330pm. Ask about combined admission to the Grand Trianon and Petit Trianon.*

Getting There: *Versailles is located about 20 km/13 mi southwest of Paris. Take RER Line C to Versailles-Rive Gauche, then it's a 15-minute walk.*

The most famous palace in Europe is now a national museum and one of the biggest tourist attractions in France.

According to legend, the young Louis XIV became green with envy when he caught a glimpse of Vaux-le-Vicomte, the sublime château that his Minister of Finance, Nicolas Fouquet, built for himself just outside Paris. The young brat-king had the miserable minister jailed for life, and the team that brought us the Vaux was set to work building the château at Versailles.

A menagerie and an orangerie were added as the first stage of a grand entry court, followed by massive construction that involved over 30,000 laborers and continued for a decade.

The Sun King moved-in in 1682 and transferred the seat of the French monarchy here from Paris. He was followed to Versailles by tens of thousands of courtiers, ministers and nobles, many of whom lived within the walls of the Palace. These were the halcyon days.

Under Louis XVI, plans were made to extend the palace further, but the French Revolution (1789-1799) put the kibosh on all that. The king was beheaded, his furnishings were sold and the palace was turned into a museum. During the Franco-Prussian War (1870-1871) the palace became a military hospital, before falling into enemy hands and becoming Prussia's military headquarters. The Versailles château owes its survival to American philanthropy, specifically to the Rockefeller family which, in the 1920s, donated huge sums for major restoration work and the return of some original furnishings and decorations.

A visit to Versailles is a full-day trip. Start with a guided tour of the **Grands Appartements**, which includes about half the rooms that are open to the public. These visits also go through the **Hall of Mirrors**, where the German Empire was proclaimed in 1871 and where, in 1919, the Treaty of Versailles was signed, ending World War I.

The elaborate symmetrical gardens are another highlight. Centered around the Grand Canal, they include a large number of sculptures, monuments and auxiliary buildings, including the **Grand Trianon** and the **Petit Trianon.** The latter dates from 1760 to 1764 and was a favorite residence of Marie Antoinette, who had an artificial rural village, the Hameau (hamlet), built on its grounds.

The highly formal **Versailles Gardens** were created by landscape architect

André Le Nôtre (1613-1700), who invented the grand style of French neoclassicism. This masterpiece is characterized by ornamental urns, statues, canals and fountains powered by water that was channeled from the Seine. In summer, the fountains are synchronized to baroque music, every Sunday from 330-530pm.

You can picnic next to the pond known as "*le piece d'eau des Suisses*," or walk five minutes into town for a decent restaurant meal. The cafeteria near the Château's main entrance is strictly for sustenance.

fONTAiNEbLEAU

Getting There: *Fontainebleau is located 40 mi/65 km southeast of Paris. Take the train from Gare de Lyon to Fontainebleau-Avon, then bus, taxi or bike (rentals at the station) to the Château. The ride from Paris takes about 50 minutes.*

Fontainebleau is basically a big, beautiful château surrounded by a big beautiful forest. A trip here is a leisurely day out of the city that's great for hiking, biking and picnicking.

The **Château de Fontainebleau** was transformed from a modest hunting lodge into a sumptuous palace by King François I in the 1500s. It was here where the Fontainebleau style of French painting developed, transmuting the hectic Italian Mannerist style into a softer, more elegant French mode.

The palace was a favorite resort of French monarchs from the 16th through the 19th centuries. Successive rulers added, modified, reconstructed and redecorated, including Napoléon Bonaparte who preferred the Empire Style.

Fontainebleau was ransacked during the French Revolution (1789-1799) but was subsequently restored by the Emperor Napoléon I, who favored it above Versailles. Today the Château's ornate interiors are a major tourist attraction.

When you're ready to rock, take to the Fontainebleau Forest, one of the wildest nature spots within easy reach of Paris. Pick up a free hiking map from the **Fontainebleau Tourist Office**, 4 Rue Royale (tel. 01.60.74.99.99), or rent a bike from the Gare de Fontainebleau (tel. 01.64.22.36.14).

Fontainebleau Château

Tel. 01.60.71.50.70. **Open** June-Sept 930am-6pm Wed-Mon; Oct-May 930am-5pm Wed-Mon. Admission €8.50 adults, free for youths under 18.

GiVERNY

Getting There: *Giverny is located 80 km/50 mi northwest of Paris. Take the train from Gare St. Lazare to Vernon, which is 4 mi/6 km by taxi, bicycle (which can be rented at the train station) or foot.*

Giverny is synonymous with Impressionist artist Claude Monet who lived here with his mistress and eight children from 1883 to 1926. A visit here is a leisurely day communing with nature and art. And it's a rare treat to experience the famous flower gardens and water lilies that influenced an entire artistic movement. Indeed, the pink-brick house and Japanese water gardens, which were donated to the Académie des Beaux-Arts in 1966, look something like an impressionist painting. It's so magical you can almost forget about all the tour busses whaling around the parking lot. Flowers bloom from April to October, and the water lilies are in abundance year-round.

The nearby **Musée Americain Giverny** shows the work of Mary Cassatt and other saccharine American artists who were drawn to France by the impressionists.

Musée Claude Monet
84 Rue Claude Monet (tel. 02.32.51.28.21).
Open *Apr-Oct, Tues-Sun 930am-6pm.*

Musée Americain Giverny
99 rue Claude Monet (tel. 02.32.51.94.65.).
Open *Mar-Nov, Tues-Sun 10am-6pm.*

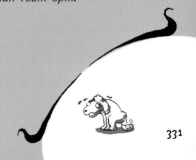

ChANTiLLY

Getting There: *Chantilly is 30 mi/48 km north of Paris. Take the train from the Gare du Nord (direction Creil-Compiegne) to Chantilly. It's a short walk or taxi ride to the Château.*

The Renaissance **Chantilly Château** is a storybook castle built with turrets and domes, and set on an island in the middle of a lake. There's a **Petit Chateau** next door, plus formal gardens by Le Nôtre and vast expanses of rolling hills. Now housing the **Musée Condé**, the Château contains the extensive art collections of its former owner, the Duc d'Aumale. It's an impressive lot that includes stellar works by Poussin, Delacroix, Watteau and Van Dyck, among others.

Chantilly is also the home of French horse racing, and the town is home to a major track and the **Musée Vivant du Cheval et du Poney**, one of the world's great dog and pony shows. Here you can visit working stables that were built to accommodate 240 horses and almost 500 hunting dogs. There are dressage demonstrations at 330pm.

Chantilly Château (Musée Condé)
Tel. 03.44.62.62.60. **Open** Mar 15-Oct 15, Wed-Mon 10am-6pm; Oct 16-Mar 14, Wed-Mon 1030am-1245pm & 2-5pm. Closed Tues. Admission to chateaux and park €7 adults, €6 youth 12-17, €2.80 children 3-11; park only €3 adults, €2 children under 12.

Musée Vivant du Cheval et du Poney
Tel. 03.44.57.13.13. **Open** Apr-Oct, Wed 1030am-600pm, Sat-Sun 1030am-630pm, Tues (May-June 1030am-530pm; July-Aug 2-530pm); Nov-Mar, Mon and Wed-Fri 2-530pm, Sat-Sun 1030am-6pm. Admission €8 adults, €6.50 youths 13-17, €5.50 youths 4-12.

dISNEYLANd RESORt PARiS

Tel. 01.60.30.60.30; www.disneylandparis.com. **Admission** €25-€107 (depending on entry for one or both parks, 1 or 3 days, high or low season, child or adult.). **Disneyland Park open** Jan 5-Feb 14 and Mar 3-Apr 4, 10am-8pm Mon-Wed, 9am-8pm Sat-Sun; Feb 15-Mar 2 and Apr 5-July 4, 9am-8pm daily; July 5-Aug 31, 9am-11pm daily. **Disney Studios open** Jan 6-Feb 14 and Mar 3-Apr 4, 10am-6pm Mon-Fri, 9am-6pm Sat-Sun; Feb 15-Mar 2 and Apr 5-July 4, 9am-6pm daily; July 5-Aug 31, 9am-8pm daily.

Getting There: Disneyland Paris is located 20 Mi/32 km east of Paris. Take the RER to Marne-la-Valée-Chessy, which stops right at the park. The ride from Paris takes about 40 minutes.

Let's hope you didn't come to Paris for Mickey and Main Street USA. But then again, maybe you have a good excuse. Attacked by a former Minister of Culture as a "cultural Chernobyl," Disneyland Paris (formerly known as Euro Disney) can be a fun day out. For a start, it's the biggest amusement park in Europe, one-fifth the size of the city of Paris. Secondly, it's so unlike the rest of France—organised, efficient, clean—it's scary. Workers actually wash daily, shave clean, and smile at you.

Like Disney's other parks, this one is built with six theme worlds, each of which puts the company's trademark spin on the Wild West, small-town life in the US and other motifs. But all the ride narrations are in French.

A single entry price includes access to all the attractions. Lines are worst on weekends and holidays, and shortest early in the morning. That's when you should make a beeline for the biggies: Space Mountain, Phantom Manor, Pirates of the Caribbean, Big Thunder Mountain Railroad, Star Tours and the Visionarium.

In April 2002 Disneyland Paris celebrated its 10th birthday by opening a new theme park next door, Disney Studios, which combines "educational" insights into animation and the history of Disney filmmaking with a live stunt show, superfast corkscrew roller-coster set to Aerosmith tunes, and a studio tour of the Disney Channel's live show, Zapping Zone. Built to resemble a Hollywood film studio, it looks a bit eerily like a California shopping mall. You can buy a three-day pass which allows unlimited access to both parks.

The Disneyland Resort also includes a number of theme-hotels, a golf course, and the Disney Village (free entry), which really does resemble an American mall/entertainment complex with its shops, Rainforest Café, Planet Hollywood and IMAX theatre. Come at night for the live music shows, dancing at the Hurrican Club or the authentic cowboy stunts at Buffalo Bill's Wild West Show.

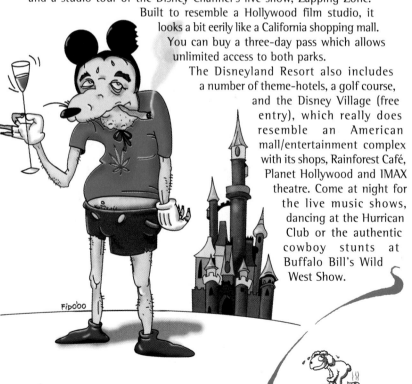

No 11

BEFORE YOU GO ESSENTIALS

PLANNING

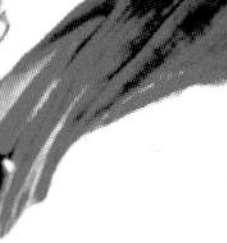

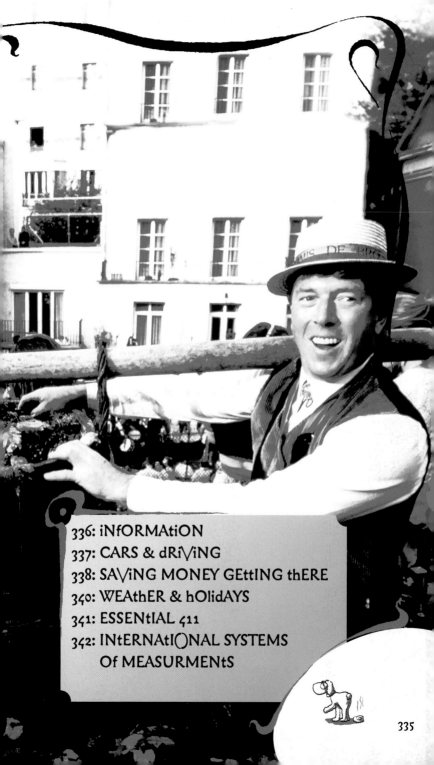

iNfORMATiON

The www.avantguide.com CyberSupplement™ is the best source for happenings in Paris during your stay. Visit for updates and links to info on current cultural events and other happenings.

Official information on events in and around Paris is offered from **French Government Tourist Offices: Australia** (tel. 02/9231-5244); **Britain** (tel. 0891/244123); **Canada** (tel. 514/288-4264); **USA** (tel. 212/838-7800 or 202/659-7779).

See Chapter 2 for a list of information sources in Paris.

For information and entry requirements, duty-free limits and other foreign concerns, see "For Foreign Visitors," below.

For Travelers With Disabilities

Paris is not very hospitable to wheelchair-bound and other disabled travelers. The terrain is relatively flat, sidewalks are smooth and most public buildings are ramped. But public transport makes almost no special accommodations and few restaurants and hotels are accessible.

It is common in Paris for theaters, nightclubs and attractions to offer discounts to people with disabilities. Ask for these before paying full-price. For information about disabled access, contact the Paris Tourist Board

Access in Paris, a painstakingly thorough English-language guide detailing wheelchair-accessible sights, theaters, cafes, shops and toilets all over town is the essential guide for disabled visitors. Order it from **RADAR**, Unit 12, City Forum, 250 City Rd., London EC1V 8AF (tel. 020/7250-3222). The book costs £6.95, including UK postage. Add £2 for Europe, £7 for rest of world.

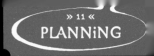

French roads are divided into *autoroute* highways (marked with an "A" in front of the route number), most of which are toll roads *(péages)*; smaller *routes nationales* roads (marked "N"); local *routes départementales* ("D" roads) and tiny, rural *routes communales* ("C" streets). The speed limit on A-roads is 130km/h (80mph); The speed limit on N-roads is 90km/h (56mph).

You don't need a car in Paris and it's a hassle to have one. Anyway, public transport and taxis can get you almost everywhere. Traffic crawls along at a snail's pace, street parking is difficult and a garage will set you back €12-€20 per day.

Some rules: All passengers must wear seat belts, children under ten are not allowed to travel in the front seat and, when drivers flash their lights at you, they're saying "keep out of my way."

If you drive your own Porche to France, be sure to pack your car's registration and insurance documents. American and British automobile associations don't have reciprocal arrangements with their French counterpart. You can buy breakdown insurance in the UK from **Europ Assistance** (UK tel. 01444/442 211; France tel. 01. 41.85.85.85).

If your car dies in the middle of Paris and you don't have insurance, call **Action Auto Assistance** (tel. 08.00.00.80.00) or **SOS Dépannage** (tel. 01.47.07.99.99).

Auto Rentals

As is usual, the big international car-rental firms are the most expensive. Rates vary, but expect to pay about €65 per day, and €250 per week, for a French-made, two-door tin can. Local rental firms are cheaper than the international chains, but their cars are decidedly worse. Try **Continental** (tel. 08.25.80.58.04), which charges about €35 per day.

At the other end of the spectrum there's **International Limousine** (tel. 01.43.80.20.45) and **American Limousines** (tel. 01.39.35.09.99), both offering chauffeur-driven stretch limos for about €95 per hour. Prices rise after midnight. All major credit cards accepted.

Company	France	USA	UK
Avis	08.02.05.05.05	800/331-1212	0990/900500
Budget	08.25.00.35.64	800/527-0700	0541/565656
Hertz	01.39.38.38.38	800/654-3131	0990/996699
National/Europcar	08.03.35.23.52	800/227-7368	0345/222525

Motorcycle Rentals

Atelier de la Compagnie 57 Blvd. de Grenelle, 15th (tel. 01.45.79.77.24), is the best place in Paris to rent a motorbike. They've got 50cc-125cc, with helmets and anti-theft guards for €29-€50 per day, and €135-€230 per week. They've got special weekend deals too. A credit card deposit is required. They're open Mon-Fri 10am-7pm, Sat 10am-6pm. Visa only.

SAViNG MONEY GETTiNG ThERE

Frankly, we don't trust most travel agents to really dig for the lowest fare. They get paid a small percentage of the price of each ticket, so it doesn't benefit them to spend *more* time trying to make *less* money. We usually make reservations ourselves, directly with the airlines, then visit our travel agent for ticketing. Here's the secret to getting the best deal: If you don't know airline jargon, don't use it. Just ask for the lowest fare. If you're flexible with dates and times, tell the sales agent. Ask him or her to hunt a bit.

THE MAjOR AIRLiNES

	France	USA	UK
Air Canada	01.44.50.20.02	800/776-3000	990/247-266
Air France	08.20.82.08.20	800/237-2747	020/8742-6600
American Airlines	08.10.87.28.72	800/433-7300	0345/789-789
British Airways	08.25.82.54.00	800/247-9297	0345/222-111
Continental Airlines	01.42.99.09.09	800/525-0280	0800/776-464
Delta Air Lines	08.00.35.40.80	800/221-1212	0800/414-767
KLM	08.90.71.07.10	800/777-5553	0990/750-900
Lufthansa	08.20.02.00.30	800/645-3880	0345/737-747
Northwest	08.90.71.07.10	800/777-5553	01293/543-511
United Airlines	08.10.72.72.72	800/246-5221	0845/844-4777
US Airways	01.49.10.29.29	800/428-4322	0800/783-5556

Budget Airlines & Consolidators

Recently we have been buying airplane tickets almost exclusively from consolidators. Also known as "bucket shops," consolidators are travel agents that buy airline seats in bulk, in return for deep discounts. This business has become so sophisticated that most of them now buy their tickets from even larger wholesalers. To find the best fare at any given time, check the travel sections of *The New York Times*, the *Los Angeles Times* or any other big-city newspaper. Bucket shop ads are usually very small, and list a lot of destinations. The US-based consolidators we use to get to Paris are **Cheap Tickets** (tel. 212/570-1179 or 800/377-1000); **Air Brokers** (tel. 800/883-3273); **Cheap Seats** (tel. 800/451-7200); **Travel Link** (tel. 213/441-3030); and **Travel Abroad** (tel. 212/564-8989).

Several cut-rate, UK-based budget airlines offer short-hop service over the Channel. **Air Jet** (UK tel. 020/7476-6000) flies from London City Airport to Paris CDG. **Air Liberté** (UK tel. 0345/228899) connects London Gatwick with Toulouse and Bordeaux. **Air UK** (UK tel. 0345/666777) flies from London Stansted and Leeds to Paris CDG.

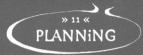

Crossing The Channel From The UK

BY FERRY Ferries crossing the Channel cost about 30% cheaper than the Chunnel. There are numerous companies for both passengers and cars from Dover to Calais, Portsmouth to Le Havre, Portsmouth to Cherbourg, Ramsgate to Dunkirk, and Newhaven to Dieppe. And there are frequent special offers.

Brittany Ferries (UK tel. 0990/360360)
P&O Lines (UK tel. 0990/980980)
Sally Line (UK tel. 01843/595566)
Sea France (UK tel. 01304/212696)
Stena Line (UK tel. 01233/647047)

BY HYDROFOIL **Hoverspeed** (UK tel. 01304/240241; France tel. 01.42. 85.44.55) flies on a cushion of air above the water from Dover to Calais, and Folkestone to Boulogne. Air-sickness bags are provided during choppy weather.

BY TRAIN The **Eurostar Train** between the capitals of Britain and France takes three hours from London Waterloo (UK tel. 01233/617575) to Paris Gare du Nord (tel. 08.36.35.35.39). Passengers are required to check in 20 minutes before departure.

BY CAR/CHUNNEL The fastest way to get you and your car from England to France is on **Le Shuttle** (tel. 01.43. 18.62.22 or 08.01.63.03.04), an undersea train link which takes about 35 minutes from Folkestone to Calais. Prices range between €200-€338 for a car and all its passengers, depending on when you go. Trains run 24/seven, up to four times per hour.

Packages vs. Tours

When it comes to travel lingo, most people confuse packages and tours. In the industry, a *tour* usually refers to a group that travels together, follows a flag-toting leader and is herded on and off busses. Obviously we seldom recommend this kind of tourism.

A *package*, on the other hand, is a travel deal in which several components of a trip—transportation, accommodations, airport transfers and the like—are bundled together for sale to independent, unescorted travelers. Many independent travelers purchase complete vacations from travel agents without ever knowing that they're buying a package. That's O.K.—packages can offer great value. Package companies buy in bulk and are often able to sell complete vacations for less than you'd pay for its components individually.

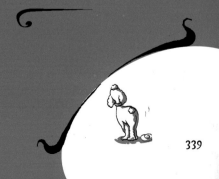

WEAThER & hOlidAYs

Weather

Situated at the junction of marine and continental climates, Paris is seldom extremely hot or cold. Spring and fall are the best seasons; both are sunny and mild. Winter is often long, wet and gray. And summers are stuffy, as pollution reaches its zenith. Come July, many locals head for the country, leaving the city to foreigners.

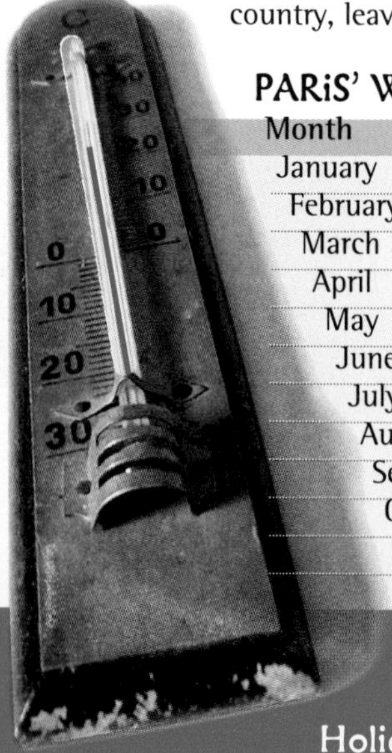

PARiS' WEAThER AVERAGES

Month	Daytime Temperature
January	8C=46F
February	7C=45F
March	10C=50F
April	16C=60F
May	17C=62F
June	23C=74F
July	25C=77F
August	26C=78F
September	21C=70F
October	17C=62F
November	12C=53F
December	8C=46F

Holidays

Holidays are particularly sacred in France as they stroke two particularly French traits: the sanctity of custom and the pleasure of not working. Many restaurants, shops, museums and businesses close on public holidays.

Aside from plenty of official holidays, French are pros at finding plenty of other occasions to play hooky from work. And the long weekend, created when a holiday falls on a Thursday or Tuesday, is *de rigor.*

While the city used to empty out in August, things are now changing. Four-week vacations are becoming scarcer as many more companies are defying tradition to stay open throughout the month. And high-end restaurants are getting so much business from rich tourists that they too are choosing money over *liberté*.

Public Holidays

New Years' Day (January 1), **Easter, Easter Monday, Labor Day** (May 1), **VE Day** (May 8), **Ascension Day** (sixth Thursday after Easter), **Whit Monday/Pentecost** (second Monday after Ascension), **Bastille Day** (July 14), **Feast of the Assumption** (mid-August), **All Saints' Day** (November 1), **Veteran's Day** (November 11), **Christmas Day** (December 25)

ESSENTIAL 411

CURRENCY EXCHANGE

See Chapter 2/Money.

CUSTOMS REQUIREMENTS

Each adult visitor from non-European Union countries may bring into France free of duty: one liter of alcohol over 44-proof, and two liters under 44-proof; 200 cigarettes or 50 cigars or 8.82 ounces (250 grams) of smoking tobacco; and up to €150) of new goods.

There are no restrictions on the movement of currency and few laws restricting the importation of plants and food; you can legally show up at Charles-De-Gaulle with a smoked mackerel.

US customs allows returning Americans duty-free import of $400 worth of merchandise, 200 cigarettes or 100 cigars and one liter of spirits. Above these amounts, travelers are assessed a flat 10% tax on the next $1000 worth of goods. When you shop big in Paris, keep the receipts to show customs officials.

DOCUMENT REGULATIONS

Americans, British, Canadians, Kiwis, Australians, Japanese and most Euros don't need a visa to enter France for up to six months; only a passport with an expiration date at least six months later than the scheduled end of your visit is required. Passport Control officials sometimes ask younger travelers to prove they have enough cash on hand before admitting them into the country. You can avoid this hassle by writing the name of an expensive hotel on your landing card. Citizens of most other countries, including South Africa, must obtain a visa from a French embassy or consulate. Poodles are welcome, of course, as long as they travel with a vaccination certificate.

ELECTRICITY

France runs on 220V, 50 cycles and a two-prong outlet that differs from the US and UK. American appliances must be plugged into converters; Most British appliances only need adapters, but some may also need a transformer if it's not already built into the device.

TAX

Unlike the United States where tax is tacked on at the register, in France Value-Added Tax (VAT) is already figured into the ticket price of most items. Restaurants usually include VAT in menu prices, but sometimes it is added to the bill, along with a service charge. The policy is usually written on the menu. There is no additional airport tax upon departure, and tax is included in all hotel rates.

TIME

Paris one hour ahead of Greenwich Mean Time (GMT+1); 6 hours ahead of US Eastern Standard Time. Daylight Savings Time moves the clock ahead one hour, from the last Sunday in March through the last Saturday in September.

TELEPHONES

To call Paris from the US, dial 011 (international code), 33 (France's country code), and the ten-digit local telephone number, minus the first "0." **To call Paris from the UK**, dial 00 (international code), 33 (France's country code), and the ten-digit local telephone number, minus the first "0." For information on phones in Paris, see Chapter 2/Telecommunications.

VIDEO

PAL standard.

INtERNAtI()NAL SYStEMS Of MEASUREMENtS

LIQUID VOLUME

1 fluid ounce = .03 liters
1 pint = 16 fluid ounces = .47 liter
1 quart = 2 pints = .94 liter
1 US gallon = 4 quarts =3.79 liter = 83 Imperial gallons

US GALLONS TO LITERS
Multiply the number of gallons by 3.79 (10 gals. x 3.79 = 37.9 liters)
US GALLONS TO IMPERIAL GALLONS
Multiply the number of US gallons by .83 (10 US gals. x .83 = 8.3 Imperial gals.)
LITERS TO US GALLONS
Multiply the number of liters by .26 (10 liters x .26 = 2.6 US gals.)
IMPERIAL GALLONS TO US GALLONS
Multiply the number of Imperial gallons by 1.2 (10 Imperial gals. x 1.2 = 12 US gals.)

LENGTH

1 inch = 2.54 centimeters
1 foot = 12 inches = 30.48 centimeters = 0.305 meters
1 yard = 3 feet = .915 meters
1 mile = 5,280 feet = 1.609 kilometer

MILES TO KILOMETERS
Multiply the number of miles by 1.61 (100 miles x 1.61 = 161 km.)
KILOMETERS TO MILES
Multiply the number of kilometers by .62 (100km x .62 = 62 miles)

WEIGHT

1 ounce = 28.35 grams
1 pound = 16 ounces = 453.6 grams = .45 kilograms
1 ton = 2,000 pounds = 907 kilograms = .91 metric ton

POUNDS TO KILOGRAMS
Multiply the number of pounds by .45
(10 lbs. x .45 = 4.5 kgs.)
KILOGRAMS TO POUNDS
Multiply the number of kilograms by 2.2
(10kgs. x 2.2 = 22 lbs.)

AREA

1 acre = .41 hectares
1 square mile = 640 acres = 2.59 hectares = 2.6 kilometers

ACRES TO HECTARES
Multiply the number of acres by .41 (10 acres x .41 = 4.1ha)
SQUARE MILES TO SQUARE KILOMETERS
Multiply the number of square miles by 2.6 (10 sq. mi. x 2.6 = 26km^2)
HECTARES TO ACRES
Multiply the number of hectares by 2.47 (10ha x 2.47 = 24.7 acres)
SQUARE KILOMETERS TO SQUARE MILES
Multiply the no. of square kilometers by .39 (100km2 x .39 = 39 sq. mi.)

CLOTHING CONVERSION CHART

WOMEN'S CLOTHES

UK	08	10	12	14	16
US	06	08	10	12	14
Euro	38	40	42	44	46

WOMEN'S SHOES

UK	03	04	05	06	07	08	09
US	05	06	07	08	09	10	11
Euro	36	37	38	39	40	41	42

MEN'S CLOTHES

UK	38	40	42	44	46
US	38	40	42	44	46
Euro	48	50/52	54	56	58/60

MEN'S SHOES

UK	08	09	10	11	12
US	09	10	11	12	13
Euro	42	43	44	45	46

TEMPERATURE

Degrees Fahrenheit To Degrees Celsius
Subtract 32 from °F, multiply by 5, then divide by 9
(85°F - 32 x 5 ÷ 9 = 29.4°C).
Degrees Celsius To Degrees Fahrenheit
Multiply °C by 9, divide by 5, and add 32
(20°C x 9 ÷ 5 + 32 = 68°F).

Indexes

NGUYEN
11
TRABBIA
PERRET
GARANCINI-IDIART

BOOk iNdEX

d

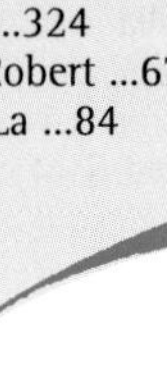

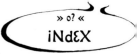

E

f

G

h

i

j

k

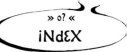

L

M

N

O

P

Q

R

S

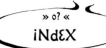

MAP iNdEX

STREET INDEX

d

e

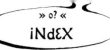

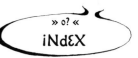

MAP INDEX

PLACES OF INTEREST

MÉTRO STATIONS